Spiritual Passages

ALSO BY DREW LEDER, M.D., PH.D.

The Absent Body

Spiritual Passages

Embracing Life's
Sacred Journey

Drew Leder, M.D., Ph.D.

Jeremy P. Tarcher/Putnam
a member of Penguin Putnam Inc. *New York*

Most Tarcher/Putnam books are available at special quantity discounts for bulk purchases for sales promotions, premiums, fund-raising, and educational needs. Special books or book excerpts also can be created to fit specific needs. For details, write or telephone Putnam Special Markets, 200 Madison Avenue, New York, NY 10016; (212) 951-8891.

Jeremy P. Tarcher/Putnam
a member of Penguin Putnam Inc.
200 Madison Avenue
New York, NY 10016
http://www.putnam.com

Library of Congress Cataloging-in-Publication Data

Leder, Drew.
   Spiritual passages: embracing life's sacred journey/Drew Leder.
     p.   cm.
   "Jeremy P. Tarcher/Putnam."
   Includes bibliographical references and index.
   ISBN 0-87477-873-5
1. Aged—Religious life.   2. Aged—Conduct of life.   I. Title.
BL625.4.L43   1997   96-6500 CIP
291.4′4′0846—dc21

Book design by Lee Fukui
Cover design by Greg Wittrock
Cover illustration, *The Miracle*, by Nicholas Roerich (1874–1947)

Printed in the United States of America
10 9 8 7 6 5 4

To my father,
Harold,
and my mother,
Gertrude:

May they find the
wholeness they sought.

Contents

Acknowledgments

THE SUPPORT AND WISDOM of many people are embodied in this book. Some of that came in the form of institutional assistance. This work was first conceived while I was a scholar-in-residence at The Park Ridge Center for the Study of Health, Faith, and Ethics. The center provided gracious assistance and encouragement, as did the Retirement Research Foundation, who funded my fellowship. I further developed my ideas during exciting "conscious aging" conferences and think-tank meetings hosted by the Omega Institute.

It's one thing to so garner ideas for a book—another to find the time to write it. This time was provided by the generous leave policy at Loyola College in Maryland.

My own ideas were particularly influenced by the work of two mentors, whom I now count among my friends: Ram Dass and Rabbi Zalman Schachter-Shalomi. The insights of these two wise and playful men inform every page of this book. And how to measure the influence of others I've met? Bob Atchley, Tom Cole, Rick

Moody, Carol Segrave, Jane Thibault . . . the list could go on and on. Such people, laboring in the vineyards of thought and research on "conscious aging," are brewing up many a fine wine.

Several friends helped midwife this book. Lynn Rosen, my agent, first encouraged me to write it. Irene Prokop has proved an ever-helpful and supportive editor. Carol Krucoff provided useful feedback on the manuscript. Lisa M. Flaherty has served as a tireless and enthusiastic research associate. Then, too, Kathleen Donofrio's spiritual companionship has been sustaining over the years. My daughter, Sarah, has embroidered this year of writing with delight, thankfully pulling me away from the computer. And finally, my wife, Janice McLane—fellow writer, philosopher, friend, and lover—I look forward to spending life's second half with you.

Introduction

TIME IS BOTH a thief and a generous soul. It can steal from us things of great value, yet lavish precious gifts in return.

For there are gifts of the ripened mind, heart, and spirit. As we grow older, we may finally *grow up*—attain the maturity that's always eluded us. We may also grow younger at heart. There's a wildness and a freedom buried inside us beneath layers of social convention. Why not let it loose? Why not play?

Then, too, maybe the fears that have bedeviled us—of our past mistakes, of death hurtling toward us from the indeterminate future—will finally disperse as we age. We can stand in the present, serene. Maybe the driven pace of our lives, whipping us about like a drunken merry-go-round, will finally slacken. We can rest inside. We can be alone with ourselves in a spirit of joyful solitude, not soul-crushing loneliness.

Even so, the soul asks for more, ever more. What loneliness we have felt is hardly the result of a sheer lack of people. We are surrounded by crowds, our days filled with collisions and conversations. But how to really let folks into our hearts? How to find that intimacy that is not just a give and take, but a *give and give*, each one fed by the other? We crave soul food, the real thing. We won't be satisfied by less.

This craving carries us beyond the meat of this world. We reach out for . . . what to call it? God, the realm of Spirit, the One that unites us? The Tao, Buddha Nature, the indwelling Christ? So many different words. They are like fingers pointing to that which, beyond the self, or within the self, will truly make us whole. Whole, holy, healed. If the passage of time does not bring us this wholeness it is nothing but idiocy—moments strung out one after another, after another, without deep meaning or purpose.

However, the world's religions share a common testimony: that with age we can become sage. There is a wholeness possible in life's second half that often evades us as callow youths. But nobody said this accomplishment would prove easy. With the passage of years, we stumble in the dark, meet with unexpected obstacles and hazards. In negotiating these, we will receive little guidance from our culture. Too often it portrays aging as a senseless event, a slip-slide toward dotage and the grave.

We need not despair, though. If we know where to seek them, we will find guides aplenty. They are there in the wise elder of Native American traditions, and the biblical Sarah, a postmenopausal mom. We can learn from a laughing Aikido master, a long-lived Taoist tree, Jesus struggling with pain, mockery, and abandonment. An old woman wears purple and kicks up her heels. Scrooge confronts his Christmas ghosts. A Hindu sage retires to the forest to seek the God within. These stories, provided by the world's spiritual traditions and the pens of artists and poets, can teach us how to age. In this book we will work through them together.

For most of us, long experience best prepares us for these lessons in midlife or our later years. Hence I focus on this period of life. However, spiritual passages have no fixed season. Many a younger reader, churned forward by life's turbulence, is already a sage in training. Furthermore, the issue of aging is not only for the "aged." It is something we are all undergoing at every moment, whether we are seventeen or seventy. The sooner we learn how to work with time's changes, the better we can negotiate life.

Several authors in our society have tried to map the landscape of adulthood. The psychiatrist Erik Erikson was one such pioneer. Refusing to restrict psychological development to childhood, he charted, as well, the stages of midlife and beyond. In a more popular vein, Daniel Levinson has written about the "seasons" of a man's and woman's life. Gail Sheehy has sketched the passages we age through, including the "flourishing forties," "flaming fifties," and "serene sixties."

The works of these and other such authors yield much of value. They provide an empirical record of what people *do* experience as they age within our culture. Moreover, they suggest something of what we *should* experience if seeking to be whole: integrity, generativity, and the like.

My own book draws on and overlaps with such themes. But, finally, it has a different purpose. Something is still missing from this focus on the psychological passages of adulthood. The soul wants more—it seeks spiritual passages to the divine. It wants to dive headfirst into that reservoir of joy and insight we dip from in our better moments. It wants a glimpse of that eternal life that stretches beyond the grave. And so this book addresses life's spiritual passages.

Where better to seek guidance than from the world's sacred traditions? (Admittedly, personal and space limits bound the selections.) Buddhism, Christianity, Taoism, Judaism, Hinduism, Native American cosmology, and more. Are these clashing systems arrayed for battle? Or are they like the many colors that separate when light is refracted through a prism? Each has its unique beauty, and also is part of the One. I prefer the latter image. The divine light refracts through the prism of culture and history. Let us gather up all its shining rays.

Each chapter begins with a *spiritual passage*—that is a passage, a story, drawn from one of the world's religions or from a contemporary source with sacred overtones. Part 1 introduces the book's overall themes. Difficult experiences—as represented by Buddha's encounter with aging, illness, and mortality—can thrust us into a heightened awareness of life and a quest for the transcendent. Hinduism offers counsel on how then to proceed. Life's second half represents an ideal curriculum for spiritual growth, if we can so use it; to do so, we must accept and work with change. Here, three Taoist sages serve as our teachers. From the Taoist perspective, the fulfilled life is that which harmonizes opposites—light and dark, male and female, assertion and yielding. This notion structures the rest of the book which presents themes in complementary pairs.

Part 2 discusses the wisdom, but also the holy foolishness, simple and direct, that can develop over the years. Either one without the other is unbalanced. In their richest form, the two interpenetrate. The wise elder, free of ego, has a playful spirit. The fool often speaks wise truths that others dare not.

Part 3 turns to the dialectic of *service* and *rest*. As ripened adults, we have much to contribute to a world seemingly gone mad. But we can't help the world if we ourselves are driven. We need to cultivate not just *doing*, but a quality of *being*: at peace in Sabbath time.

How to find this holy balance of wisdom and playfulness, service and rest? We don't become enlightened simply by piling on the decades. With the passing of time, there are inner passages we must make. Along the way we're likely to encounter our demons, but we can convert them into angels, trusted companions for our journey.

This journey takes us both into the past and future, the dual focus of part 4. Material from our personal history may cry out for healing. We can do so through acceptance, forgiveness, and amends. Then, too, we know death lies somewhere on the road ahead. Too often we're haunted by macabre images—the grim reaper, rotting corpse, and hollow skull. Don't look away, spiritual traditions counsel. On the contrary, look closer. Stare your own death in the face, and you will see something curious happen. The horrible death mask dissolves to reveal the shining face of the Deathless Divine.

Coming to terms with death frees us to live life to the fullest. We can plunge into both its *sufferings* and *joys*—the topic of part 5—drawing on each for spiritual renewal. Let's not deny it: age is the sword of a thousand small cuts. But in wounding us it also opens us up to the giving and reception of love. And these wounds may yield the labor pains of joyous rebirth even in life's second half. With a divine midwife we deliver a new self, red, wet, and raring to go.

Psychological passages are often portrayed as unfolding in predictable sequence. Not so these spiritual passages, a disorderly lot. We go through them as we are thrust into them by life's traumas or led by the urgings of spirit. And our movement is not only linear, but circular, as we revisit certain issues time and again.

For such reasons, feel free to use this book in a way tailored to your needs. The first three chapters function as an integrated introduction. A narrative flow guides the rest of the book. But you may choose to read chapters out of sequence. If a particular theme seems most relevant to your current life issues, personality, or spiritual calling, don't hesitate to leap ahead and work in depth with that chapter. But when the time is right, look into its complementary opposite; do it even (especially?) if you have resistance to the topic. You may feel drawn to the joyful story of Sarah, but not to that death-and-suffering stuff. If you are action oriented, you might rush to the chapter on later-life service, not the one on contemplative rest. Remember, though, that the wholeness we seek involves harmonizing all of who we are, including the parts that are underdeveloped or unwanted.

To help you work personally with this book I supply questions, interspersed within each chapter. It's one thing to scan generalities in a text, quite another to really apply these to your life. The questions invite you to reflect on your past and to image a future, design a healing ritual, make a list of amends, mine pains and losses for the riches they can yield, contact sources of intuitive guidance, and more. It's helpful not just to think through the questions but to *write about them* in a separate journal. The writing process lends focus and depth to our reflections.

There are also truths the linguistic brain cannot access. The visualizations at the end of each chapter tap into another part of the mind where those truths unfold.

Of course, it's not necessary to do these exercises. The text can stand on its own. (I must confess, I'm an inveterate exercise-skipper.) By using them, however, you convert this book into an interactive tool for self-transformation. It becomes a work you are writing yourself. The subject: your own spiritual passages. Your guides: Buddha, Jesus, Sarah, and other learned companions. The goal: nothing less than your awakening, enlightenment, and fulfillment. Why think small when we want the All?

Part I Awareness and Acceptance

Awakenings:
The Story of Buddha

When Siddhartha was born, so this story runs, his father summoned fortunetellers to find out what the future held for his heir. All agreed that this was no usual child. His career, however, was crossed with one basic ambiguity. If he remained with the world he would unify India and become her greatest conqueror, a Cakravartin or Universal King. If, on the other hand, he forsook the world he would become not a king but a world redeemer. Faced with this option, his father determined to steer his son into the former destiny. No effort was spared to keep the prince's mind attached to the world. Three palaces and forty thousand dancing girls were placed at his disposal; strict orders were given that no ugliness intrude upon the courtly pleasures. Specifically the prince was to be shielded from contact with sickness, decrepitude, and death; even when he went riding runners were to clear the roads of these sights. One day, however, an old man was overlooked or, as some versions have it, miraculously incarnated by the gods to effect the needed teaching experience of the moment; a man decrepit, broken-toothed, gray-haired, crooked and bent of body, leaning on a staff, and trembling. That day Siddhartha learned the fact of old age. Though the king extended his guard, on a second ride Siddhartha encountered a body racked with disease lying by the road; and on a third journey, a corpse. Finally on a fourth occasion he saw a monk with shaven head, ochre robe, and bowl; on that day he learned the possibility of withdrawal from the world. . . .

Once he had perceived the inevitability of bodily pain and passage he could not return to fleshly pleasure. . . . He determined to quit the snare of distractions his palace had become and follow the call of a truth-seeker. One night in his twenty-ninth year he made the break, his Great Going Forth. . . . Gautama shaved his head and "clothed in ragged raiment" plunged into the forest in search of enlightenment.

Huston Smith, *The World Religions*

THIS WONDERFUL MYTH tells how Prince Siddhartha began the awakening process that transformed him into Buddha (literally, "the Awakened One"). After leaving the artificial kingdom constructed by his father, Siddhartha spent many years studying under Hindu masters. He pursued their ascetic disciplines: torturing his body, he tried to overcome its hold. He merely ended up exhausted and near death. At last he discovered what Buddhists call the Middle Way. Neither indulging the body nor destroying it, he tried to quiet its hold over the mind. This practice freed him to explore in meditation the basic nature of consciousness. Why does the mind produce such suffering? How can we escape it? Finally, sitting through the night in an explosion of meditative energy, he blasted past all mental barriers. He had the experience that Buddhists call nirvana. He became aware of a great reality that transcends the separate self and the passage of time. This was bliss. The Buddha spent almost the next half century travelling through India trying to teach others how they too might awaken from their tormenting dream.

We'll focus on the beginning of Buddha's spiritual journey. Though he was a young man at the time, his story provides some exquisite lessons for life's second half.

PARENT AND CHILD

First, let's look at Buddha's father. Hearing that his son will become either a world redeemer or India's universal conqueror, he does everything possible to steer things down the latter, more practical path. You can imagine him musing, "World redeemer? Where's the future in that? Saviors don't make too good a living. Ah, but universal conqueror, now there's a job! Untold riches. Power galore. Respect, oh, you'll get plenty of respect (and so will I, your aging father). Job security's not bad either. Who dares challenge a universal conqueror?"

In your own youth, someone may have tried to steer you down a certain path. Perhaps your parents wanted you to be a doctor, a lawyer, or an accountant, or to marry someone well-to-do. Or maybe the pressure came not so much from your parents as from the world at large. After all, everyone seems to value material success. The message screams at us from TV, magazines, advertising: "Have stuff, lots of stuff, and you'll be happy. Pleasure, power, profit, prestige—that's the ticket!" We suck this message like baby food from the culture's breast. Sometimes it seems like we're force-fed it whether we're hungry or not.

Amidst all this pressure, maybe there were dreams we set aside. Siddhartha almost lost sight of his true calling. Maybe, to some degree, we have as well. Are there parts of the self that we left undeveloped? In our youth, did we feel drawn to something—the arts, nature, travel, spirituality—that we lost sight of along the way? Were there any life or career dreams that we abandoned? The great psychiatrist, Carl Jung, suggests that restrictive choices are inevitable in the first half of life as we build up the ego-self. We are seeking to define ourselves and succeed as individuals. But life's second half, he suggests, has a different purpose; we reach for psychospiritual wholeness. To do so, we need to develop the parts of ourselves that have been repressed or neglected. We need to honor what lies hidden within our souls.[1]

As well as with Siddhartha, we might also identify with his father. Now in life's second half, we may have certain parental roles:

raising children, teaching students, or mentoring young colleagues. Siddhartha's father surely meant well as he steered his son toward practical matters. Have we tried to do something similar with those we mentor? That's not necessarily a bad idea. It's a harsh world out there, and the young need to ground their dreams in prudent realities. But there's a problem with the father's approach: he's not seeking to assist the realization of his son's dream, but to impose his own. "World conqueror, that's the way to go." *But he never asked Siddhartha.* Maybe that's not the boy's wish or *dharma* (duty, place of fulfillment).

Maybe then, when Siddhartha left the nest, it was not only the son but the father who awakened—awakened to the fact that he had to learn to let go and accept that his child had his own dreams and destiny. He couldn't protect him, control him, or run his life. This awakening can be painful yet healing. As Kahlil Gibran writes in *The Prophet*:

> *Your children are not your children.*
> *They are the sons and daughters of Life's longing for itself.*
> *They come through you but not from you,*
> *And though they are with you, yet they belong not to you.*
>
> *You may give them your love but not your thoughts,*
> *For they have their own thoughts.*
> *You may house their bodies but not their souls,*
> *For their souls dwell in the house of tomorrow, which you*
>   *cannot visit, not even in your dreams.*
> *You may strive to be like them, but seek not to make them*
>   *like you.*
> *For Life goes not backward nor tarries with yesterday.*[2]

Were there desires of your youth that you learned to put aside while "growing up"? Do you still harbor some unrealized dreams or goals? Write these down. Then, using this list, and your own reflection, ask yourself what parts of yourself you might develop in life's second half. How could you give these unrealized talents, feelings, and desires fuller expression?

Were there times you acted like Siddhartha's father, being overprotective or overcontrolling? Were there times you practiced the opposite—the letting go, the empowering of others? How have these two experiences differed, both for yourself and the other people involved?

THE OLD MAN

One of the first things excluded from the artificial kingdom constructed by Siddhartha's father was any sign of human aging. Within our own society, don't we attempt to construct just such a dream kingdom? Open almost any mass-market magazine, or turn on prime-time TV, and what do you see? Beautiful young bodies, hard and tanned, cavorting through life. If you were an alien landing on our planet and surveying such images, you might conclude that the human life span ends at thirty-five. Now and then you see an older person in an ad for cosmetics, or laxatives, or vacation cruises, but the point is that these products can keep that person youthful. You never have to become the old person that Siddhartha sees—broken-toothed, crooked, and trembling.

Not only in ad images, but in reality, we try to exclude such sights. We have retirement communities and nursing homes that older people willingly join, or into which they may be placed. Some of these locales are quite congenial. (In fact, many a retirement community is like an artificial kingdom itself, walled off from the troubles of the outside world.) There are often good health and safety reasons to enter such places. Yet isn't it true, too, that society wants to hide away those judged decrepit? That many are more comfortable when broken-toothed and crooked oldsters are institutionalized out of sight?

This is not just a matter of manipulating externals but of altering our inner awareness. Siddhartha's dream kingdom also represents the illusions of our mind. In life's first half, we rarely imagine that we will ever get old. That's something that happens to other people; *my* future is limitless. We may even use vitamins, cosmetics, weight-lifting, aerobics, anything, to preserve the fantasy of eternal youth.

Like Siddhartha when he witnessed the old man, in life's second half we experience painful awakenings to our own aging process. That pulled muscle—it just doesn't heal the way it used to. My lack of energy . . . why do I always feel like I need a nap midafternoon? I used to go all day without stopping! And my company, I notice, no longer seems to be fast-tracking me like the new kids. But *I* used to be the new kid! Wrinkles under the eyes. Thinning hair. Where'd that come from? I'm beginning to look like my parents.

These signs of aging are natural, but that doesn't make it easier when it's happening to us. The moments when we feel our age can be painful. They may involve very real losses, "little deaths," as we let go of parts of who we were. And as with any death, it is helpful to acknowledge the loss and sadness, and give ourselves time to grieve.

We may know people who are overinvested in their youthful identity and have a hard time accepting life's changes. We laugh at the stereotypes: grandma in a miniskirt, or the aging jock who overdoes it on weekends. Beneath the exuberance there is often a lot of fear and denial about getting old.

Like Siddhartha's fantasies, woven of palaces and dancing girls galore, our dream of perpetual youth can be seductive. But Siddhartha recognized that his illusions were golden chains that kept him bound to a false world. They also assured that he would suffer when the truth emerged. Surely he grieved when his illusions were shattered. But he didn't stop there. He also used this experience as a tool of awakening. Seeing the signs of "bodily pain and passage," he became a determined truth-seeker.

And his story suggests that the truth will set us free. He discovered that aging was not the *only* truth; he sought and found the eternal. As the story goes, he had an experience of nirvana—Buddha Nature—that drew him beyond the separate self and its decaying flesh.

Here our own beliefs doubtless come into play. What, if anything, underlies, but outlives, the aging body? The term "God" might come to mind. Or "eternal Soul." Or the "cycle of nature," the "continuity of generations," the "body of Christ," the "Tao." Whatever we believe, Buddha's story embodies a profound teaching. It suggests that the aging process can help us wake up to a larger reality, a spiritual connectedness.

To be sure, it's a rude awakening, and often we'd rather linger in our dreams. But sages throughout the centuries testify to the benefits of rolling out of bed. As we awaken to the Greater Reality, we often experience a calming of our fears, a sense that all is taken care of. We don't need to run the universe; forces greater than ourselves have things well in hand. Even suffering plays a part in the larger harmony, like the minor keys of a rich concerto. And we don't have to curse our aging body. Our true self, we know, connects to something larger, untouched by the passage of time.

※　　※　　※

What are some of the painful moments and changes that have awakened you to your own aging? Have you taken time to acknowledge and grieve the losses

properly? Can you also see benefits of this awakening? How have these moments stimulated your own journey toward "enlightenment," whatever that means to you?

The Sick Man and the Corpse

Siddhartha also came across a sick person, and then a corpse; again, we can see analogies with our culture. Like Siddhartha's father, we too try to hide away sickness and death, with our hospitals and mortuaries. Death, no longer a part of everyday life, is a kind of hushed obscenity. We seek to defeat the grim reaper with every medical means at our disposal. When we "fail," we immediately spirit the corpse away and give it to the undertaker to make it look lifelike.

We don't even like to pronounce the word "death." We say "Aunt Sheila passed away last summer. We were so sorry to lose her." Or, with animals—"We had to put poor Fifi to sleep." These are euphemisms. You can almost hear Buddha saying, "Let's get real. We're talking about dying."

But death is scary. Especially when we realize that, as with aging, it applies to *ourselves.* Of course, we know intellectually that we will one day die. But don't we also have a deep-down resistance to that truth? Leo Tolstoy writes in *The Death of Ivan Ilych:*

> In the depth of his heart [Ivan] knew he was dying, but not only was he not accustomed to the thought, he simply did not and could not grasp it.
>
> The syllogism he had learnt from Kiezewetter's Logic: "Caius is a man, men are mortal, therefore Caius is mortal," had always seemed to him correct as applied to Caius, but certainly not as applied to himself. . . . "Caius really was mortal, and it was right for him to die; but for me, little Vanya, Ivan

Ilych, with all my thoughts and emotions, it's altogether a different matter. It cannot be that I ought to die. That would be too terrible."[3]

Don't many of us experience the same denial? Our self-awareness often works to keep us in Siddhartha's dream kingdom. In life's second half, we often awaken from this dream. We may not want to. In a materialist world view, death seems to threaten everything—our pleasures, our relationships, our identity. We are taught by our culture to be terrified of death.

However, sages throughout history have suggested the benefits of looking death squarely in the eye. The twentieth-century German philosopher Martin Heidegger wrote that an authentic awareness of our death was life-transforming.[4] As long as we believe we have limitless time and choices, we may not take them seriously or use them well. Why enjoy today's glories—the warm sunshine, the willow tree swaying in the wind, the brief encounters, the quiet moments alone? They'll be here tomorrow, and tomorrow, and tomorrow.

The truth is they might not be. If we really let this truth in, how we might suck the marrow from today! And how we might reshape our lives. Now, we tend to think, "I hate my job. Someday I'll find a new one." "I've always wanted to see Paris. Sooner or later I will." "Things aren't going great with my husband. But we'll get around to fixing it." Meanwhile time and opportunities drift by. As the saying goes, "Life is what happens to you while you're busy making other plans."

As a solution, Carlos Castaneda's Don Juan suggests keeping your own death near you as an advisor.[5] A strange concept. But remembering your death (whenever it might come) reminds you that opportunities are limited, each moment precious. It helps to clarify what is really worth focussing energy on, and what is a waste of time.

Buddha also sought that which is *beyond* time. If it's a delusion to believe we will never die, Buddha discovered through years of searching and meditation that death was also a delusion of sorts. He felt he had awakened to that which encompassed but also reached beyond death and decay. The materialist vision of the world was not the only picture.

Again, your vision of the transcendent may differ from that of a Buddhist. But the awareness of death, which often heightens in midlife and beyond, certainly places the issue before us.

In this way, life (or karma, or God) operates as an ideal teacher. How so? Such a teacher would seek to challenge us with ever-harder questions as we advance, each one preparing us for the next. In life's first part there are plenty of tricky problems. Who am I? How am I separate from Mommy and Daddy? How should I relate to them, and to other people? What is special and different about me? What are my proper tasks in life? To use a phrase from spiritual teacher Ram Dass, we are in "somebody training." Then, having mastered being somebody in childhood and young adulthood, we are ready for an even harder problem. Now that I am aging, how do I go beyond the somebody I thought I was? The body, roles, and relationships I based my identity on are all changing. What's left? Who am I really? And what, if anything, will remain after my death?

While these questions gain prominence in life's second half, they can seize our attention at any time. Buddha, after all, was a young man when he first confronted the specter of mortality, and so are many of us. An accident, an illness, or a loved one's death may suddenly propel us on a spiritual journey though we're still wet behind the ears.

This lesson was vividly taught to me by a strange incident many years back. I was in my late twenties, thoughts of aging and death far from my mind. In the midst of a vigorous swim in the Long Island Sound I suddenly felt a spasm of pain through my chest. Like any medical student, I possessed that dangerous thing: a little knowledge. Could this be a heart attack? I was seized by fear. But I also knew of "medical student syndrome" (you're sure you have every disease you're studying), so I laughed at myself as I swam on.

"I'm young, healthy, I live right—it can't be a heart attack. Surely, it's just a muscle pull." My calm returned but was immediately shattered again when a searing pain shot down my left arm—a second classic sign of a heart attack. The nerve pathways connected to the cardiac region are such that the pain of an infarction is often referred down the arm. No longer laughing, I climbed out of the water in a carefully controlled panic and drove to the nearest emergency room. I was led into a room, laid flat on a table, and hooked up to an EKG machine that would monitor my heart's electrical patterns for abnormalities.

My arrival had coincided with a car accident that was shortly to flood the ER with its victims. Physicians bustled about in preparation. They had little time for me. I lay there connected to a machine patiently recording patterns no one was available to read. Suddenly the crushing chest pain returned. Simultaneously, the EKG machine started screaming bloody murder. I knew it was programmed to make this noise when the heartbeat turned irregular. I frantically searched with my eyes for help. A physician rushed into the room, and I tried to get his attention. Oblivious, he merely grabbed the wall phone to discuss another case. Before I could catch him he vanished again.

I'll never forget the thoughts and feelings of that moment. It all seemed like one of those black comedies you enjoy in the movie theater, but not in real life. Here I lay surrounded by medical personnel, perhaps to die for lack of medical attention. And there was nothing I could do. I was tethered to the machine, immobilized, in an isolated room, seemingly in the midst of a heart attack. My thoughts turned inward. Was this death? If so, could I cope with it?

Answers struck me with clarity and force. Yes, I could cope with it, if I was really dying. Soon it would all be over. A heart attack seemed a quick and easy way to go. At the time I had no spiritual beliefs concerning an afterlife. When I am dead, I felt, I won't really be there to experience it.

On the other hand, what if I was having a heart attack, but *didn't die?* That seemed a very different sort of threat. It would mean that my most vital organ was dangerously weak. I'd live the rest of my days under a shadow: having had an episode at such a tender age, the possibility of a second, fatal attack would never be far from my thoughts. Any joy, any love I experienced could be seized from me at any moment. Could I live like that? I wondered. No. I simply didn't have the inner resources. I couldn't face this indeterminate death sentence.

Then, I was struck, clear as a bell, by an insight. To cope with this situation I'd have to find spiritual help. I had no idea exactly what that would look like. But I sensed that nowhere else could I find my needed strength. I had a promising career, a wonderful girlfriend, plenty of money, but it wasn't enough. Not in the face of death. I would need contact with the Transcendent—nothing less would do.

In many ways, I date the beginning of my serious spiritual journey to that moment in the emergency room. As with Buddha, it brought me face to face with my own mortality. It impelled me to a quest that continues to this day. This book records some of the sights I have seen along the path and some others I anticipate in my future. Perhaps it's appropriate that the process began in an emergency room. It was, after all, a place of *emergence,* as my spirit expanded and danced.

When I finally secured medical attention, it all came clear: I was perfectly O.K. The chest pains were the result of a muscle pull brought on by the strenuous exercise of swimming. The shooting pain down my left arm? I'd been stung by a jellyfish. The ER doctor informed me they were rampant at that time of year. What of that resurgence of chest pain in the ER, coupled with the screaming EKG machine? Simple. The cramping muscle had caused me to turn slightly, dislodging one of the EKG leads. But I was fine, perfectly fine. The machine, reconnected, signaled no abnormalities.

What a weird series of coincidences. Or had Spirit orchestrated it all for my edification? Can God use a jellyfish? Why not?! Whatever its source, I'll be forever grateful for that convergence of events.

A confrontation with death came to me at a young age. There's no settled timeframe for the actions of spirit. But as we age, we will experience many such moments, each with the capacity to shock us awake. Like Buddha we will vision a sick person, an old person, a corpse. But let us not avert our gaze. These figures, who first seem so ugly, may prove messengers sent for our aid.

�֎   ✖   ✖

Think of examples in your own life, or the lives of those around you, of illness, disability, or death. Which experiences were particularly powerful for you? (For example, discovering a breast lump? A chronic illness? The death of a parent or close friend?) Can you see ways in which such experiences awakened you and changed your priorities?

Have you been able to hang on to this awakeness in your daily life? If so, how does that still manifest? If not, how might you incorporate more fully into your life any truths you once realized?

✖

❈ *Guided Meditation* ❈

USING DEATH AS YOUR ADVISOR

(Note: You might wish to read this, and the other visualizations I supply, into a tape recorder; you may be able to enter more deeply into the experience as you listen to a tape with your eyes closed.)

Visualize yourself in a physician's antiseptic examining room. There is a scale for taking weights in one corner, a white porcelain sink in another. You are sitting half-dressed on the examining table. It's a little chilly. The physician, a middle-aged woman, strides in. After a long pause, she says, "I don't know how to break this to you, but the melanoma has proved malignant. I believe you only have one to two years left to live." You sit there, shocked.

Now imagine yourself at home, later, after you've had time to absorb the bad news. You are sitting in whatever room, whatever chair or sofa, feels most comfortable. You are deciding what you will do with that year or two remaining. Allow yourself to ponder the question. What experiences will you seek out? What other experiences will you refuse to waste time on anymore? What is really most important in your life? Most pleasurable? Most valuable? What dreams can you no longer postpone? Whatever thoughts come to mind, allow them.

When you are done, imagine yourself back in the doctor's examining room. You have been hastily called in. Imagine the physician striding in, somewhat red-faced. "I'm so sorry, and I'm embarrassed," she says. "Pathology mixed up the reports. Your lesion was completely benign. There were no signs of cancer. You'll live out your normal life span."

Now slowly bring the visualization to an end. Allow your awareness to return to the room you are now in, the present moment. For a brief time you had death as your advisor. Though the experience has receded, can you still use any of the teachings you received? Did it give you any guidance you can apply in your life?

❈   ❈   ❈

2

Loss as Liberation:

The Hindu Life Stages

When a householder sees his skin wrinkled, and his hair white, and the sons of his sons, then he may resort to the forest.

Abandoning all food raised by cultivation, and all his belongings, he may depart into the forest, either committing his wife to his sons, or accompanied by her.

Taking with him the sacred fire and the implements required for domestic sacrifices, he may go forth from the village into the forest and reside there, duly controlling his senses.

Let him offer those five great sacrifices according to the rule, with various kinds of pure food fit for ascetics, or with herbs, roots, and fruit. . . .

Let him always be industrious in privately reciting the Veda; let him be patient of hardships, friendly towards all, of collected mind, ever liberal and never a receiver of gifts, and compassionate towards all living creatures. . . .

In summer let him expose himself to the heat of five fires, during the rainy season live under the open sky, and in winter be dressed in wet clothes, thus gradually increasing the rigour of his austerities. . . . Making no effort to procure things that give pleasure, chaste, sleeping on the bare ground, not caring for any shelter, dwelling at the roots of trees.

But having thus passed the third part of a man's natural term of life in the forest, he may live as an ascetic during the fourth part of his existence, after abandoning all attachment to worldly objects. . . .

Let him always wander alone, without any companion, in order to attain final liberation, fully understanding that the solitary man, who neither forsakes nor is forsaken, gains his end.

He who has in this manner gradually given up all attachments and is freed from all the pairs of opposites, reposes in Brahman alone.

All that has been declared above depends on meditation; for he who is not proficient in the knowledge of that which refers to the Soul reaps not the full reward of the performance of rites.

The Laws of Manu, ed. Max Muller, trans. G. Buhler

THE STORY OF Buddha taught us that age can be the agent of awakenings. To learn how to work with these, how to systematically extend our awareness once we have been jolted awake, we can turn to a Hindu model for guidance.

The ancient *Laws of Manu* (collected around 100 B.C.–100 A.D.) lays out a comprehensive vision of the human life span. We have here only an excerpt; the text as a whole proposes a four-stage development. The first stage (*asrama*) is that of the student (*brahmacarya*), learning sacred texts and good habits of character from the master. Next, beginning with marriage, comes the householder (*grhastha*) stage. This is the time to pursue a profession and raise a family. So far, these life stages sound pretty familiar, even if described in foreign terms. We are reminded of our Western sense of childhood/adolescence and midlife, each a period of growth. But we tend to see later life as a downhill slide, whereas from the Indian perspective it's quite the reverse.

The true aim of life, in the Hindu view, is spiritual union with God. And the first two stages alone just won't get you there. Admittedly, the duties of the householder ground society and call a person beyond narrow self-interest. In that way this stage has a clear spiritual dimension. Yet it also has its limits: we are tied down by responsibilities and private concerns. To awaken fully we must transcend the ego-self.

We truly reach toward this spiritual adulthood in the third stage, the forest dweller (vanaprastha). "When a householder sees his skin wrinkled, and his hair white, and the sons of his sons" he, alone or together with his wife, is expected to leave career and family to live in the forest. (The asramas were prescribed for *men* of the three highest castes; hereafter I'll discard this gender and class bias.) The forest dweller is then free to devote him- or herself to the performance of ritual, the reciting of sacred texts, and the observation of rigorous austerities designed to free one from the body. All energies are directed toward union with Brahman, the divine ground of the universe.

After a period of retreat, the individual then enters the fourth stage, that of the wandering ascetic (sannyasa). Time to abandon all attachments, even those to the forest hut. Meditation and austerities increase, with the goal of attaining full enlightenment. If it is achieved, the ties to life and death are simultaneously broken. The person has escaped the wheel of reincarnation and experiences the bliss of union with God.

THE (LIKE IT OR NOT) ASCETIC

What does this model have to say to us? Maybe we can identify with some of the signs of aging mentioned: wrinkles, white hair, or grandchildren may be with us, or approaching in the not so distant future. But the instructions do not sound very appealing. Go live in the forest; "during the rainy season live under the open sky, and in winter be dressed in wet clothes . . . making no effort to procure things that give pleasure." "Thanks, but no thanks," most of us would reply.

On closer examination, the Hindu model, suitably reframed,

has much to offer us. Like it or not, we may fall prey to many of the same austerities that the forest dweller and wandering ascetic willingly choose. Just as the Hindu renunciate (considering stages three and four together) lets go of his/her profession, so do many of us in the West. This loss can be the result of company downsizing, forced retirement, or personal choice. With the job, a lot else can disappear—the associated prestige and security, and, often, the nice paycheck padded with years of seniority. So we may face some lifestyle cutbacks. Not as extreme, one hopes, as those of the Hindu ascetic "sleeping on the bare ground . . . dwelling at the roots of trees." Still, it can be a bitter pill to have to get by on less. We may have to forsake some accustomed comforts and pleasures. Then, too, these might be stolen by the aging process itself. The morning stiffness of arthritis; the petty humiliations of a weak bladder; an old back injury turned chronic—aren't these austerities even a Hindu might appreciate?

In both cultures, the years can also bring interpersonal losses. The Indian renunciate decides to be chaste. As we age, we may find that the diminishment of our drives or of available partners reduces our sexual activity. We may fear this loss. And whereas the Hindu leaves home and family, Westerners often face home and family leaving them. After all, the kids do grow up. One's parents may pass away. Even though perfectly "expected" and "natural," all this leaves a gaping hole. In addition, work relationships vanish when one leaves a job, and good friends die and move away. We may come to feel, as much as the renunciate, like one who "always wander[s] alone, without any companion." And just as the Hindu takes to forest and road, we may relocate. Perhaps we choose or are forced to move from our big old home to a more "sensible" alternative. Such changes may come quite late in life, or much earlier, as we confront limitations.

Here we see a paradox: what the Hindu seeks out seems like a horror to the Westerner. Losing a job, the kids gone, sexual diminishment, chronic aches, lifestyle cutbacks, leaving home, seeing friends and family members die—what worse fate could the gods impose? It's as if the very self is being blown to bits.

But this dissolution is, in a way, just what the Hindu wants. The self we've so identified with may be blocking us from our spiritual Self. When we blow up the ego-self, what's left is more than a pile of ashes. Rising from it, like a phoenix, can be a vastly expanded sense of who we are. Different cultures use different words to express this phenomenon. "I am the Divine Self, one with All." "I am a child of God." "I have an immortal Soul."

To the Hindu, aging is more than a series of meaningless losses. There are modes of liberation contributing to spiritual growth. If age strips away pride, pleasures, and profit, all the better. This process is a part of the karmic curriculum, challenging the little self. If our responsibilities are diminished, the time available to explore the sacred expands. Let us not flee these changes, but embrace them, utilizing them to the utmost.

Imagine yourself, like the Hindu renunciate, going off to the forest to pursue enlightenment. What things in your life would you definitely leave behind? (Think of particular chores, distractions, and habits of mind or emotion you'd like to be free of—paying the bills, perhaps, dealing with car problems, always feeling rushed, et cetera.) Make a list of these burdens and then put a line through the list to symbolize your renunciation.

Now make a second (hopefully smaller) list of things you'd bring with you to your forest retreat, just as the Hindu brings ritual implements. What would you want with you? Certain spiritual books, perhaps? A particular person to serve as friend or guide? Special objects from art or nature that help to ground your awareness? List the things you would take along.

Now ask yourself: Is there a way to create such a space of renunciation in my life? You probably can't troop off to the forest. But is there a place or time you can set aside to escape the things you wish, and to work with the healing presences you've listed?

❋

The Perceptual Flip

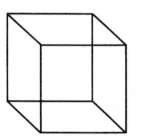

Let's further explore this shift of perspectives using a visual image. The diagram illustrates an object referred to in cognitive psychology as a Necker cube. If you look at it long enough, you'll see it undergo a perceptual flip. First one side seems to be coming out of the page toward you. You visually interpret this as the "front" of the cube. But suddenly, everything switches, and the same side now appears to be the "back." Where before the cube was pointing up to the left, now it seems to point down to the right, or vice versa. It's the same cube on paper, but not in your experience. All the lines and surfaces reverse meaning.

The Hindu model suggests this sort of reversal. Imagine the changes of aging as lines on the cube. Interpreted in a Western mode as loss and diminishment, they all lead one way. But what if we apply the perceptual flip? What if these changes can take on an opposite significance, representing modes of challenge, freedom, and growth? Suddenly our eye is led in the opposite direction. We find the gain even in the midst of loss.

For example, imagine a woman in her mid-forties, married, a successful medical technician. Her career is on the upswing, and she's the logical person to be promoted to an administrative position recently vacated. It doesn't happen. Company cost cutbacks do away with the position. Suddenly she feels frozen and frustrated in her job. At least this is balanced by a happy marriage—that is, until tragedy strikes some months later. Her husband, in his fifties, dies unexpectedly of a heart attack. What now for the widow?

She feels herself falling into depression. A chasm opens up that threatens to swallow her whole. So many losses. For a solid year she grieves. Finally, the seeds of life begin to bloom in the rich, black soil of her sadness. The loss of an old life bids her find herself anew. If she is not just her profession, not just a wife, who is she then?

Her quest takes her outward into new relationships and activities. She strengthens her friendship with three other women in her life. With one, she takes a class in yoga to loosen up her tired body and spirit. She also finds herself taking long walks alone. In the fading sun of the late afternoon, outward movement deepens into inward search. She discovers herself talking to her departed husband. "Why did you leave me?" she almost shouts. More quietly, in prayer, she asks the same of God. This first attempt at prayer is filled with complaint and self-pity. "Why did you do this to me? Where are you now that I need you?" She's got to speak what's real. But getting these feelings out makes room for something else to enter. How to describe it? As the late afternoon light deepens into the soft blue of early dusk, she feels the beginnings of peace. It's as if God's touch brushes gently across her forehead. Maybe she is not alone.

Over time, these spiritual baby steps deepen into a real faith journey. While valuing time spent with good friends, she also grows to love solitude. It's a time to write, think, pray, build a relationship with God. She'd never felt the need so strongly when her life was filled with husband and professional ambitions. One weekend a month she goes on retreat at a local spiritual center. There she finds inner direction that leads her down new paths: volunteer work at an AIDS clinic, a class in watercolors, God knows what else in the future. *She* surely doesn't. But she rests open to the delightful unknown.

Like the Necker cube, in this woman's transformation the meaning of events was reversed. Her losses guided her not only downward to depression but upward into the Spirit's embrace.

When we first look at a Necker cube, it often seems to reverse

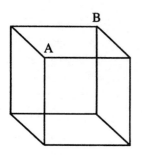

back and forth spontaneously. We're not sure why, and we feel little mastery over the process. But there are techniques we can use to help choose our perspective. For instance, when we focus on point A, as shown, this point will probably seem to come toward us from the page. Refocusing on point B can enable us to reverse the cube's direction.

In the same way, the meanings we find and the emotions we experience often depend on where we choose to place our focus. As Henri Nouwen and Walter Gaffney write, "Is aging a way to the darkness or a way to the light? . . . Ultimately, it can only be discovered and affirmed in the freedom of the heart. There we are able to decide between segregation and unity, between desolation and hope, between loss of self and a new, recreating vision. Everyone will age and die, but this knowledge has no inherent direction."[1] For a time the woman may see nothing but her losses, pushing against them like a tongue with a sore tooth. Not surprisingly, pain increases. But with time, she can refocus on the possibilities her losses offer: new closeness with friends, her inner self, her God. Point A or point B—so much depends on this choice. This book is meant to help you see a number of points in a way that can reorient your experience of aging toward positive and illuminating perspectives.

Certain caveats are in order. First, this mastery can't be gained just by the intellect. The sacred teachings in this book are reasonably easy to understand but hard to realize—make real in our lives. It takes work, and time, and not least of all, divine help. The whole self—body, mind, spirit, emotions, and actions—must be engaged.

Second, we must beware of seeing things in either-or terms. Just as the Necker cube really incorporates both perspectives, so life includes both misery and contentment, loss and liberation. To acknowledge this fact only enriches our vision. After all, our depth vision arises because we have two eyes taking in different perspectives. We risk reverting to a one-dimensional view if we try to see only the positive. "Cheer up! Your husband's death is your perfect karma. Isn't it wonderful?" We'd rightly give such a person a swat.

The losses are too real for that Pollyanna treatment. A deeper spirituality keeps life's suffering in view, while also finding the grace. If we deny our grief, it will only keep us frozen.

Rachel Naomi Remen, a physician, tells the story of a patient with bone cancer whose leg was removed at the hip. Just twenty-four, he felt bitter at the injustice of his fate. For over two years he worked through his despair and rage, using painting, imagery, and psychotherapy. He was able to help others who had suffered physical losses, sharing his own pain and healing. He and his physician sat down to review their work together.

> He showed me one of his earliest drawings. I had suggested to him that he draw a picture of his body. He had drawn a picture of a vase, and running through the vase was a deep black crack. This was the image of his body and he had taken a black crayon and had drawn the crack over and over again. It was very, very painful because it seemed to him that this vase could never function as a vase again. It could never hold water.
>
> Now, several years later, he came to this picture and looked at it and said, "Oh, this one isn't finished. . . . He picked a yellow crayon and putting his finger on the crack he said, "you see, here—where—it is broken—this is where the light comes through." And with the yellow crayon he drew light streaming through the crack in his body.[2]

Few of us will ever face this man's particular disability. But as Ralph Waldo Emerson said, "There is a crack in everything God has made."[3] As we age, the cracks begin to show. Are they just about darkness and brokenness? Or are they also a place for the light of Spirit to stream through? The truth is they're both. Let's embrace it all.

Think of some of the changes of aging, particularly those you've experienced as loss. (A friend moving away? Being laid off from a job? A degenerative physical problem?) You might write these down along the top lines of the Necker cube.

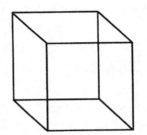

Ask yourself: What negative thoughts and feelings have I had around these events? (Sadness, fear, loneliness, rage?) Look at the Necker cube, and see the lines leading one way.

Now ask: How have I been, or could I be, spiritually matured and freed up by these events? What are the hidden gifts? (Even if it seems artificial, let yourself play with this idea and find what you will.)

Now look at the Necker cube and see the lines reverse direction.

MODELS OF AGING

In today's society, people are growing old in unprecedented numbers. At the turn of the century in America the average life expectancy was about forty-seven. Now it's over seventy-five. Two-thirds of all the increase in the human life span since time immemorial has occurred in this century! The result has been an ever-growing population of elders. Since 1900, the number of Americans over sixty-five has shot up from three million (4 percent of the population) to thirty-three million (13 percent).

What are we to do with these later years? For some, this is a very present question. Even for those of us who are younger, it is an issue well worth pondering. The sooner, and the better, we prepare for our aging, the more likely we are to meet it on our terms rather than being buffeted by time's gale-force winds.

So far I've discussed two responses to the challenge of aging. The current Western model focuses on diminishment and loss, the Hindu on spiritual expansion. But this contrast is oversimplified. In fact, there are ideas circulating in our culture of how to build a good old age; I'll examine three before returning to the Hindu perspective. First, in what I'll call the *sociomedical model* of successful aging, much used by professional gerontologists, aging represents a series of social and medical problems to be addressed. The focus is on applying the appropriate personal, professional, and governmental remedies. There are diseases and disabilities of age. Also, older people often face economic quandaries—how to pay for shelter, food, and increasing health care costs, just when their earning power may be going down the tubes. Finally, there are psychosocial problems; for example, the sense of loneliness and uselessness that plagues many of the elderly.

Within the sociomedical model, a variety of solutions are presented. The liberal might focus on building an adequate social welfare network. The conservative emphasizes the role of the private sector, the traditional family, and personal responsibility in helping us avoid these afflictions. The holistically-minded might stress disease prevention through diet, exercise, and the like, while medical researchers develop new forms of treatment. Still, these are variations on a common theme: aging as a series of problems to be solved.

Much good has surely come from this approach. Who would want to do without the safety net of Medicare, for example, or preventive measures for the diseases of later life? The sociomedical model clearly has its role. However, as Betty Friedan argues force-fully in *The Fountain of Age*, this model has also done its share of harm. Because it highlights the losses of later life, not the creative possibilities, age comes to seem like a litany of diminishments—of health, attractiveness, cognitive ability, income, status—the list goes on and on. Admittedly, the sociomedical model tries to remedy such dysfunctions. But at the same time it reinforces the sense of aging as dysfunction, a kind of grim disease.

Many popular books, however, say quite the opposite, present-ing what I call the *productive model* of aging. We don't need to fo-cus on dysfunction, they argue. Once we put aside ageism, we discover that older people can be just as active and productive as anyone else. Inspirational examples are given of octogenarian ac-tivists, artists who excelled in later life, lovers who performed in the sack well into their nineties. The message is clear: No slowing down! The good old age is busy and engaged. There are causes to support, groups to join, books to write, house repairs to oversee. We can keep going until the day we drop. As Betty Friedan writes, "Maybe I would be lucky enough to die with life, as Maury did, a page half written on my open pad, with a sudden heart attack or in an airplane crash."[4]

Clearly, this model, too, has done its share of good. We all ben-efit by countering stereotypes of old-age incapacity. But it also has its downside. It's not really a model of the elder years so much as of a midlife indefinitely prolonged. There's a dream that somehow we can conquer nature, overcome all the frailties of later life. We can be like the Eveready Bunny—just keep going and going. What hap-pens when we find out it just isn't so? We may become fearful, or enraged. We may sink into depression or feel guilty for having failed. The productive model didn't prepare us for life's losses.

This model is linked to the Western capitalist focus on produc-tivity. We learn to measure our worth by how much we can make or do, not just who we are. Over the years we internalize the pressure. With the empty nest and retirement looming, we feel our self-worth profoundly threatened. The solution? Get busy with a dozen new worthwhile projects.

Is this all the later years are about? Don't we yearn for some relief from the constant rush and demands? Some retired individuals complain that they've never been so busy since they stopped working. What of the rest and enjoyment they long for?

A third picture of the good old age, which I call the *consumer model,* is, again, apparently the reverse of the one before. Here the elder is viewed as happily rid of work requirements, freed up for a life of pleasant leisure. Time to finally curl up in front of the fireplace with a good, long novel. Or maybe we want to move to a new area for the weather, or companionship. If we wish, there's many a retirement community offering nice housing, fun activities, well-prepared meals, all spiced up with outings to malls and museums. What's not to like?

Rather than a serious alternative to the productive model, the consumer model is more its flip side. It too flows from the values of our economic system. It encourages us not to produce but to consume, treating life like a commodity for pleasure.

Many are left without the financial resources to play. Those images of tanned and tennis-filled years can seem but a cruel joke if you're struggling to make ends meet. Even those fortunate enough to play, though, may not find the game that fulfilling. A life devoid of responsibilities can also lack significance. One older individual I know compared his retirement community to a cruise ship. To live there seems pleasant for a time but can finally grow trivial, boring, disconnected. The ship is heading for no particular port. Missing is the call to social contribution and psychospiritual growth.

These models share a common problem. Though they seek to design a positive old age, they don't help us find deep meaning in later life. What's our expanded life span for? They variously answer: it's a time to stave off afflictions; to keep busy and productive; to kick back and enjoy. There's some merit to each response when suitably applied. But none of them seems to truly satisfy. They are not powerful enough to fulfill the longings of the human spirit. We sense something more is at stake, that the long trajectory of life shouldn't culminate in such a fizzle. Surely the later years have a meaning of their own, one that involves a sense of wholeness and fruition.

Here the Hindu account proves its worth. Leaving out some of the specific details—Vedic recitations, fire sacrifices, and the like—Hinduism proposes an alternate paradigm, which I'll call the *spiritual model* of aging. According to this model, the later years are not simply a time to battle one's decline or keep oneself occupied with business and pleasures. Rather, life's second half provides unique opportunities for soul-expansion. Even the losses associated with the passage of years can provide modes of liberation. As the story of Buddha suggested, such losses can help us awaken. They thrust us against the limits of our ego-self, and invite us to go beyond. They provide the impetus, the maturity, the leisure, to plunge into the spiritual quest. For some, this transition to renunciation can come early, maybe in our thirties, forties, or fifties, provoked by life's upheavals. For others, it will be associated with retirement or the approach of death. But it is never too soon to begin the work of "aging gracefully" by contacting the source of grace.

Clearly we need not make this turn toward the sacred. Even in ancient times, the four-stage prescription was an idealized construct; there is no evidence that many people followed its prescriptions fully. We are tempted now by any number of distractions. In many ways, it's much easier to go to the doctor's office, or the workroom, or the tennis court, than to set off on a forest retreat. But if we do go to the forest, we may be surprised at what we find there. Concealed in the midst of its wild regions are the infinite riches of Spirit.

✳ ✳ ✳

Currently, which model of aging seems to have most power in your awareness? Probably the spiritual model has some allure, or you wouldn't be reading this book. But how about the others? Do you focus a good deal on the sociomedical issues surrounding your aging (health maintenance, financial planning, and so on)? Are you the sort more drawn to consumerist pleasures as you age? Or to continued high-level productivity?

Whatever model seems to have most power in your life, can you see positive opportunities and experiences it opens to you? Conversely, can you see its limits? Are there experiences, sides of yourself, that are **shut off** *by the model(s) of aging you've been using?*

※

❋ *Guided Meditation* ❋

THE FOREST RETREAT

Imagine that you have come to that time in your life when it is right to go off on a forest retreat. You may return when the retreat's purpose is achieved. But for now it's time to depart on an adventure.

Friends and family members have gathered around you in a circle to mark this special moment. If you can, visualize who you want to be present. These are some of the most important, and loving, people in your life. They are there to honor all you have meant to them, but also to celebrate your freedom. You are setting out to *expand* your spirit. So you must let go of much of who you "thought you were."

Imagine yourself placing in the center of the circle, one by one, a piece of clothing or an object—each a symbol of a role or identity that has been yours. Are (were) you a businesswoman? Perhaps place your briefcase or business suit in the circle center. An avid runner? Place your running shoes there. A devoted father? Lay down the baseball glove you used to play with your son. One by one, imagine laying aside symbols of who you have been. Continue, until you feel you are almost naked, like the Hindu renunciate. This is the only way to go on retreat.

You may feel sad to let go of all you have been. But notice in each case: the symbol is not *you*. You still remain as someone separate from all your roles and identities. Experience the joy of that, and the freedom in your release.

Now imagine yourself saying goodbye to all the people in the circle, goodbye to all the objects in the circle. You turn around to begin your walk toward the forest. What does it all feel like? Is there fear? Grief? Loneliness? Do you have a sense of purpose and excitement? Know that the forest is not a cold, forlorn place. Waiting there will be the thing you most want. Let yourself imagine what that might be. What truly awaits you in that forest of your soul?

❋   ❋   ❋

3

Embracing Change:
The Yin and Yang

Master Ssu, Master Yü, Master Li, and Master Lai were all four talking together. "Who can look upon inaction as his head, on life as his back, and on death as his rump?" they said. "Who knows that life and death, existence and annihilation, are all a single body? I will be his friend!"

The four men looked at each other and smiled. There was no disagreement in their hearts and so the four of them became friends.

All at once Master Yü fell ill. Master Ssu went to ask how he was. "Amazing!" said Master Yü. "The Creator is making me all crookedy like this! My back sticks up like a hunchback and my vital organs are on top of me. My chin is hidden in my navel, my shoulders are up above my head, and my pigtail points at the sky. It must be some dislocation of the yin and yang!"

Yet he seemed calm at heart and unconcerned. Dragging himself haltingly to the well, he looked at his reflection and said, "My, my! So the Creator is making me all crookedy like this!"

"Do you resent it?" asked Master Ssu.

"Why no, what would I resent? If the process continues,

33

perhaps in time he'll transform my left arm into a rooster. In that case, I'll keep watch on the night. Or perhaps in time he'll transform my right arm into a crossbow pellet and I'll shoot down an owl for roasting. Or perhaps in time he'll transform my buttocks into cartwheels. Then, with my spirit for a horse, I'll climb up and go for a ride. What need will I ever have for a carriage again?

"I received life because the time had come; I will lose it because the order of things passes on. Be content with this time and dwell in this order and then neither sorrow nor joy can touch you. . . .

Suddenly Master Lai grew ill. Gasping and wheezing, he lay at the point of death. His wife and children gathered round in a circle and began to cry. Master Li, who had come to ask how he was, said, "Shoo! Get back! Don't disturb the process of change!"

Master Lai said, "A child, obeying his father and mother, goes wherever he is told, east or west, south or north. And the yin and yang—how much more are they to a man than father or mother! Now that they have brought me to the verge of death, if I should refuse to obey them, how perverse I would be! What fault is it of theirs? The Great Clod burdens me with form, labors me with life, eases me in old age, and rests me in death. So if I think well of my life, for the same reason I must think well of my death. . . . Where could he send me that would not be all right? I will go off to sleep peacefully, and then with a start I will wake up."

Chuang Tzu, *Basic Writings*, trans. Burton Watson

MASTER YÜ'S DOING FINE. Admittedly, his body isn't. He's suffering from a crippling condition that leaves him hunchbacked and dragging. Some sort of scoliosis? Arthritis? Osteoporosis? He doesn't have the tools of modern medicine at his disposal. But he seems to have access to something even more valuable, for he remains "calm at heart and unconcerned." How so? Whence his ability to laugh with his friends in the midst of this tragedy?

And what of Master Lai, facing death? Surely we can understand why his wife and children are in tears. Their loss will be immeasurable when he dies. But how much more so his own loss, for to die is to have one's whole world dissolve. Not just the body is threatened with extinction, but the joy of a cool breeze in the early evening, the look of the stars, the wonderful novels one has read or never gotten to, the grandchildren one so longs to see—all is swirled away into death's black hole. So much to grieve for at once. What heart can withstand it?

In the last chapter we spoke of the ability to flip our vision of loss and find liberation. How does one accomplish this alchemy? The Taoist masters can help us. What they go through in this story—bodily distortion, disability, and decay, we may have to face as well. Yet they do not grieve, but face their fate with equanimity, even a sort of contemplative delight.

The masters' secret, it turns out, is nothing secret; this Taoist story lays everything bare. The illness of these two men is the occasion for them to present their teachings clearly and succinctly. After all, they have no time to waste. As winter strips trees down to their essential frame, so the elder and sage get right to the point; no frills obscure the message.

"If I think well of my life," says Master Lai, "for the same reason I must think well of my death."

We may feel that the more we love our life, the more we should dread and despise that which destroys it. But Master Lai states that if life and death are opposites, they are not locked in mortal combat but joined in intimate embrace. From the moment you are born, you begin to die. Furthermore, from Lai's perspective, death is the gateway through which new life arises. "I will go off to sleep peacefully, and with a start I will wake up."

Here, then, is the first teaching: nature's opposites, such as death and birth, sleep and waking, are like two sides of a coin. It is foolish to affirm one and deny the other. Admittedly, we sometimes do. My young daughter often wails when it's time for her nap. No matter how tired she is, she fights against sleep. She doesn't want to miss a thing. As a father, I know that her wakeful moments are enhanced by a good rest, and that, conversely, good rest flows from an active day; the two are mutually necessary and harmoniously conjoined. As she grows up, she will come to understand. Lai proclaims this grownup knowledge, combined with the trust of a child. "Where could [the Creator] send me that would not be all right?" Life and death, wakefulness and sleep, are part of the universal harmony.

The first "secret," then, is the need to accept this complementarity of opposites. This leads directly to the second secret: the need to flow equably with life's changes. Youth gives way to age; morning to evening; health to illness. If we cling to one and resist the other, we must always suffer.

Don't we often do so? In the midst of summer's heat we long for the cold breezes of winter. When winter comes, we would trade all the snow piled on our doorstep for one piña colada sipped in the tropical sun. We desire most that which we don't have. Sometimes this perversity seems stamped on human nature. But this Taoist story suggests it is not. We can cultivate the ability to affirm that which the universe presents us with *now*. If it is winter, let us cavort in the snow and recognize its shining beauty. A single spider's web coated in frost can be more precious than diamonds to the discerning eye. If it's summer, well, then, let us glory in sweat! What better opportunity to fling a football through the air; bicycle to the lake's age and stand, regarding; or snooze away the afternoon, a novel upended over our eyes, shading us with its pages. Let there be winter in winter, summer in summer. So this is the sage's secret? How simple.

But again, what's easy to understand can be hard to apply, especially when facing Master Yü's predicament: a crippling disease. Though the story doesn't provide details, we can imagine all that his illness has robbed from him. Perhaps he loved to take long walks in the country. Now, "dragging himself haltingly," he no longer can.

Perhaps he was once a master wheelmaker. (Maybe this is why he imagines his buttocks transformed into cartwheels.) But his crooked body is no longer sufficient to the work. Perhaps not long ago he was regarded as rather an attractive catch by women of the village. Now his grotesque appearance has driven them away. Any change entails losses—something old makes way for the new—but with certain changes, the losses are particularly evident, and they squeeze us like a fist around a vital organ.

Who wouldn't scream out in pain? Only someone well culti-vated in embracing change. Someone, in short, like Master Yü. His focus is not on what he has no longer—his youth, good health, his strong, straight body. When all that was around, thanks to the Cre-ator, he made the most of what he was given. But now the Creator has brought a new gift; that too, must be gratefully accepted. Being free of lamentation, self-pity, and resentment, Master Yü can find the hidden graces even in his losses. If his left arm is turned into a rooster, he'll keep watch on the night. If his right arm becomes a crossbow pellet, all the better for hunting. These are playful exam-ples, but the principle is clear. No matter what distortions his ill-ness imposes, he will find ways to accept them, work with them, and embrace the new possibilities they present.

The personal account of a Maryknoll sister provides a contem-porary example. She was struck by rheumatoid arthritis, a progres-sive, crippling joint disease, with consequences not unlike those borne by Master Yü. At first, she raged against her illness. She was the principal of a Peruvian school, and the disease, against her will, forced her to return to the States for treatment. Finally, praying be-fore a statue of Christ in the hospital, she came to embrace her own stigmata.

> I remember thinking that even though my hands were going to
> be broken and crooked, they would still be sacred to me. I'd
> use them to bring something to somebody, I didn't know what.
> My hands could be the compassionate hands of Christ as
> much as the hands of the doctors and nurses.

So I sought to be able to enter into the world of the sick, and to live with the mystery of suffering. . . . I returned to Peru at a lower altitude. Almost everything had changed, especially my attitude toward the people I was working with. I could feel their terrible poverty and pain in a whole new way. . . . How often I'd rushed around trying to solve people's problems without really seeing them—the pain in their faces, the insecure eyes, the nervous hands, all expressions of the hurt inside. It was only when suffering had actually touched me that I began to feel their condition. . . .

And so my ministry changed. It became the ministry of walking together. Some of us with physical disabilities joined together to share our experiences. . . . Our pain and weakness and deformity proved to be teachers of a great mystery, a small introduction into the kind of dying from which new spirit is born. . . . Having been brought low, it was just a matter of standing humbly before others, and presenting a visible sign of hope by some silent testimony.[1]

We see here someone enabled by effort and grace to work with the changes that life has brought. "So the Creator is making me all crookedy like this!" After passing through her period of desolation, this woman found a way to affirm her new life. The illness deepened her inward journey, and carried her out of herself.

❊   ❊   ❊

Master Yü proclaims, "So the Creator is making me all crookedy like this!" Where in your life have you felt points of crookedness—some disability, perhaps, some physical or emotional weakness, or an unfortunate turn of fate? (These crookednesses need not be associated with aging—some are with us even from birth.)

✳

Master Yü then talks playfully of the uses of his crookedness—"perhaps in time he'll transform my right arm into a crossbow pellet and I'll shoot down an owl for roasting." How have your own points of crookedness yielded surprising uses? (Think of how they might have deepened you as a person, opened up new options, stimulated new talents or associations.) Can you celebrate, with Master Yü, even crooked gifts? (If you don't really feel that, better to be honest and explore your true feelings.)

✳

THE YIN AND THE YANG

The wisdom of a Master Yü or Lai does not arise in a vacuum. Few of us can attain psychospiritual heights without climbing on the shoulders of others—that is, being trained in a preexisting tradition. Any scientist-in-training begins by absorbing an existing body of knowledge, and so does the spiritual seeker in need of direction. There is a tradition that these masters draw on, a world view that underlies their joyful acceptance even of aging, illness, and death.

Master Lai explains: "A child, obeying his father and mother, goes wherever he is told, east or west, south or north. And the yin and yang—how much more are they to a man than father or mother!" The key lies in this notion of yin and yang.

According to ancient Chinese cosmology, the universe arises out of, and everywhere manifests, the interplay of these two powers. The term "yin" first designated the shaded, or northerly, side of a mountain, and "yang" referred to the side facing the sun. During the "Spring and Autumn Period" of Chinese history (722–481 B.C.), the terms were often used in their root meaning, but by the latter part of that era they had come to incorporate a wide variety of other associations. Yin was identified with the cool and dark, yang with the warm and bright. Yin was understood as the female principle associated with the earth, yang was male and associated with heaven. Yin represented passivity; yang, activity; yin, the moon and water; yang, the sun and fire; and so on. The ancient Chinese were fascinated with such classificatory systems, and the lists can seem endless. But a general principle underlies this play: that the universe is structured through a harmony of opposites.

The yin-yang symbol helps us to understand this principle. It has become a pervasive, somewhat trivialized icon in Western culture. (I recently saw it used in an ad run by tobacco companies!) But the symbol encodes an entire world view.

The first thing we notice is a circle divided into two parts. The dark side represents the yin, or female, principle; the light side, the yang. However, we also see a small spot of light at the heart of the dark half, and vice versa. The dots suggest that yin and yang are not mutually exclusive. Rather, they intermingle, each one arising from its opposite. The universe yields a plethora of examples. In the middle of the brightest afternoon (yang), the sun has reached its apex and is just beginning to set (yin). So yin arises from the heart of yang. The converse is true as well. Let me illustrate this idea with a personal example. My birthday happens to be December 22, right at or around the winter solstice, the time when the sun is farthest from the equator, yielding (in the Northern Hemisphere) the shortest day of the year. Winter officially begins in this cold, dark (yin) time. But the winter solstice also marks a turning point; from here on, the days begin to lengthen. Yang is in ascent. Hence ancient winter solstice festivals celebrate rebirth, an association preserved by the timing of Christmas. Yang is birthing right at the heart of yin.

My daughter's birthday, it just so happens, is June 22, the summer solstice. It's the longest day of the year, but henceforth the days shorten. Here yin arises from out of yang.

According to this principle, then, the universe oscillates rhythmically between opposing poles. This movement is captured in the yin-yang symbol's circular outline. Trace the circle to the right and sooner or later you find yourself travelling back to the left. Go up, and reaching the peak, you find yourself travelling down. So day gives rise to night, summer to winter, birth to death, activity to rest, and vice versa, the world in circular movement. Hence, Master Lai's confidence in facing death: "I will go off to sleep peacefully, and then with a start I will wake up." Everything gives rise to its opposite.

To be honest, most of us wouldn't be quite so trusting. In general, we're all right with being alive. But when the aging process carries us around the circle toward death, we may scream and kick against the current. How else to account for the huge health care expenditures relating to the last few months of life? We are fighting a hated enemy.

Even in day-to-day life, we tend to value certain states (for example, happiness and good health) and scorn others (sadness, illness). We want to be good and not bad, loved and not left, winners and not losers; the list goes on and on. We have a hard time accepting the notion that opposites are necessary to one another and complementary.

In fact, would we even know what happiness was if we didn't have sadness to contrast it with? And it would be boring if every day were sunny, never a drop of rain. (My apologies to southern Californians.) Nor could one always be pleasantly sated with food, or sex, or rest. The pleasure of each is dependent on the relief of an associated lack (hunger, horniness, exhaustion). We know this intellectually. But other parts of us often say *"Naaah!*—I want it all, *now,* and *constantly."*

Even when we try to restrain this voice we may end up with one-sidedness rather than yin-yang harmony. Western philosophy and religion is filled with examples. Plato, for instance, was far from a greedy sensualist, but in criticizing such values, he created his own series of static dualisms. In his more extreme moments, he made it clear that he thought the soul was to be cultivated and the body squelched. We should seek heavenly Forms, and escape this imperfect world. Hence, death was finally superior to life, reason to emotion, and the eternal to that which changes.

We might term such views (somewhat ponderously) hierarchical dualism. We can picture such a structure by looking at the diagram in the margin, juxtaposed to the yin-yang symbol. In hierarchical dualism, two terms are seen as in opposition. There is no seed of one in the other, as with the yin-yang symbol. A rigid line indicates that "never the twain shall meet" except to do battle along the front that separates them. For example, a religious enthusiast may preach good versus evil, God versus Satan, spirit versus flesh, humility versus pride. The one is seen as thoroughly opposed to the other. Moreover, in each case, it's clear which half of the duality is better. Hence the term *hierarchical* dualism—there is a definite hierarchy of values. The diagram pictures this as the ascendancy of the light over the dark.

The yin-yang symbol portrays a very different relationship. The line dividing yin and yang is never rigid. The one principle curves into the other, and each overlaps its boundaries. Neither yin nor yang is ranked above the other. Though we may have particular desires at particular times, summer is not better than winter, day than night, life than death, reason than emotion, spirit than flesh, or male than female. According to this view, hierarchical dualism simply misunderstands the universe. It denies that opposing terms are interdependent, that the good resides not in X-versus-Y but the harmonious whole that incorporates both. "Who knows that life and death, existence and annihilation, are all a single body? I will be his friend!"

This principle can sound like facile relativism. On a given day, why live rather than die, why do anything rather than anything else, if everything is equally part of the whole? In the Chinese tradition, however, the notion of yin-yang is used to provide definite direction. To explain, I'll return to the very first appearance of the terms, in the *I Ching* ("Book of Changes"). Possibly the oldest book in existence, the *I Ching* is a tool of divination, based on a system of sixty-four hexagrams (six-lined figures). Each one represents a unique combination of broken (yin) and unbroken (yang) lines. Together, the constellation of yin-yang energies embodied in a hexagram designates a particular state in the universal flow, as well as the responses appropriate to it.

An example: one begins by posing a question to the *I Ching*—say, "Is this the right time to expand my business?" One then throws the *I Ching,* using yarrow sticks (an ancient method) or, more simply, coins, generating the hexagram's lines one by one. Imagine that six throws yield the hexagram pictured here, which is entitled "Stagnation." Like all hexagrams, it is seen as composed of two trigrams (three-lined figures) whose interaction determines the hexagram's meaning. The problem here is the sharp disjunction between the upper trigram, composed entirely of yang lines (the sign for "heaven"), and the lower trigram, entirely yin (signifying "earth"). In the words of one ancient interpreter, "The creative (heaven) and the receptive (earth) do not intersect forming the condition for Stagnation. An enlightened person, therefore, is reserved in his behavior and in that way avoids misfortune."[2] According to the hexagram, now is clearly no time for ambitious plans. The universe would not cooperate. Better to wait until conditions change; they will, as yin-yang energies shift.

Do you believe in this stuff? Maybe so, maybe not. For my purposes, what matters is the world view implied. The *I Ching* portrays a universe constantly in flux; if a person's actions are to succeed, they must be appropriate to the time. It would be self-defeating to expand one's business when conditions are aligned against it. On the other hand, when circumstances shift, one must be ready to act. To be too yin (passive) in a yang moment allows opportunity to slip past. The wise person knows to go with the flow. As Ecclesiastes says, "For everything there is a season, and a time for every matter under heaven."

We see this flexibility demonstrated by the two sages of our story. If "the Creator is making me all crookedy like this," then Master Yü knows how to flow with it. No state is devoid of creative opportunity: one simply accepts its restrictions and embraces its potentials. In the same way, Master Lai adjusts to impending death: just another point on the yin-yang circle.

✸ ✸ ✸

Can you think of some times when your life underwent an important shift? (Perhaps this shift was an inner change, physical or emotional. Or perhaps it involved something external—moving to a new home, having a baby, starting a new job, et cetera.) Make a list of just a few of these key change-points.

✸

Taking them one by one, ask yourself: Was I able to "embrace the change"— go with the flow and make the best of it? Identify parts of your personality that assisted you in this process—for example, being "easy-going" or an "optimist."

✸

*Now, for each change, try to identify your **points of resistance.** What can get in the way of change for you? Lack of trust in the universe? Difficulty grieving loss? Being "set in your ways"? Fear of the unknown? Don't condemn yourself for what you find, or immediately try to fix it. Just see what you see.*

✸

JUNG AND OLD

How can we apply this wisdom to the aging process? Some suggestions are provided by a decidedly Western source, C. G. Jung. Originally a disciple of Freud, he broke with traditional psychoanalysis to pursue his interest in collective archetypes of the human spirit, often represented in myth and religion. Whereas Freud focused primarily on childhood development, Jung was equally sensitive to life's later stages. He wrote:

> A human being would certainly not grow to be seventy or eighty years old if this longevity had no meaning for the

species to which he belongs. The afternoon of human life
must also have a significance of its own and cannot be merely
a pitiful appendage to life's morning.[3]

Here the Chinese world view provides a vocabulary. We might
say that life's "morning" is a *yang* time. The sun is in its ascent, and
so are the ego's powers, as the young man or woman sets out to pop-
ulate and conquer the world. Within our own society, these yang
values are particularly rewarded. We read admiring tales of aggressive entrepreneurs, of "superwomen" balancing children and careers, or successful actors or sports stars who have reached the
pinnacle of success. Every month boasts some technological breakthrough that enhances our (yang) mastery of nature. Faster
computers, new medical procedures, state-of-the-art audio equip-
ment—the list is endless. Even when it comes to our bodies, yang
is in. Who wants soft curves anymore? *Hard* is where it's at, firm
muscle suggesting youthful power and discipline. God forbid anything should sag!

But the Chinese message is that yang needs to be comple-
mented by yin. Whether in Chinese medicine, psychology, or politics, unbalanced energies pose a danger. And perhaps we can see
that in our own society. The overpraise of masculine, yang values
has done damage to men and women alike. When competition is
valued more than caring, aggression over accommodation, everyone
suffers. And our yang attitudes toward the body set us up for frustration. We may declare "No sagging!" but nature has other plans.
Our battle to conquer nature also has more global dangers: acid
rain, the loss of the ozone layer, soaring cancer rates, deforestation.
In the words of the *Tao Te Ching*:

> Do you think you can take over the universe and improve it?
> I do not believe it can be done.
>
> The universe is sacred.
> You cannot improve it.

> If you try to change it, you will ruin it.
> If you try to hold it, you will lose it.[4]

There is a social value to aging. The sun may be descending in life's afternoon, but that also means that yin is growing; and this is the energy needed to rebalance our culture. If growing older helps us to grow in acceptance and tolerance (yin energy), what better contribution could we give the world? If the later years also lead us to slow down, all the better. As I discuss further in chapter 7, our rush-rush-get-it-done-yesterday world is in need of a healing pause. So instead of honking at the slow driver ("Speed up, old man!") maybe we do better to emulate his pace. And so what if we don't keep up with the latest software package? Perhaps nature (and we) would be better off without our heedless plunge into each new technology.

Maybe it's time to say *"Yin is in!"* and value the virtues of life's second half.

On the other hand, we need to consider personal differences, not just an overarching theory. Aging, in a general way, may be about yin over yang—slowing down, contemplation, gentle wisdom, and the like. But this is not always true for the individual.

Jung, as well as the Taoists, was particularly attentive to the importance of gender difference. He believed that every human being had a store of both "feminine" (yin) and "masculine" (yang) traits. However, "in the first half of life, unequal use is made."[5] We emphasize those parts of the psyche that are "appropriate" to our biological sex. (See chapter 5 for a further discussion.) From childhood, the boy is taught to "be a man" and suppress all effeminate characteristics. "Don't cry. Don't be weak. Tough it out. Don't be a *girl.*" Conversely, the little girl is discouraged from being too "masculine"—that is, aggressive, risk-taking, self-concerned. In life's first half, we can grow entrenched in our gender roles. They seem so crucial to "who I am."

Jung suggests that, as we age, this imperative is left behind somewhat. With the loss of muscle mass, the passing of the reproductive years, hormonal shifts, and the like, the bodies of men and women grow more similar. So do their psyches, according to Jung. In life's second half, repressed parts of the soul demand their due. The aggressive businessman, hitting fifty, may feel the need to downshift—relax, make time. Yang energy changes over to yin. Perhaps he starts spending weekends in the garden and playing with his grandchildren. Conversely, his wife, who was rather gentle and submissive, might now allow her "masculine" side to emerge. She wants to do what she never did before—perhaps manage her own business. And she pursues this dream with an aggressiveness that surprises both her husband and herself. She will no longer be defined as Mrs. Somebody Else. Yin is shifting over to yang. In fact, Gail Sheehy asserts that this pattern is found repeatedly even in widely disparate cultures: "Each sex [in later life] adds some of the characteristics that distinguished its opposite in First Adulthood, women becoming more independent and assertive, men more expressive and emotionally responsive."[6]

Though there is much truth in such a scenario, we also must be wary of stereotyping men and women. Both the Jungian and the yin-yang system do so to a degree. While neither identifies "male" or "female" as better, they both associate the genders with stereotypical characteristics: aggression versus submission, hard versus soft, and so on. Happily, we have come to question these dichotomies. Clearly there are tough women and soft men in every stage of life.

Leaving aside rigid gender categories, the Jungian and Taoist message remains powerful. In life's second half we strive toward psychic wholeness. What was unbalanced seeks correction. If we were yang in early life, now our yin self calls out for expression. If we were yin, maybe it's time to beef up the old yang.

However, even this schema is a bit oversimplified. It tends to draw a monolithic contrast between life's first and second half. Clearly that's not how people work. We don't have one set personality until age forty, then undergo a magical shift, living out opposite traits until the day we die. Like the yin-yang symbol, all lines are curved, all figures interpenetrating. Movement is slow and organic and turns round and round the circle.

Even in life's second half we can expect many changes. We may, for example, go through an active phase, then find ourselves growing contemplative. Perhaps for a good six months we withdraw into the self. We refuse social engagements, go to the office less, and spend more time just walking and thinking. Then a day comes when whatever soul work we were doing feels complete. With a burst of energy, we start calling up friends, signing up for courses, reengaging in business. Yin has given way to yang; we sense the hexagrams shifting.

The *I Ching* teaches us that this shift is to be expected. It does not advocate yin rather than yang, contemplation rather than activity, or the reverse. Rather, it suggests that you align yourself with the changing constellations of energies and events. As we saw, the hexagram of *stagnation* arises when yang and yin are too rigidly separated. The psychic wholeness to which Jung refers includes a fluid equilibrium of activity and contemplation, reason and spirit, assertion and yielding, joy and sorrow, death and rebirth.

From such concepts flows the structure of the rest of this book. Hereafter, each part presents paired, complementary chapters. Their themes are, respectively, wisdom and the holy fool; service and rest; looking backward and forward; suffering and joy. In each pairing, one chapter has a female lead character, the other a male (not necessarily corresponding to yin or yang). There is opposition within each pairing, but we also find in each pole a seed of its complement. For example, our model of "wisdom" has a delightful innocence: our playful "fool" is also wise. We give service to a frantic world in our very ability to rest. Through coming to terms with our past, we can better accept the death that lies in our future. Though suffering, and dying to the self, we prepare the way for a joyful rebirth. These are spiritual passages all, paired and interpenetrating.

Would you characterize yourself as primarily a yang or a yin person, or a mixture of both? How so? Which of your character traits do you identify with one or the other of these cosmic energies?

Given your portrayal of yourself, can you see imbalances that need correction either in a yang or yin direction? Do you have any sense of what this correction might look like in your life? (For example: "I need to take more time for myself; really leave work behind when I come home at night; do a retreat at least twice a year," et cetera.)

�֎ *Guided Meditation* ✷

THE LAUGHING TAOISTS

Imagine you are walking down the road with the four Taoist masters. You are there when Master Yü falls ill and declares, "The Creator is making me all crookedy like this!" You laugh as he makes his playful predictions: "Perhaps in time he'll transform my left arm into a rooster. In that case, I'll keep watch on the night. . . . Or perhaps in time he'll transform my buttocks into cartwheels. Then, with my spirit for a horse, I'll climb up and go for a ride."

You are still laughing when you realize that you, too, are suddenly growing all crookedy. You proclaim to your road-mates, "Oh my God, I'm getting older!"

"Do you resent it?" asks Master Ssu.

"Why no, what would I resent? The Creator is making me age like this. If. . . ."

Imagine yourself completing the sentences that follow. Give as many responses to each one as you like; allow these to be playful, but also serious; keep to the positive in what you imagine.

If I develop arthritis, I'll _____

If I lose friends and loved ones, I'll _____

If they don't want me at work anymore, I'll _____

If I have fewer things I *must* do anymore, I'll _____

If I need others to take care of me, I'll _____

If I feel death approaching, I'll _____

Then imagine you and your Taoist friends interlocking arms and laughing. You proclaim together, "How marvelous the Creator is!"

✷   ✷   ✷

Part II

Wisdom
and the
Holy Fool

The Wisdom of Age:

An Aikido Master

The train clanked and rattled through the suburbs of Tokyo on a drowsy spring afternoon. Our car was comparatively empty—a few housewives with their kids in tow, some old folks going shopping. I gazed absently at the drab houses and dusty hedgerows.

At one station the doors opened, and suddenly the afternoon quiet was shattered by a man bellowing violent, incomprehensible curses. The man staggered into our car. He wore laborer's clothing, and he was big, drunk, and dirty. Screaming, he swung at a woman holding a baby. The blow sent her spinning into the laps of an elderly couple. It was a miracle that the baby was unharmed.

Terrified, the couple jumped up and scrambled toward the other end of the car. The laborer aimed a kick at the retreating back of the old woman but missed as she scuttled to safety. This so enraged the drunk that he grabbed the metal pole in the center of the car and tried to wrench it out of its stanchion. I could see that one of his hands was cut and bleeding. The train lurched ahead, the passengers frozen with fear. I stood up.

I was young then, some twenty years ago, and in pretty good

shape. I'd been putting in a solid eight hours of Aikido training nearly every day for the past three years. I liked to throw and grapple. I thought I was tough. The trouble was, my martial skill was untested in actual combat. As students of Aikido, we were not allowed to fight.

"Aikido," my teacher had said again and again, "is the art of reconciliation. Whoever has the mind to fight has broken his connection with the universe. If you try to dominate people, you are already defeated. We study how to resolve conflict, not how to start it."

I listened to his words. I tried hard. I even went so far as to cross the street to avoid the chimpira, the pinball punks who lounged around the train stations. My forbearance exalted me. I felt both tough and holy. In my heart, however, I wanted an absolutely legitimate opportunity whereby I might save the innocent by destroying the guilty.

"This is it!" I said to myself as I got to my feet. "People are in danger. If I don't do something fast, somebody will probably get hurt."

Seeing me stand up, the drunk recognized a chance to focus his rage. "Aha!" he roared. "A foreigner! You need a lesson in Japanese manners!"

I held on lightly to the commuter strap overhead and gave him a slow look of disgust and dismissal. I planned to take this turkey apart, but he had to make the first move. I wanted him mad, so I pursed my lips and blew him an insolent kiss.

"All right!" he hollered. "You're gonna get a lesson." He gathered himself for a rush at me.

A fraction of a second before he could move, someone shouted "Hey!" It was ear-splitting. I remember the strangely joyous, lilting quality of it—as though you and a friend had been searching diligently for something, and he had suddenly stumbled upon it. "Hey!"

I wheeled to my left; the drunk spun to his right. We both stared down at a little, old Japanese man. He must have been well into his seventies, this tiny gentleman, sitting there immaculate in his kimono. He took no notice of me, but beamed delightedly at the laborer, as though he had a most important, most welcome secret to share.

"C'mere," the old man said in an easy vernacular, beckoning to the drunk. "C'mere and talk with me." He waved his hand lightly.

The big man followed, as if on a string. He planted his feet belligerently in front of the old gentleman, and roared above the clacking wheels, "Why the hell should I talk to you?" The drunk now had his back to me. If his elbow moved so much as a millimeter, I'd drop him in his socks.

The old man continued to beam at the laborer. "What'cha been drinkin'?" he asked, his eyes sparkling with interest. "I been drinkin' sake," the laborer bellowed back, "and it's none of your business!" Flecks of spittle spattered the old man.

"Oh, that's wonderful," the old man said, "absolutely wonderful! You see, I love sake too. Every night, me and my wife (she's seventy-six, you know), we warm up a little bottle of sake and take it out into the garden, and we sit on an old wooden bench. We watch the sun go down, and we look to see how our persimmon tree is doing. My great-grandfather planted that tree, and we worry about whether it will recover from those ice storms we had last winter. Our tree has done better than I expected, though, especially when you consider the poor quality of the soil. It is gratifying to watch when we take our sake and go out to enjoy the evening—even when it rains!" He looked up at the laborer, eyes twinkling.

As he struggled to follow the old man's conversation, the drunk's face began to soften. His fists slowly unclenched. "Yeah," he said. "I love persimmons, too. . . ." His voice trailed off.

"Yes," said the old man, smiling, "and I'm sure you have a wonderful wife."

"No," replied the laborer. "My wife died." Very gently, swaying with the motion of the train, the big man began to sob. "I don't got no wife, I don't got no home, I don't got no job. I'm so ashamed of myself." Tears rolled down his cheeks; a spasm of despair rippled through his body.

Now it was my turn. Standing there in my well-scrubbed youthful innocence, my make-this-world-safe-for-democracy righteousness, I suddenly felt dirtier than he was.

Then the train arrived at my stop. As the doors opened, I heard the old man cluck sympathetically. "My, my," he said, "that is a difficult predicament, indeed. Sit down here and tell me about it."

I turned my head for one last look. The laborer was sprawled on the seat, his head in the old man's lap. The old man was softly stroking the filthy, matted hair.

As the train pulled away, I sat down on a bench. What I had wanted to do with muscle had been accomplished with kind words. I had just seen Aikido tried in combat, and the essence of it was love. I would have to practice the art with an entirely different spirit. It would be a long time before I could speak about the resolution of conflict.

Ram Dass and Paul Gorman, *How Can I Help?*

YOUNG MIND

At first it's hard to find fault with the young man in this (true) story. He wants to do good. The passengers on his train are in jeopardy, including an old woman, a mother, and her baby. He prepares to utilize his martial arts skills, honed over years of practice, to "save the innocent by destroying the guilty." Most of us would cheer him on and wish we had the courage and skill to do likewise.

But the narrator, now twenty years older and wiser, can see through his own youthful pretensions. We can almost hear him chuckling at his earlier self. Yes, he had tried with fresh enthusiasm to "make-this-world-safe-for-democracy." But now he recognizes the self-righteousness involved. His attitude was that he was right, the laborer wrong. He was "tough and holy," the laborer was a no-good sleaze. The crisis offered him a chance to build up his ego at another's expense.

The situation also provided a "legitimate" excuse to unleash his own violence. If ever there was a time to use his martial arts skills, this was surely it. A drunken man, out of control—what other recourse than to level him? Only with the purest intentions, of course.

We may recognize ourselves here. When we were young we probably showed some of the same traits. And they're not all bad: passion, courage, commitment, high ideals—nothing wrong with that. In our earlier life, we may have dreamed of building a better world, marched in protests, declared we'd never "sell out." We felt things deeply and were sure of our beliefs. We, like the Aikido student, might have even been willing to put life and limb on the line. Our society desperately needs that youthful passion. The train passengers were surely glad when the young man stood up.

But maybe we can also identify with the young man's vices. When we professed our beliefs (whatever they were—conservative or leftist, religious or secular, business-oriented or artistic) wasn't there a tinge of self-righteousness? Were we quick, when young, to divide the world into "us versus them"? Maybe we looked down on the poor. Maybe we looked down on those who looked down on the poor. In the end, it's not that different: we were in the business of separating and judging.

We might call this a feature of "young mind." After all, in life's first half, our sense of self is still tenuous. We struggle to establish who we are, as opposed to someone else. That's why, as adolescents, we delighted to find our parents wrong, or someone in high school even dorkier than ourselves. "I'm not just Daddy's little girl. And I'm not some geeky loser like Maureen." We tried to build a positive self-image through distinguishing ourselves from others.

This feature of young mind is not simply a function of chronological age. Due to psychic traumas and spiritual disconnection, young mind can last a lifetime. Still insecure, we want to be the best parent around—"not like that other mother I saw dragging her kid down the street!" In work, we want to outdo fellow employees. After all, in the economic rat race we're all pitted against one another. A kind of adolescent sibling rivalry infects the adult world—and so do adolescent attitudes toward authority. We want the boss, or our doctor, or our president, to fix everything like a magical parent. When they fail, we feel self-righteous contempt. Our boss is an idiot, our political leaders all crooks and incompetents. We could surely do it better. Unfortunately, no one manifests such attitudes more than certain oldsters long set in their ways. We know the routine: "The world's gone to the dogs! Why, when I was young. . . ." Little does the person realize they *are* young—still manifesting young mind.

The story illustrates the drawbacks of this mindset. The young Aikido student, with all his good intentions, ends up little different from the drunk. The laborer is intoxicated on liquor, the student on himself. In each case, there is a loss of clear vision. The laborer doesn't "see" the people he's terrorizing. With clarity of mind and heart he wouldn't attack a mother holding her baby. But she is a mother no longer, not even really a person—just some symbol at which he strikes out blindly. In the same way, the laborer is only a symbol to the Aikido student. The student doesn't really "see" his grief, his self-loathing, his humanity. The drunk is just a cut-out figure standing in for evil. The student prepares to "take this turkey apart," matching violence with violence.

This behavior may solve the immediate crisis, but what of its long-term effects? The laborer's defeat would only add to his own shame and violence. And who would be the recipient of that violence? Perhaps the next trainload of passengers. His blows might rain down even heavier with no defender to repel them. In the words of the Compassionate Buddha, "Hatred never ceases by hatred. Hatred only ceases by love."

�֎ ✖ ✖

When you were younger, who were some of the people or institutions you felt superior to? You might want to make a list of some of these, and how and why you felt "better than."

Can you see some ways this self-righteousness was hurtful to yourself or others? Did it undercut some work you were trying to accomplish, damage relationships, or keep you at a distance from others? That is, can you see (as the Aikido student did) the dangers of young mind?

✖

In what areas of your life are these attitudes still operative? Where do you find yourself most judgmental? (At work? With your children, parents, spouse? Talking politics or religion? Or with yourself, perhaps?) Don't attack yourself for what you find—that itself is a judgmental attitude. Just take note.

✖

ELDER WISDOM

We've been focusing on the young Aikido student. But the story's hero is really "a little, old Japanese man . . . well into his seventies." He's the one who brings healing resolution. If we saw young mind in the student, this man exemplifies what I'll call elder wisdom.[1]

It's worth noting the difference between the terms "elder" and "elderly." The latter fairly reeks of the sociomedical model of aging. Hear "elderly," and what do you think of? Perhaps someone stooped over, decrepit, in need of help. "That poor elderly woman who lives across the street. We really should visit her. It would give her *something* to do." On a broader scale, "the elderly" are portrayed as a dire social problem. Politicians and economists debate what to do about their growing numbers, and the drain it will impose on our resources. With all these negative messages about the elderly, is it any wonder that we dread joining their ranks?

The term "elder" can have different connotations. The elders of traditional societies often received great respect, even veneration: the elder is a guardian of the tribe's traditions. Through the blessings of long life, he or she remembers, gathers, and preserves that which is of value from the past. Such a person also has the perspective to be farsighted about the future. His or her own proximity to death is seen as a mark not of limitation but of closeness to the divine. For all such reasons, elders lead the tribe in its ritual observances, and they are entrusted with important communal decisions. In chapter 6 I discuss a Native American example. We see this principle, as well, in ancient Hebrew culture, and traditional African societies, where elders take on religious, juridical, and political duties. Reverence for age is also encouraged in Japan, the setting of our story. The Japanese celebrate a national "Honor the Aged Day." One's sixtieth birthday is also marked by special ceremony. With family and friends gathered, and donning ritual garments, one hallows the transition to elderhood.

My use of the term "elder" is meant to recall such meanings. As for "wisdom," the term comes from a family of roots meaning "to know" or "to see." For example, it's related to the Sanskrit *Vedas* (sacred books of knowledge) and the Latin *videre* (to see), from which we get words like "video" and "television."

What kind of sight does wisdom involve? Few would think of modern-day television (literally, "to see across a distance") as being a transmitter of wisdom. It's too superficial. Just as the screen is flat, yielding a two-dimensional image, so the contents are often equally shallow. The nightly news gives us world events wrapped up in three-minute segments. How complex an understanding can that yield? Wildlife shows present the wonders of nature, but reduced to cute camera shots sandwiched between ads. Television helps us see, but not in depth; it doesn't penetrate to the heart of things.

Neither does the vision of the Aikido student. As if watching a TV shoot-'em-up, he sees a two-dimensional world of heroes and villains. But the old man has *insight*—literally, the ability to "see in." This power does not originate with his eyes—nor even his intellect: we have no reason to believe he was schooled in abnormal psychology. No, his insight first arose from the heart. He sees deep into the laborer because he sees him with *compassion*. Etymologically, this term means "to suffer with" (*passio* and *com*). The old man suffers with the laborer, feels for his plight rather than judging it. Admittedly, one is old, the other young; one sober, the other drunk; one calm, the other violent. So what? These are surface distinctions. The heart-to-heart link cuts through all that like a knife through butter.

The result is multidimensional in-sight. For one, the old man sees past the immediate present. Right now, the laborer is a drunken menace. But that now is only the tip of an iceberg whose farther reaches are submerged in the past. Gradually they're brought to light. It turns out that he has lost his wife, his home, his job, and with them his self-respect. "I'm so *ashamed* of myself." The suffering he now inflicts is simply an expression of the suffering he has undergone.

If the past is part of the present moment, so is the future. The Aikido student can't imagine the laborer as other than he is right now, but the wise elder knows something different: the present is but a way station, a pathway to further miseries or the miracles of healing grace. The old man sees all the hidden potential. Like the persimmon tree in winter, the laborer is damaged but far from dead. "Our tree has done better than I expected," rejoices the old man, maybe planting a seed in the other's mind. The future can always bring renewal. Winter is followed by spring. By the end of the train ride, there's been a radical change of seasons. The stormy laborer lies at peace in the old man's lap.

This closeness itself is an expression of more that the elder sees. As he penetrates into the heart of the laborer, he does not find just an individual, particular in history and potential. He also uncovers something mysterious that binds the two men, and all people, together. The term "Aikido" itself captures this truth. *Ai* means "harmony"; *ki* means "spiritual energy"; and *do* is the Tao, or "way." Aikido, then, is the way of harmony that arises from realizing the spiritual energy that unites us. Though a martial art, it is not a tool of aggressive intent. It is a path to unify one's own mind and heart and defuse the roots of conflict with others. Based on a blend of Shinto and Buddhist religion and practice, Aikido was founded by Morihei Ueshiba (1883–1969). He said:

> All people share the same divine origin. There is only one thing that is wrong or useless. That is the stubborn insistence that you are an individual, separate from others. Give thanks and show gratitude. Work for the paradise on this earth. In this way, your true nature will continually unfold.[2]

The old man's wisdom makes him a master of Aikido, even if he never formally studied the art. He seeks points that will link the other's spirit to his. If the laborer is drunk, the master reaches out: "You see, I love sake too." The laborer begins to respond in kind. When the old man speaks of his treasured tree, the other echoes, "Yeah, I love persimmons too." The old man's affection for his wife is matched by the laborer's: he sobs as he speaks of her death. Love of nature, love of others—these are expressions of underlying spiritual connection. When the master taps into that, all separation melts. He has seen past the division between self and other, as well as that between saint and sinner. In the words of Morihei Ueshiba, "Within divine love there is no good or evil, no happiness or unhappiness. There is only constant giving."[3]

At the same time, this giving must be guided by practical insight. After all, the train passengers are in dire jeopardy, the laborer and student about to come to blows. There's no time for sentimentality. But the old man's wisdom helps him to see how best to distract the laborer, then draw him out and awaken his better self. The results are powerful. Though in his seventies, small and weak, he accomplishes more with a well-timed "Hey!" than the young student could have with his rippling muscles.

In the words of the *Tao Te Ching,* "Therefore the Master acts without doing anything / and teaches without saying anything."[4] Without doing anything forceful, the old man single-handedly disarms the drunk, defuses a crisis, and maybe forestalls others yet to come. His teaching skills are no less formidable; without saying anything to the student, he delivers a profound lesson to him also. It still resonates for the student some twenty years later. And not just for him: we, the readers, also receive a teaching from this man. He gives us an example of elder wisdom at work, radiating insight, compassion, and power.

As you survey your current life, in what particular areas or relationships have you been able to bring "elder wisdom" to bear? (With a family member or friend? At work? During some recent conversation?) At such times, can you see aspects of the Aikido master in yourself?

What is it that allows us to enter into elder wisdom at such times? (Prayer? A spirit of compassion? Sticking to the truth?) Seek the keys that unlock the door for you.

EMPTYING OUT

The old Japanese man's wisdom is not always particularly associated with the second half of life. We surely know young people who strike us as "wise beyond their years." Some have had their maturity accelerated by external factors. A hardscrabble life, deaths in one's family—such things can force us to grow up in a hurry. Or, more gently, a loving mentor may take us under his or her wing. Spiritual teacher Eknath Easwaran considers his grandmother his guru—it was she who introduced him to profound spirituality when he was just a boy. Or maybe we're the sort who simply matures rich and early, apparently impelled from within. Believers in reincarnation might label such a person an "old soul." He or she has already progressed far in previous lives and thus shows uncanny insight in this one. Therefore, it's never too soon to seek out elder wisdom, and recognize the traits within ourselves.

Just as younger people can possess this wisdom, older people may clearly lack it. It's not hard to think of examples. The "elder statesmen" on the political scene often show no more insight than their younger colleagues. On a personal note, perhaps we have an Uncle Henry or Aunt Sophie we'd do anything to avoid. Age has hardly polished their luster. On the contrary, they seem to have gained an uncanny ability to talk for hours on end without ever listening; to point out others' faults without seeing their own; to lay down guilt trips and demands, but deny they're doing so. Yes, age also has its vices. You don't get to be an elder just by living a long time.

Yet there is truth to the link between age and wisdom. We may see this truth manifesting in our own lives, as the passage of time leads to spiritual passages. We also see this association in cultures throughout the world. I've already discussed the revered status of the elder in traditional societies. In addition, archetypes appear in religion and mythology. In the Judeo-Christian tradition, God is often imaged as a wise old man. The wise elder appears as the "sage" or "master" in Taoism and Confucianism. The "crone" or "wise woman" is a recurring figure in Goddess traditions. Wisdom was particularly associated with postmenopausal women; their supposedly retained menstrual blood, described as "wise blood," was considered to be a source of their insight.[5]

How can we understand, in modern terms, the association of age and wisdom? For one thing, age is an *adding on*. The growth of years brings the opportunity for growth in experience, perspective, and understanding. Over time, this can lead to what might best be called practical wisdom. The Greek philosopher Aristotle recognized this wisdom as a form of intelligence distinct from that born of theory and study. The person of practical wisdom (*phronesis*) knows how to handle himself or herself in the real world: when to act, and when to stay quiet; how to negotiate a solution to conflicts; how to take in the many features of a situation and respond appropriately, avoiding rash extremes.

We see this exemplified in the Japanese man. He may not be a whiz at philosophy or physics, but he knows how to handle a crisis. This practical wisdom probably developed with age. The young student meant well, but he had never been in such a situation before. He's coping with the unknown. Not so the old man. He's probably seen many fights and had the chance to gauge the success and failure of different tactics. Beyond that, age has given him more time to observe the human condition. He knows the pervasiveness of suffering, so he is not so quick to judge those in pain. He has probably explored his own shadow side—how rapidly his own pain can turn to rage—so he knows better what motivates the laborer.

This elder wisdom, developed over long years, is not easily captured by psychological tests. Traditionally these have pointed to decreases in cognitive ability in old age. Lately there's been a reassessment of such studies. They largely focus on "pure," contextless cognition—the memorization of nonsense syllables, and the like. At such tasks, young people indeed do better. But these tests do not measure the practical reasoning at which older individuals excel, and may even penalize it.

In one example, test takers were asked about the amount of lawn to be mowed on an imaginary plot. Would it change if the houses on the land were moved into a different configuration? The correct answer is that the total lawn area would be unchanged. It's the same square footage, just rearranged. However, older respondents were less likely to give the "right" answer. They noted that it was harder, and would take more time, to mow several small grass plots than one large lawn.[6] These respondents were drawing wisely on their life experience. As Adlai Stevenson said of the mature adult, "The knowledge he has acquired with age is not a knowledge of formulas or forms of words, but of people, places, and actions . . . the human experiences and emotions of this world, and of oneself and other men."[7]

Life's passage helps us acquire experience and perspective. However, spiritual practices like that of Aikido also suggest another paradigm: I'll call it the "emptying out" model. In this model, wisdom is not simply something we acquire over time, like water poured into a cup, but is something always already there, intrinsic to our human/divine nature. We have a natural knowing that includes a sense of connection and access to intuitive guidance. Yet this inborn wisdom can be obscured. There are also forces of ignorance within the human condition—selfishness, greed, and fear, for example—that cloud over the sun of truth. Our access to wisdom is cut off. Life experience gives us the opportunity to clear away those clouds. Aging can strip us of illusions, empty us out, so that we better express the divine.

> In the pursuit of knowledge,
> every day something is added.
> In the practice of the Tao,
> every day something is dropped.[8]

What do we need to drop? Perhaps we can cluster it all under the notion of "self." Not the divine Self, that authentic, playful, expansive being we discover when expressing our true nature; that's the fount of elder wisdom. But on the way to that, a false but tenacious ego-self must first be stripped away. Imagine the soul as a beautiful piece of rosewood furniture covered by a layer of cheap paint. Life has its way of pouring on the solvent until the paint bubbles up, then going at it with a scraper. The process can be abrasive, but the results well worth it. A wise elder gleams in her insight and joy like rosewood in the autumn sun.

In stripping away the false self, first to go may be our *self-righteousness*. As the Aikido story suggests, life often tears apart our youthful dream of heroes and villains. Over time, we find that those with whom we disagree in politics or religion may turn out to be pretty nice folks after all. Conversely, our "allies" sometimes disappoint us. And we discover that we ourselves often fail to live up to our own standards. We're not so quick to judge, lest we be judged.

That kissing cousin of self-righteousness, *self-centeredness,* may also have to go. Ever notice how a toddler assumes it's the focus of the world? A friend of mine has a two-year-old who recently marched around the house declaring, "Hannah's doll" and "Hannah's kitchen." The culmination came when she opened the door, looked around, and proclaimed it "Hannah's outside!" Of course, what's endearing in a child can be aggravating in an adult. No one wants to be around a self-centered mate or colleague, or be thought one. So we all learn to politely ask, "How are you doing?" But secretly, haven't we often marched through life thinking something like (substitute your own name) "Hannah's spouse," "Hannah's job," "Hannah's government," even "Hannah's God." We want people, organizations, even deities, to do our bidding, things to unfold according to plan. *Our* plan. Thus self-centeredness gives rise to *self-will,* as we try to engineer a desired outcome. Sometimes we're crude and demanding about it. Do what I want, or else! Other times, we manipulate sweetly. After all, you catch more flies with honey than vinegar. But whatever the tactics, the goal is the same— "Hannah's flies!" We want our way, and so does everyone else, setting the stage for massive conflict.

Happily, life has a way of challenging all this. We may like to think the universe revolves around us, but over the years evidence mounts to the contrary. Perhaps we lose a valued relationship. We didn't pay enough attention to the other person's needs. Ouch. Older now, we don't turn heads on the street the way we used to. Ouch, ouch. We're passed over for a desired job; someone else is just more of a go-getter. Ouch, ouch, ouch. All this destruction of our narcissism can lead to midlife depression. But it can also be the start of elder wisdom. Life is weeding our garden, but to cultivate new growth. Over the years it can bear fruit in deepened humility, realism, and compassion.

For that to happen, we must let go of control. It's tempting to want to run the world; after all, God needs some help, doesn't She? Again, experience teaches us how often self-will doesn't work. Despite dire threats and cajoling, our students don't do the reading we assigned. Our teenage daughter seems to revel in whatever music and boyfriend we like least. We finally see our favorite politician win, but soon there's a voter backlash that elects the other side. Frustrating! It seems the more we try to force our will on others, the more they fight back, and the less is accomplished. Elder wisdom involves a learning to let go. Not to bail out of proper responsibility—just to recognize the true limits of our reach, and accept a universe that lies in God's hands, not ours.

A Sufi story provides a nice example.

> Nasrudin was now an old man looking back on his life. He sat with his friends in the tea shop telling his story.
>
> "When I was young I was fiery—I wanted to awaken everyone. I prayed to Allah to give me the strength to change the world."
>
> In mid-life I awoke one day and realized my life was half over and I had changed no one. So I prayed to Allah to give me the strength to change those close around me who so much needed it.
>
> Alas, now I am old and my prayer is simpler. 'Allah,' I ask, 'please give me the strength to at least change myself.' "[9]

This man has let go of *self-importance*. The self-important person is eager to fix others, but not himself to be challenged and changed. Unfortunately, this is a stereotype of age: "You can't teach an old dog new tricks." A true elder is quite the opposite. He or she is far more educable than even a puppy. A Western archetype exemplifies this aspect of elder wisdom: the figure of Socrates in later life. The oracle of Delphi labels him the wisest man in the world. How one might preen to hear such golden words! But Socrates' reaction is quite the opposite. Aware of his own limitations, he can't believe his ears. He has spent his life trying to acquire wisdom. But life has also taught him how far he has to go, how limited the human mind. His pursuit of truth, he realizes, must continue up to and beyond the grave. Sentenced to death, he spends his last day discussing with friends the immortality of the soul. What does he hope lies on the other side? Endless opportunities to grow further in wisdom.

Elder wisdom is characterized by this stance of the perpetual learner. In contrast to young mind, which can be infected with know-it-all self-certainty, I call this trait beginner's mind. Zen teacher Shunryu Suzuki labeled it crucial to the practice of Zen or, truly, any spiritual practice. "In the beginner's mind there are many possibilities, but in the expert's there are few," he writes. We can probably identify. When entering a new field, we feel excited, inquisitive, open to the new. "In beginner's mind, there is no thought 'I have attained something.' "[10] As a result our progress can be rapid. As soon as we become an expert, things grind to a halt. No one is less teachable then people who think they have all the answers.

Looking back over your life, can you see experiences that have helped to strip away your false self? For example, what moments, what events, have helped to strip away (try to list one or two experiences for each):

   1. Self-righteousness

   2. Self-centeredness

   3. Self-will

   4. Self-importance

In general, how did such experiences feel? Liberating and joyful? Painful and traumatic? Or a mixture of both? In any case, can you see ways in which they made you a wiser person, nurturing your insight, realism, compassion?

�֍

TRAINING FOR WISDOM

How do we develop the traits of elder wisdom? It's not enough to wait passively for life to do its work. We have to actively cooperate with our "wisdom training." Otherwise, the danger is that we'll just grow old, without any true soul-growth.

The young Aikido student is an elder in training. Exhibiting young mind, he starts off being superficial, judgmental, and self-righteous; but he is no longer so at the story's end. He has been transformed by what he witnesses. What opens him so to life's teachings? The answer lies in his *practice.*

A serious student of Aikido, he's trained eight hours a day for three solid years. He's not simply pursuing a physical skill; this martial art, and the philosophy to which it's tied, is his path toward wisdom. He is self-righteous, but it's the Aikido training that enables him to admit his own mistake. Through a martial art where he submits to a teacher, is thrown as much as he throws, he has learned a certain humility. He has also learned enough Aikido philosophy to recognize the master. He knows that true mastery lies in the spirit of reconciliation and giving. Though he fails to live up to it himself, he responds powerfully to its presence in the old Japanese man.

It's helpful to remember that any spiritual practice is, after all, a *practice:* a repeated exercise to improve one's skill. Happily, we don't need a "perfection." But like the Aikido student, we all need repeated exercises and methods that open us up to continued growth.

Practices can take many forms. Socrates, for example, pursued a path of the intellect, one that appeals to many of us as we age. For example, there's been a burgeoning interest in Elderhostel courses held on campuses and field sites around the world. Elders are studying medieval poetry, the ecology of the rain forest, the late works of Beethoven, quantum mechanics—whatever and wherever their passion leads them. Then, too, hundreds of Institutes of Learning in Retirement (ILRs) have sprung up at colleges. Why should education all be wasted on the young? Any teacher knows that older individuals often possess a wealth of experience, interest, and appreciation that is usually lacking in teenagers. And ILRs are not just about listening to "the sage on the stage." Older individuals gather to share experience and expertise with one another, wearing the mantle of teacher as well as student.

If we take Socrates' path, we must bear in mind a caution from his life. He was not seeking merely to satiate curiosity and stimulate the mind. We risk shooting too low if this is all we ask of learning in life's second half. For Socrates, learning was a way to liberate the soul. His intellectual endeavor served a deeply spiritual quest. He sought answers to the most fundamental questions: How are we to live? What awaits us after death? What is the place of the sacred in human affairs? He lived his life according to the answers he received, and that is why his example transformed others' lives. Any of the subjects just mentioned—poetry, ecology, music, physics— can be studied in this Socratic vein. They unlock for us the mysteries of art and nature, and so can lead us to the divine. But study can also become idle play. So much depends on whether we are seekers of distraction or of genuine wisdom.

Many of the more mundane pursuits we are drawn to as we age can also become our wisdom practice. A recent newspaper article talked about the prolonged period of retirement we can anticipate with our greater longevity. The researcher comments, "Now you're looking at twenty or thirty years without active, meaningful engagement. That's a lot of golf." A hell of a lot of golf. An unappetizing prospect for most of us. Golf, after all, is the very stereotype of a fun but ultimately meaningless activity. Yet even golf can be an opportunity for quiet meditation; communion with nature; one-pointed attention. Michael Murphy's *Golf in the Kingdom* recounts the spiritual possibilities of this practice.

Spiritual teacher Ram Dass (who has lately become an avid golfer) tells of how, many years ago—back in the late sixties—he was speaking to an audience of avid seekers. It was a young crowd, hip to hallucinogens and Hinduism, except for one elderly lady sitting in the front. No matter how esoteric Ram Dass's spiritual teachings, she would sit there and nod in agreement. How had she learned all this? Ram Dass had to know. It was driving him crazy. He, himself, had studied with a guru in India, meditated at length, performed austerities. What practice had lifted her to such heights of awareness? Her answer: "I crochet."

So it's not the particular practice we use, but the way we use it. Golf, crocheting, college courses; meditating, church attendance, Sufi dancing; withdrawing into solitary retreat; volunteering in a busy soup kitchen—each can be a pathway to elder wisdom when we know how to use it. This book itself is designed as one such pathway, if you engage with it in depth. It is also meant to give a taste of the great variety of paths provided by the world's spiritual traditions. If any image or story particularly touches you, it might suggest a practice to pursue in depth through further reading, meditation, and contact with teachers.

Who are one's teachers? Again, they can come in a variety of shapes and sizes. There are, of course, accredited "masters": clergy, yogis, and the like. But we shouldn't overlook the teachers of elder wisdom we have contact with in our daily lives. Such a person may be a relative of ours—parent, grandparent, aunt, or uncle. Or the master may come in the form of an older friend, a mentor, even a public figure we admire from afar. Not to say that such people are perfect. They undoubtedly have human flaws. But the light of elder wisdom shines even through flawed glass. It might manifest in the form of simple joy: the aunt who loves, above all, to putter in the garden on a breezy spring day. It may be a teaching of compassion: the grandmother who keeps track of everyone's birthday. It might be a matter of insight and humor: the friend who always gets us to laugh at our crises and remember they will pass. At such times, we're in the presence of wisdom. We receive a teaching that helps us in our current life and helps prepare us for our own elderhood.

So it is for the Aikido student. He recognizes the older man as his teacher, though he has no formal credentials. Their brief encounter is enough to leave a lasting impression. It is not the result of words exchanged or sermons delivered. When Gandhi was asked by a reporter what message he had for the world, he replied, "My life is my message." Similarly, it is who the old man *is*, not what he says, that impresses itself on the youth. In just such a way is elder wisdom *transmitted* from giver to receiver. We see the marks of it in the young man twenty years later, now telling the story for our benefit. He, too, has become a man of insight. He sees deeply into his own heart, and that of the laborer and the old man, observing all with laughter and compassion. So the storyteller is the story's hidden sage. It's easy to forget him; he never calls attention to himself. But isn't this characteristic of elder wisdom, that gives better for having emptied out the self?

❋   ❋   ❋

As discussed, we all need certain practices to continue to grow in mind, heart, and spirit as we age. What have been your preferred practices so far? You may wish to make a list of them. Next to each one, you might note how it has contributed to the development of elder wisdom. (For example, has it increased your sense of compassion, open-mindedness, serenity, joy, or spiritual connection?)

❋

As you imagine the future, do you think you will continue with such practices, or perhaps develop some new ones? Allowing yourself to free-associate, write down some new wisdom practices you could imagine becoming involved with as you age. (Painting? Meditation? Elderhostel courses? A certain kind of volunteer work?) Don't feel pinned down to what you write. Just see what comes to mind.

Finally, think about exemplars of elder wisdom you have known. Whether family members, friends, teachers, or public figures, make a list of the people who come to mind. Next to each name, you might want to note the particular lessons you associate with that person. Do they exemplify a trait you admire—humility, perhaps, or compassion, or sound judgment?

Know that these individuals are outer personifications of your own elder wisdom. For you to recognize and value a trait in another, you also must have it within yourself. They just help give you access to that part of you.

❋ *Guided Meditation* ❋

THE INNER ELDER

Imagine that within you there is a personal guide and mentor, your "inner elder." No matter what your age, this person is older and wiser than you and so is able to act as your teacher. Gradually allow an image of the person to come to mind. They may be male or female, of any race or culture, looking whatever way you picture them. Let their image become clearer in your mind's eye. What does their face look like? As they gaze at you, what kind of expression do they have—one of compassion, humor, peace, or joy? Note any other details that strike you; for example, their clothes, posture, or the surroundings you find them in.

You need not tell them all about yourself—they know you through and through. All your life they have been observing you with compassion. Drawing on their store of elder wisdom, they are ready to help you with any issues in your life.

In your mind, begin to talk to this person. There may be a particular question you are wrestling with. If so, ask your inner elder for advice. What do they see that you may be missing? What perspective or solution can they provide?

Or you may be caught in a problem that has you stymied. If so, share it with your inner elder and imagine their response. It may or may not come in the form of words. Allow yourself to sense their response, however it arrives.

Finally, make a little time for open exchange. Is there anything else this elder wishes to communicate to you? Some message of love or guidance perhaps? A reminder of some truth you have lost touch with? Is there anything you want to say, or even do together with them? Allow yourself to image this scene.

When the time seems right, imagine you are saying goodbye to one another. Communicate in whatever way seems appropriate—hugs, or respectful bows, or laughter. Know that you will meet again. Your inner elder is there to help whenever you need assistance; all you need to do is go inside to find them. Know also that as time progresses, the two of you will only grow closer. For this person represents your own elder wisdom, which will grow deeper and richer as the years progress.

✻   ✻   ✻

The Freedom of the Fool:
An Old Woman in Purple

Warning

When I am an old woman I shall wear purple
With a red hat which doesn't go, and doesn't suit me.
And I shall spend my pension on brandy and summer gloves
And satin sandals, and say we've no money for butter.
I shall sit down on the pavement when I'm tired
And gobble up samples in shops and press alarm bells
And run my stick along the public railings
And make up for the sobriety of my youth.
I shall go out in my slippers in the rain
And pick the flowers in other people's gardens
and learn to spit.

You can wear terrible shirts and grow more fat
And eat three pounds of sausages at a go
Or only bread and pickle for a week
And hoard pens and pencils and beermats and things in boxes.

But now we must have clothes that keep us dry
And pay our rent and not swear in the street

And set a good example for the children.
We must have friends to dinner and read the papers.

But maybe I ought to practise a little now?
So people who know me are not too shocked and surprised
When suddenly I am old, and start to wear purple.

Jenny Joseph, Selected Poems

WHAT'S WITH THIS WOMAN? She's looking forward to growing old, an unusual sentiment in our culture. And when she gets there, she will do foolish things: wear unmatched clothes; waste needed money on frivolities; make a public nuisance of herself; eat in a decidedly unhealthy way.

There's a danger to identifying age exclusively with wisdom. In a chapter entitled "Long Live the Old Fool!" Jungian analyst Adolf Guggenbühl-Craig argues this case. The archetype of elder wisdom may make us feel pressured to heroically overcome our deficits, hang on to power, serenely rise to all occasions. After all, we're supposed to be wise! But the fool is blessedly set free from these burdens. Guggenbühl-Craig writes, " 'We demand the liberty to be fools' would be a suitable slogan for a political demonstration by the old."[1]

Perhaps this liberty is what so attracts us about this poem. The book whose title is taken from Jenny Joseph's first line, *When I Am an Old Woman I Shall Wear Purple,* has been wildly (and unexpectedly) popular. The poem is reprinted time and again. It rarely fails to evoke a laugh and a spark of recognition. Joseph reminds us that the good life, at any age, includes humor, freedom, daring to be ourselves.

We often associate aging with opposite characteristics: sobriety, restriction, conservatism. Isn't it, after all, the young who wear purple? As we age we may become "more serious." Our wilder clothes are stuffed into giveaway bags. We cut our hair in a professional style; after all, we just can't look too weird at the office. Spur-of-the-moment late-night jaunts with our buddies fade into distant memory. We're just not up to it anymore. Besides, we've got responsibilities at home. Can't go running off at a moment's notice. The upshot? Bit by bit we settle into a confined routine. The coffin at the end of the line merely finalizes this narrowing compass of our life.

However, Jenny Joseph suggests the opposite is possible: that life's second half can be a time of joyous freedom.

AGING INTO FREEDOM

"But now we must have clothes that keep us dry/ And pay our rent." Such, to use Hindu terms, is the dharma (duty) of the householder, with which we're probably all too familiar. We may have young children to raise—that is, clothes to wash, homework to read over, rides to organize, and shopping to do. At the same time, we may have to care for aging parents with their own social and medical needs. And let's not overlook the fact that all this takes money. So we're often working an extended day, and trying to do the extras that help career advancement. The result? We may feel like we're in one of those action movies where the hero is trapped in a small chamber, all four walls closing in at once. Job, kids, relatives, mortgage, boss, bills, *aaaiiieee!*

Somehow the hero always escapes in those movies, though, and Jenny Joseph suggests that aging itself can help us make our escape. "When I am an old woman," the children will be grown up and out on their own; job pressures may finally let up. At last we'll be able to say in good conscience, "I shall sit down on the pavement when I'm tired." We don't have to keep racing anymore.

The passing of years can also free us from certain social constraints. None of us wants to just be conventional—think, dress, talk as others do. So why do we so often end up there? The pressures toward conformity are strong when we are young. Almost every teen wants to fit in with the gang, and it's not much different as we enter adulthood. When we go out on a date, we want to seem attractive. We wish to make a good impression at work. Unspoken rewards and punishments also keep us toeing the line. Your body doesn't look like the current ideal? Maybe no one will ever ask you out. You don't "dress for success" and cultivate the right contacts? You're passed over for a key promotion. As much as we hate to admit it, we're bombarded and controlled by these social messages.

However, they can lessen as we age. Joseph imagines herself finally able to do all those inappropriate things—wear purple, eat three pounds of sausages, go out in slippers during the rain. How does she get away with it? One answer: 'cause nobody really cares anymore! Older folks are deemed irrelevant in our youth-biased culture. They just don't seem to matter as much as the sexy young thing or the rising executive. Moreover, if we behave strangely, people will probably chalk it up to the debilitating effects of age. Imagine the response when the old Jenny Joseph presses alarm bells and picks other people's flowers. "Poor old dear. Getting dotty, you know. Can't really hold her accountable." Again, the ageist assumptions. Joseph's poem teaches us a creative jujitsu by which we turn this energy of attack to our advantage. Finally, we can get away with what we've always wanted! Social condescension is turned into a zone of freedom.

This freedom comes not just from the changing attitude of other people; it also derives from changes within ourselves. We've had it with living as others tell us to. For better or worse, we've climbed the ladder of success or gotten stuck on a bottom rung. We've pleased everyone around us, or suffered through their disappointments. Either way, we've "been there, done that" when it comes to the social game. Some of us have this experience earlier in life, others later. Either way, we're now ready to move on.

Joseph's poem implies that age can help give us *freedom from* certain practical and social constraints. But the more interesting question is: What are we *freed up for?* What new possibilities await us?

Joseph envisions her future self as free to pursue her true desires. If she wants to dress wildly, drink brandy, get fat, so be it. "It's sad," the neighbors might say, "how she's let herself go." But isn't this exactly the point? She's letting go into her natural wants that had long been artificially hemmed in.

If we're free to express our sensuality, so, too, our politics. Joseph longs to "press alarm bells / and run my stick along the public railings." Sometimes there are fires going on in society that burn away unaddressed: poverty, racism, ecological devastation (add your own). Someone needs to press the alarm bell, make a racket. As we grow older, we may grow more willing to speak our mind undeterred by "public opinion."

In short, age frees us to be ourselves. Joseph envisions growing old as a time to discover and assert her true wants, beliefs, and character. Earlier I discussed elder wisdom as the fruit of an emptying out of self. But Joseph emphasizes the *claiming of self* that is possible as we age.

Contradictory messages? In the yin-yang spirit, we can view these opposites as complementary and interpenetrating. A movement toward one finally carries us around to the other. For example, when we embark on the path of self-negation, we don't end up a vague nobody. On the contrary, the most selfless spiritual masters are often the ones with the most vivid personalities. Tales abound of laughing or loving gurus, Zen masters, saints, and sages, each one radically unique. Having let go of their ego-selves, they become ever more their own persons. The wise Aikido master provides a wonderful example. In every gesture he expresses, unselfconsciously, who he really is—playful, caring, a lover of beauty. In fact, he may even remind us of Joseph's character. The two of them might get along fabulously—sniffing flowers and debating the merits of sake versus brandy!

Jenny Joseph's poem is funny, earthy, outrageous. But spiritual? I think so. The old woman's claiming of self can finally be a path to wisdom and the sacred. In a famous Hasidic tale, Rabbi Zusya, shortly to die, surveyed the meaning of his life. He said, "In the coming world, they will not ask me, 'Why were you not Moses?'

They will ask me, 'Why were you not Zusya?' "[2] God does not demand of us that we walk another person's path. We are only asked to fulfill our own unique calling, become the person we are truly meant to be. To wear purple, spit, and drink her brandy is part of Joseph's character becoming herself. She's daring to be the person Spirit fashioned, in all her sensuality and specialness.

When is the right time to get on with this work? For reasons I have touched on and will further explore, Joseph identifies it primarily with later life. But she was in her early forties when she penned this poem. Even in flourishing midlife we can seize the freedom to assert and enjoy our true selves. "Maybe we ought to practise a little now," no matter what our age.

�֎   �֎   ✖

"In the coming world, they will not ask me, 'Why were you not Moses?' They will ask me, 'Why were you not _____?' " Write your own name in the blank. Imagine this question being posed to you. In what ways have you really been **yourself** *in your life? List some of the ways you have expressed your true self, whether in your relationships, jobs, hobbies, personality. Now make a second list of ways you have* **not** *been yourself. What pressures (from within or without) were you giving in to?*

✖

Are there ways you have "aged into freedom"? What liberties (with your emotions, your time, your relationships, your job, et cetera) have you claimed for yourself as the years have passed? You might list and reflect on these. Have these freedoms come from changes in the expectations of others, or changes within yourself?

✖

WOMAN FREEDOM

Jenny Joseph does not simply write "When I am old. . . ." Her message is more specific: "When I am an old *woman*." One freedom that age can grant us is some release from confining gender roles—both female and male.

Many writers have noted that a sort of straitjacket descends on girls around early adolescence. Up to this point they've often enjoyed a certain spontaneity, playfulness, and self-confidence that allows a young girl to be herself in the world. But around age twelve that can come crashing down. In Gloria Steinem's words, girls are then taught to be "female impersonators." Their behavior is increasingly constrained by social messages about proper femininity. "You have to look nice or boys won't want you." "Don't you think you could use to lose some weight?" "Don't worry if you're not too good in math. You're not expected to be." "Be nice. No one likes a girl who's too aggressive." Inner wants are gradually drowned out by these messages from outside. Often, nobody needs to state them directly. They're there in the magazine ads filled with pencil-thin models, the sexist attitudes of certain teachers, the peer pressure to fit in as a "desirable" girl.

As a girl slips into this role she risks losing herself, for the role involves subjugating her wishes to those of others. The "good" girl (or woman), we are taught, is the one who places herself constantly in service—as wife, office worker, mother, daughter. Service, of course, can be a high spiritual ideal. But not when it is coerced, and lived out at the expense of your true desires and callings. As in the Hasidic story, Zusya then never becomes Zusya. This kind of self-denial can be soul-killing. Nor is it very healthy for the body: the ideal of feminine attractiveness—unnaturally slim—can lead to obsessive dieting and exercising, even life-threatening anorexia or bulimia. At the end of it all, most young women still can't produce the ideal. "Look at that fat on my thighs. My little breasts. My big tummy. God, how I hate my body!"

It doesn't help that messages about female sexuality contradict each other. One voice says, "You have to be sexy to attract guys. Don't be afraid to show some skin." The other voice scolds: "Don't be a slut. Sex is something guys want, not girls—don't let them have it." Huh? How to be both a vamp and the Virgin Mary at the same time? Such messages place women not just in a bind, but in a *double bind*.

Aging can help release women from all that. Postmenopausal women are often not as sexualized in our culture. They may no longer fit the cultural ideal of what's attractive to men: young, lean bodies, firm breasts, wrinkle-free faces. Of course, there's a terrible downside to this dismissal; it can lead to low self-esteem and despair. But, again, we can use it to claim a zone of freedom. As Steinem says, "The role of female impersonator doesn't lift . . . (hopefully this will change) until the time we turn fifty."[3] At this time, liberated from the demand to be a sexual object, the woman may better discover her own desires. Jenny Joseph knows. She'll "wear terrible shirts and grow more fat / And eat three pounds of sausages at a go." So what if her behavior and looks don't match the ideal of femininity?

The freedom to be other than just a sex object does not mean that older women have no sexuality. Quite the contrary. Less objectified, one can be more the *subject*. That is, women can become more *themselves* in bed, not the creature of someone else's fantasies. Hormonal changes can also further this liberation. Cathleen Rountree writes, in *On Women Turning Fifty*:

> In our late forties and early fifties, with the onset of menopause, we enter a season in which we no longer need concern ourselves with unwanted pregnancy and birth control. We become more concerned with female production rather than reproduction. Many women have informed me that it wasn't until their fifties that they began to enjoy sex in a more liberating and carefree manner, partly because of this factor.[4]

In chapter 11 I say more about the celebration of sex in later life. But let's recognize that, for older women, this liberation is just one part of a many-faceted celebration of *self*. The focus no longer needs to be simply on serving others. The mature woman can overcome the internalized voice that demands such self-denial. And outer demands lessen with the passing years. Job pressures may decrease, kids grow up and move away. While the empty nest syndrome is supposed to be a time of sadness and regret, it is more often so for men. Many of them lament not having been more present as fathers now that the window of opportunity is closing. But women often experience this juncture as a time of liberation. "Finally, I can get back to *me*. Who am I, after all? What shall I do with my time?" The doors are everywhere opening.

For some, it's a chance to undertake an introspective quest. Others develop new friendships. Many women consider novel career moves. In any case, the stereotype of the older woman as experiencing sad losses—of children, looks, self-esteem—belies a far more complex reality. Gail Sheehy does report that a psychological "pit" is common for women in their middle to late forties. However, she states:

> Around 50 they begin to take off. Straight through their fifties the women studied showed gains in inner harmony, mastery, and life status as they register—with considerable surprise— that they are more fulfilled and enjoy greater well-being than at any other stage of their lives.[5]

So Jenny Joseph is not so bizarre in wanting to age. She's looking forward to this liberation.

MAN FREEDOM

This vision need not speak only to women. Just as girls are taught to be female impersonators, so boys learn early to impersonate males. Transmitted by parents, the media, teachers, and peers, the messages are relatively clear. "No crying. That's for girls. You're a little man now. You've got to be tough." If the "good girl" ideal is about self-negation, this masculine image has much to do with *self-assertion,* no matter what the obstacles. The "true man" does not give in—to pain, weakness, the demands of others. He's a conqueror. With aggressive courage and leadership he asserts his will in the world. "And may the best man win." Indeed, the "best man" is, by definition, the one who wins, achieving the pinnacle of power and success.

As there are positive aspects to the feminine ideal of service, there are some to this heroic masculine ideal. It can help men develop a healthy assertiveness and self-confidence. The result can be real accomplishments in the world.

But like the female impersonator role, the masculine ideal can also do damage. For example, each time the boy remembers not to cry, a sheath hardens over his pain. Denied expression of emotions, gradually he loses touch with them. And what you can't feel, you can't heal. Instead, the untreated suffering may turn into rage and violence. As philosopher Glen Mazis writes, "This wounding of the other allows the male to take the pain he has kept locked in his chest and to heave it 'out there,' like garbage."[6] Sometimes this wounding is socially sanctioned, as with aggressiveness in business or sports, or the out-and-out killing of warfare. Sometimes the violence is illegal—wife-beating, rape, homicide, and the like. Women and men both bear the brunt of the dysfunctional aspects of "masculinity."

Men can also become cut off from intimate relationships; they call for an openness to the other, and to one's own dependency and vulnerability, that rarely comes easily to guys. We all know the stereotypes. At the barbecue, the women discuss what's going on in their relationships and inner lives, and the men cluster around the TV. "How could that jerk have missed the tackle?!" may be as intimate as anything gets. It's not that men don't crave closeness. That football game is a way to bond. But the male ideal of aggressive self-assertion does little to develop the skills for deep sharing. For that one needs the ability to listen, identify, trust, open up. Not really the stuff men are taught.

Paradoxically, male self-assertion, no less than female self-denial, finally leads to a loss of self. Over the years, you lose touch with entire sectors of your identity.

The aging process challenges the settled habits of masculinity no less than those of femininity. Gail Sheehy writes:

> It would seem, from the intensity of their concern, that losing their hair is for men the first public sign of weakening, almost like walking around with an exposed ego wound that everyone can see, as if hair were what Samson believed it to be: the symbol of a man's power and sexual prowess.[7]

Balding, like menopause, can make one feel less desirable. Even men who hang on to their hair may sense their "virility" declining with age. This is not to deny that, in some ways, men have it easier. Male movie stars (more than female!) can remain sex symbols well into their later years, and powerful older males dominate corporations and politics. Nevertheless, aging clarifies for men, no less than women, that they're no longer on top of the hill. The young boys are up and coming. Sexier, hungrier for success, more energetic, physically strong, more "cutting edge" in knowledge and skills, they're gathering to overthrow the aging king.

The older man stands at a crossroads. He can fight back with every weapon at his disposal. As Sheehy writes,

> instead of taking the risk of change, many men in middle life keep hanging on to every vestige of power and pursue every opportunity for one-upmanship, even with their children, even when it makes them look ridiculous.[8]

However, the aging king can also do the opposite: he can cheerfully cast off his crown. You take it! I don't want it anymore. That is, a constructive response is possible. The older man is freed up, within our culture, to be more androgynous, more complete. Now that he's not as identified with aggressive virility, and is matured by life experience, he can explore other parts of his humanness. The worldly man may now give deeper thought to a spiritual life. The hard man may be called to express his softness. Many a grandfather coos over a toddler in a way he couldn't with his own children. The serious man may be liberated to play. The purposeful march of a focused career gives way to retirement experiments leading who knows where. Freed from the hero archetype, a man can begin to explore others: the sage, the magician, the trickster. He is shifting direction, freeing up the self.

Let's imagine a male equivalent to Joseph's poem. It would be different for each man; here's one version I've penned:

> *When I am an old man I shall throw off my tie.*
> *No more business suits, alarms set for six a.m.,*
> *Boots to lick, mouths to feed, rage to choke on with my*
> *cereal.*
>
> *No, when I am an old man I shall set off for the fields.*
> *I'll wander here and there, never knowing where I'm going.*
> *I'll linger over a cattail in the pond,*
> *And skip stones along the surface, laughing with the*
> *waterbugs.*
>
> *When the sun sets, I'll go with it to the west,*
> *And feel its orange heat melt my stone-hard surface*
> *Into a thousand, tingling points.*
>
> *I'll roll over and laugh with the crow,*
> *Cry with the jayhawk,*
> *And sing my song to the listening mountains.*
>
> *But maybe I ought to practice a little now?*
> *So people who know me are not too shocked and surprised*
> *When suddenly I am old, and throw off my tie.*

Think about some of the gender traits you've absorbed. In what ways have you learned to be a female or male impersonator—a "real man," perhaps, or "truly feminine"? How has this gender role restricted you? What other parts of your personality have you shortchanged over the years?

Now ask yourself whether, over time, you've escaped some of these gender messages. As you've matured, as outside pressures have (maybe) lessened, have you managed to broaden who you are? In what ways? And in what ways can you imagine going further with this process?

The Old Fool

A special kind of freedom is embodied in Jenny Joseph's poem. Jung, Joseph Campbell, and others have ferreted out the many archetypes—repeating figures and themes—that surface throughout world mythology and organize our own interpretations of life. There's the freedom of the *hero,* who sets off to conquer enemies and retrieve a great prize. But Joseph's old woman is hardly cut from this mold. Nor is hers the freedom of the *king* or *queen,* able to impose their regal will. Is it, then, the freedom of the *magician* who taps arcane powers? Or that of the *lover,* transported by romance? Nope, nope. Not this old woman.

If anything, hers is the freedom of the *fool.* I don't mean that she's simply foolish. The holy fool, the wise fool, is a recurring presence in mythology and literature with quite a distinguished pedigree. Sometimes referred to as the *trickster* figure, the fool can do, speak, and be what others cannot. S/he sows wonderful seeds of chaos that can renew a stagnant world.

A suggestion of this archetype appears in the poem's first lines: "When I am an old woman I shall wear purple / With a red hat which doesn't go, and doesn't suit me." The fool, a standard figure in the courts and culture of medieval Europe, was distinguished by motley garb, garments that sported bright, clashing colors. As in Joseph's poem, this dress symbolizes the nature of the one who wears it. It proclaims, "True, I don't have it all together. Nor do I fit in with everyone else. But I am who I am: wild, funny, outrageous. I won't be overlooked."

In the Middle Ages, people recognized a class of "natural fools," including the congenitally idiotic or insane. Unable to grasp social rules, they could hardly be expected to obey them. Instead, they were seen as innocent and free. Walter Kaiser writes, in *Praisers of Folly*:

> The idiot performs his natural functions naturally, without sophistication or the usage of custom: when he is sad, he cries; when he is happy, he laughs; when he is hungry, he eats. Unconscious of the rules of propriety, he says and does whatever is natural for him to say or do at any given moment.[9]

For this reason, the fool could get away with what others couldn't. This glorious freedom was then appropriated by the "artificial fool," familiar to us as the Shakespearean jester and the like. Such a person was no idiot, yet under the guise of playful simplicity could criticize the church, the throne, and social customs. Even the rich and powerful were fit subjects of the fool's satire. They could not object to a fool's foolishness. But such a person voiced the hidden sentiments of others. As Kaiser writes, "because the fool is not expected to *know* anything, he readily became an expression of all the mischievous and rebellious desires in man which society attempts to control or frustrate."[10]

Joseph's old woman is just such a fool. She speaks for the mischievous and natural self. She sits down when tired, gobbles her food when hungry, spends her pension on brandy. Let loose, Joseph seems to say. Be foolhardy. Listen to the wild fool who resides in your heart, not the stuffed-shirt pragmatist who inhabits the head.

Whence comes her association of the fool with old age? Well, let's face it head-on: in our culture older folks are often seen as fools. Nursing home attendants address them in baby talk. Their own children patiently chastise them as if reprimanding a toddler. The hard of hearing are treated as if they cannot think; the weak of body, as if they were feebleminded. We pay lip service to the archetype of the wise old crone and the sage gray-bearded man, but it's often the image of the *old fool* that determines our actual treatment of elders. Joseph teaches us to transform this image. Like the medieval artificial fool, we can grab this freedom as we age and milk it to the max. Old fool am I? Great! I'll do what I want, say what I think, and have a good laugh while doing it.

Is this pursuit merely self-centered? Not necessarily. After all, medieval kings valued a good jester as much as they did their best soldiers and confidants. Why? Because such a person made them laugh. Relief is desperately needed from the gravity of state affairs. Laughter lightens the mood, puts things in perspective, heals the troubled heart. Isn't this one reason we love Jenny Joseph's poem? It makes us laugh. Her old woman teaches us to see through our own pretensions. And the more we take ourselves lightly, the more our spirit soars.

So let us age into laughter. It may be the greatest gift we can give to others, and it can also heal us. When Norman Cousins was diagnosed with a chronic and incurable disease, he didn't sink into despair. He watched Marx Brothers movies and old episodes of *Candid Camera* and laughed himself back to health.[11] While this case is unusual, studies suggest that positive emotions can indeed stimulate the immune system and healing.

Even if it doesn't cure all diseases, laughter can help us cope with them better. For example, one older gentleman I know of developed bad arthritis of the knees. It would cause his legs to collapse under him, leading to unexpected falls. You can imagine the fear, anger, and humiliation he might have experienced. It could have led him to withdraw from life, cursing his frail body all the while. But his reaction was quite the opposite. He made a game of the problem, and decided to enjoy falling. What a delight to let go into space! You just have to know how to do it correctly. He began to make an art out of falling and took joy in teaching it to others. All the while, he proudly sported his T-shirt: "Better To Be Over the Hill Than Under It!" We need such elder-fools as mentors, just as we do wise old men and women.

We will, no doubt, face our own losses and diminishments. For many, even worse than physical ailments is the specter of losing pieces of our mind. We're frightened to lose mental acuity, memory, orientation. In short, we're terrified we'll turn into fools. The extreme form is no laughing matter. Anyone who's nursed an individual with advanced Alzheimer's knows that well. But the more minor cognitive losses we can embrace with humor. Rather than curse our folly, let's celebrate it. Laughter removes the sting. Ram Dass likes to quote a greeting card poem that provides a wonderful example:

> Just a line to say I'm living,
> That I'm not among the dead
> Though I'm getting more forgetful,
> and more mixed up in the head.
> For sometimes I can't remember
> when I stand at the foot of the stair,
> if I must go up for something
> or if I've just come down from there.
> And before the fridge so often
> my poor mind is full of doubt.
> Have I just put food away
> or have I come to take some out?
> And there are times when it's dark out
> with my nightcap on my head,
> I don't know if I'm retiring
> or just getting out of bed.
> So, if it's my turn to write you

there's no need in getting sore.
I may think that I have written
and don't want to be a bore.
Remember I do love you,
I wish you were here,
and it's nearly mailtime
so I'll say goodbye, dear.
There I stood beside the mailbox
with my face so very red;
instead of mailing you my letter
I have opened it instead.
I love my new bifocals,
my dentures fit me fine,
my hearing aid is perfect,
but, Lord I miss my mind!

Many of us, no matter what our age, can identify with this poor soul. We grow spacey and forgetful. But how wonderful to embrace it all in laughter, rather than react with despair!

Think of certain diminutions time has brought you—of mind, body, lifestyle, et cetera. Maybe you've lamented them. Now imagine yourself as the fool, turning it all to laughter. Can you see the humor in any of your "losses"? Like the gentleman who fell in love with falling, can you imagine celebrating something you've resisted?

THE HOLY FOOL

To learn to laugh is not merely a secular pleasure; it opens onto the sacred realm. Spiritual traditions from around the world teach us not to take ourselves too seriously. In fact, sober reverence for dogma and holy figures can stop us from experiencing our own awakening. In the words of Zen master Feng, "The Buddha is a bull-headed jail-keeper, and the Patriarchs are horse-faced old maids!"[12] Sometimes it is better to laugh than to pray; and laughter itself can become a kind of prayer. Native American traditions have rituals to celebrate the "sacred clowns," bawdy, outrageous trickster figures. For example, in the Cherokee "Booger Event," the clowns enter a circle farting, then gyrate like madmen and spray spectators with water from large pseudopenises concealed beneath their clothes. The wild forces of nature and the human spirit are celebrated. The Islamic tradition reveres the fool Nasrudin, whose escapades express crazy wisdom. We see this playfulness in the Christian tradition as well. St. Francis referred to himself and members of his joyful order as jesters of the Lord. They followed in the footsteps of St. Paul, a self-proclaimed "fool for Christ." What, in Paul's eyes, could be more "foolish" than God come to earth in a lowly form to hang out with prostitutes and rip-off artists, only to meet an ignoble end? Ridiculous! Yet "the foolishness of God is wiser than man's wisdom" (1 Cor 1:25).

The notion that even God can be the "fool" goes against many of our most ingrained images. I remember one of my first spiritual experiences, far from somber and reverential. I was meeting my ex-girlfriend in New York's Washington Square Park about a year after our breakup. Though not a drinker, she had started using the Twelve Step program, pioneered in Alcoholics Anonymous, for help with her emotional problems. Clearly it had been working. She seemed fresh-faced, happy, more fully alive. With some hesitation (we had both been agnostic), she told me that the changes were due to God. At that time, I'd had no personal experience of that Power. But I was open to her words—the evidence stared me in the face.

Right then a very strange thing happened. A voice boomed from the heavens, *"This is the Lord. Wake up!"* No, I'm not kidding. My friend and I looked around for the source. A drunk lay on the ground nearby (not an unusual sight in Washington Square Park), and a patrol car had chosen that moment to pull up. It was the officer who had delivered the rousing call over his car's loudspeaker: *"This is the Lord. Wake up!"* Reluctantly, the drunk stirred, while my friend and I shared a good laugh.

However, I also sensed the event was more than a droll coincidence. Here I was listening to a tale of God's power when suddenly the "Lord" spoke from overhead. And how appropriate the message! At the time I was a lot like that drunk in the dirt. This wasn't the result of alcohol—I was not much of a drinker. But I had been beset by emotional difficulties, which—like an alcoholic with booze—I seemed powerless to resist. But now my friend sat across from me and proclaimed a miracle. The exact same program that had fixed incurable drunks had turned her life around and might do so for mine. *"Wake up!"* God said, using the NYPD. That message, and its follow-through (which I address more later), may have saved my life.

I also learned right then that God had a sense of humor. The message may have been deadly earnest, but it also made me laugh. Yes, "the foolishness of God is wiser than man's wisdom." Over the years, I've been guided by many a comical coincidence and light-hearted inner voice. I've often learned to trust those messages more than the weighty and guilt-ridden pronouncements of "conscience." When I mentioned this experience to a friend, she confirmed it. A horsewoman, she'd had repeated experiences of God speaking to her through *manure*. "I once asked God if he had a sense of humor," she told me. "Then I heard him say, 'Where do you think you got yours?!' "

Humor is invaluable as we trudge the spiritual path. It can help to remember that as you read through this book. Any of its themes can become just another burden: "Have I really become a wise elder yet? Have I come to completion on my life, prepared for my death? I know I should meditate more . . . I feel like such a failure!" But the spirit of humor reminds us to lighten up. That will bring us closer to en-lighten-ment than any amount of self-flagellation. So better to *play* with this book than grimly "work" on it. In joy we feel God's supporting hand—even if, now and then, it sticks a whoopee cushion under our butt.

Have you had any spiritual experiences that were tinged with humor and delight? Think back on them with a joyful spirit. Do they help you relate to the image of the divine as "foolish"? Of yourself as a "fool for God"?

Guided Meditation

A POEM OF AGING

Sit quietly in a comfortable place and position. Imagine that you are an "old woman" or an "old man" who has fully embraced freedom. Joseph proclaims the things she would do—wear purple, eat sausages, sit down when tired. What would you let yourself do? Allow images of it to enter your mind: images of your true desires; of the person you really are under your social veneer; of the holy fool within, having a coming-out party.

If not purple, what do you see yourself wearing? What kinds of activities are you engaging in? Are you alone or with others? Indoors or out? Are you hearing music, or the sounds of nature, or blessed silence? Allow your mind to scan a number of scenes where you live out your freedom. What emotions accompany these?

When you are done, why not weave what you have witnessed or thought into a poem like Jenny Joseph's? You might begin it with the phrase "When I am an old woman" or "When I am an old man." You might end it in the same way she does in her last stanza: "But maybe I ought to practise a little now." But let it be very much your own poem, the poem of your wild and foolish elderhood.

Part III Service and Rest

6

Caring for Our World:
The Eagle Clan Mother

I am an Eagle Clan Mother of the Onondaga nation. In my nation, that position is chosen by the clan people. It used to be the eldest female in any given clan was entitled to that position, but over time we have been robbed of many of the people who would have been eligible as clan mother. Those who have turned to Christianity, or to the American form of government, cannot be involved as a clan mother. She must be someone who is able to perpetuate and teach the ways of our Longhouse. She must stay within our own governmental structure, and take a position on the different issues as they come up. So today, it's not always the eldest female, but the eldest *eligible* person who is chosen. This is a lifetime position.

People choose a clan mother by watching how she has lived her life and cared for her family. She has to be someone who has a family and knows the responsibilities of being a mother, because that's evidence that she will take care of all the people as if they were her children. Those are the qualifications. The duties of a clan mother are many, beginning with being a counselor. She has to be there for people in times of family crisis, or for their own personal problems. She must be someone who is able to give advice on how to handle difficult situations.

Clan mothers also have the duty of selecting a candidate for leadership chief in the clan. . . . If a chief has to be replaced for behavior that is unbecoming to his position, it's our responsibility to find someone to take that place. If we see him going on in a way that is not acceptable, we must approach him and remind him of his responsibilities. In our language, it's called "bringing him back to his feet." This does not happen often, but it has happened a couple of times during my lifetime.

One of my deepest concerns right now is about our youth. We live so close to the city—we are one of the nearest of all our nations of people to a big city—which makes it hard for the teens to keep in mind the importance of being who they are. These are the years they usually get into trouble and it's especially hard because they have this other culture coming at them from all directions. . . . If they can just make it through those years remembering our laws and ceremonies, then they will make the right decisions. I keep pointing out that, in what we call the "Great Law," we have all of the rules and guidelines for living.

I tell them, if you find yourself in a position where you have to make a major decision, think about the things that are taught in the Longhouse, and ask yourself, "Is this going to bring harm to myself, or to any other living thing?" Basically, that's what we call respect—respect for yourself, respect for people around you, and respect for the earth.

Audrey Shenandoah, as told to Sandy Johnson, *The Book of Elders*

NOW BASED NEAR SYRACUSE, New York, the Onondagas are one of the six Iroquois nations of the northeastern United States. These nations joined in peaceful federation several hundred years ago, and they are bound by allegiance to the ways of the Longhouse. The term "Longhouse" refers to the large meeting place in which the community gathers for sacred festivals, social events, and political discussion. But more than that, it stands for a traditional way of life through which the individual, community, and cosmos are harmonized.

The Onondagas are divided into nine clans. Each has sacred ties with a totemic animal. Each operates as a political unit, its chiefs participating in tribal government. Furthermore, each clan functions as an extended family; for example, you cannot marry within your own clan.

It is in this context that the clan mother serves her many roles. She is a kind of mother to the extended family; a politician charged with selecting leaders; a transmitter of Longhouse ways.

To whom would one entrust such crucial duties? We hear the Onondaga response: it falls to the oldest eligible female. Women, in Native American traditions, are seen as playing a central role as wisdom-keepers and community-builders. So, too, do the tribal elders—guardians of ancient ways, and of the fruits of long life experience. But elderhood is not simply a matter of chronological age. Even those in midlife may be recognized as elders if they manifest maturity and wisdom.

The image of the aging fool can help to liberate us from social convention and free us up for sacred play. The image of the Eagle Clan Mother reminds us that as elders (or elders-in-training) we also have responsibilities to our world. Of course, we can't simply appropriate the example of the clan mother lock, stock, and barrel; this position is embedded in a rich cultural matrix foreign to most of us. But it can provide inspiration for elder roles that might be possible in our own setting. I'll address three such roles—that of the "mentor," the "cosmopolitician," and the "guardian of ritual."

THE MENTOR

"One of my deepest concerns right now is about our youth." For Audrey Shenandoah this concern is not just a personal interest but also a sacred obligation. The Eagle Clan Mother functions as a kind of mentor, passing on Longhouse traditions.

A "mentor" is defined as "a wise and trusted teacher or counselor." We've already introduced some in earlier chapters. Though their meeting was brief, the Aikido master acted as a mentor for the younger student. The young man received a profound teaching on the true essence of Aikido. Jenny Joseph's old woman in purple serves as a kind of imagined mentor. Speaking from the future, she teaches the younger poet how to grab hold of life.

Who comes to mind for you when you hear the word "mentor"? A teacher who turned you on to a subject, and the possibilities of your own mind? A caring grandmother who initiated you into the mysteries of gardening? Someone who helped take the place of a missing father? A professional woman who showed you it was possible to shatter the "glass ceiling" and keep on rising? We may not have thought about such people in a while, but even a brief survey reveals the profound effect they have had on our lives.

We may have affected theirs as deeply. After all, the mentor relationship is mutually rewarding: the mentor gains the satisfaction of helping. The fruits of life experience are preserved and put to use. Rabbi Zalman Schacter-Shalomi gives a computer analogy.[1] Think of losing a computer file you've labored over before you can save it. It's a sickening feeling. But isn't this like what happens if we die without passing on our wisdom? There's so much we've learned, so much we want to save before death pulls the plug. Mentoring gives us a way to "download" and preserve the best of who we are.

We can do the same thing through having children. But as spectacular and spirit-filled as this relation can be, it has inherent limitations. The very intimacy of the nuclear family may breed power agendas, conflict, and rebellion. "Don't download on me!" the kids seem to say. They may even do their best to erase any files snuck in there when they weren't looking. In a sense, it's nothing personal. They just need to make sufficient space to enter files of their own.

Sometimes it's easier to give and receive in a mentoring relationship. It can incorporate aspects of the parent-child relationship, including differences of age, experience, and power, but without all the parent-child tensions. In an atmosphere of mutual care and respect, there's a transfer of wisdom, a nurturing of potential, a cross-pollination across the generations—in short, a magical exchange.

In my own life, two examples leap to mind. When very young, I had a mentor named Sally Coleman who lived, for many years, as a maid and nanny with our family. She taught me something about love. I liked to spend time in the kitchen with her as she cooked dinner, slipping me bites of the meal to come. But mostly I ate up the atmosphere that surrounded her. It was free of the tension that pervaded other rooms of the house, formed of marital disputes, sibling rivalries, and adolescent rebellion. Here, in an oasis of calm, you could be yourself. There was no pressure to perform. Love was there just 'cause it was.

Another very different mentor was Ed Casey, a philosophy professor of mine in college. I did my senior thesis with him, and when I returned years later to study medicine he made himself available to continue our work. I don't know how, in the midst of an overly busy life, he could find time to meet privately with an ex-student. He just did; and that changed my life. I ended up pursuing a doctorate in philosophy (with Ed as my advisor) and embarked on a new career.

Ten years ago I was married, on a day of torrential rains. My mother, father, and brother were long since dead and buried. There was a hole in that memorable day. But there was also Sally, standing in for my mother. Next to her stood Ed, taking the father's role in the ceremony. They'd become part of my extended family, mentors who'd made all the difference.

What goes into being a mentor? There's no pat set of answers. But drawing on mentors I've known, like Sally and Ed, and the ideas of Rabbi Zalman Schacter-Shalomi (himself quite a mentor in the conscious aging field), I'll venture a rough sketch—not so much of "rules," but of paradoxes that characterize successful mentoring.[2]

1. The mentor stays focused on giving. That's why s/he receives.

As different as Sally and Ed were, they exhibited something in common that attracted me. They were there *for me,* not just to fulfill their own agendas. They cared about my well-being and growth and would do what they could to advance them.

Such other-centeredness is a part of "elder mind." Hopefully, we're no longer caught in youthful self-absorption. And as older individuals, we've found ways—through career, family, spiritual practice—to satisfy our own emotional needs. This condition frees us up to be more genuinely giving. We're not just mentoring for the ego gratification of feeling smarter and needed. Nowhere, for example, do we sense this in the Eagle Clan Mother's work. Nowhere does she say, "Hey, what's in it for me?"

The paradox is that we receive more back as a result. In giving without a lot of strings attached, we too are freed up to experience fulfillment. We feel a sense of purpose, usefulness, and all the joy of the outflowing of spirit to others—which also fills us up from within. Don't we hear this joy implicit in the clan mother's story?

2. The mentor usually focuses on a specific area of help or guidance. But in doing so, s/he addresses the other person *as a whole.*

In most cases, mentoring relationships do center around particular foci. Sally was caring for my physical and emotional needs. Ed was teaching me philosophy. The clan mother counsels on family crises and personal problems, and teaches the young the traditional ways. Our own mentoring also will often have a practical focus. We may pass on skills to a young business associate; teach conflict resolution to a troubled juvenile; or take our grandchild to the state forest for a hike.

To the mentor, this activity is never just technical training. Whatever pursuit is shared becomes the ground from which to address the other as a whole person—body, emotions, intellect, spirit.

A skill is being taught because it will enhance a life. When I teach philosophy, it is not just to transmit a body of knowledge. I try to awaken a spirit of questioning, a search for the good, that can genuinely improve all of a person's choices. I do not always see immediate results. Yet a seed may be planted that only germinates years later.

In this wish to impact a life, our own lives become part of the teaching. Do we live up to what we say? Do we embody wisdom, rather than just preach about it? As she tries to transmit Longhouse ways, the main teaching instrument of the clan mother is herself.

3. The mentor often teaches most by *not* acting the teacher— but by being the listener and learner.

As mentors, we may be so happy to find someone who values our wisdom, and so enthralled by our own knowledge and authority, that we fall in love with the sound of our own voice. "Let me tell you . . . let me show you," we say at every turn. "No, no, that's all wrong! Here's the correct way to do it." Of course, we may be sincere in our efforts to help our students. But the upshot can be subtle harm. If we are so superior, what does that make them? Dependent, ignorant, lesser. No one likes to be put in that position. The tendency is to shut off such a teacher or try to escape, and so one should. The *authority* looms like a large tree, hogging all the sunlight, making it harder for young plants.

As *mentors* we act more like gardeners. Our job is to help the young plant to grow. We may need to water it with our skills and experience. By challenging the other's settled beliefs, we can till the soil, making room for expansion. At the proper time, we're even willing to lay out manure—that is, confess our own mistakes and ignorance. This action too can help the one we're mentoring. Throughout the process, we remember that the plant has a principle of growth from within; we merely need to encourage its unfolding.

We can often do that best by listening. How empowering to a young person to find themselves listened to—respected, encouraged, even admired—by someone they admire in turn. Ed Casey taught me something of this skill. Though he is a world-renowned scholar in his field, Ed rarely dwelled on his own work. "Tell me what *you're* working on," he'd say, and he'd listen with great relish. Then he'd throw references my way, suggest connections, stimulate me to new ideas. I'd leave a conversation feeling all my batteries recharged. I know dozens of other students who had the same experience, yet each one left him feeling special. In Ed's presence, you discovered not his gifts, but your own. That was his greatest gift.

4. The mentor relationship has its limits, but that frees up both parties.

Though Sally and Ed were, in some ways, parental figures, they were not my real mother and father. Thank God. A second set of parents was the last thing I needed as I struggled to find myself. Through the mentoring relationship, we met across differences in age, background, and interests. Our relations were constrained by our respective roles. Nor are we now as close as we once were. Though we'll be friends for life, I live hundreds of miles away from both Sally and Ed, and I speak with them only intermittently.

And that's all right. That there are limits to the mentoring relationship paradoxically frees up the participants. The mentor need not feel overwhelmed by demands. The one mentored can preserve independence, the room to flower as a unique self. When work together is completed, both parties are able to let go. Such distance can allow an optimal space for intimacy.

These paradoxes make mentoring challenging and delightful. But what if it seems we have no one to mentor? In a world that doesn't value elder wisdom, youth hardly beats a path to our door. We may discover, though, if we look a little closer, that opportunities surround us. As grandparents, godparents, uncles, and aunts, we can mentor our younger relations. Even parents can adopt more of this role as the kids grow into adulthood. How much healthier than clinging to old patterns: "Suzy, my love, did you remember to wear your heavy coat?" "Mom, I'm *thirty-five years old.*" Maybe it's time to forge a new way of relating.

Our professional lives provide another arena. We can take an interest in the progress of younger colleagues. An older dentist might pass on to a young partner tips and techniques gathered over a lifetime. An older woman who has learned to cope with a sexist workplace may be a godsend to a new female hire.

We can also mentor through our spiritual practices. Major religious traditions have long recognized the role of older congregants in providing guidance and leadership. We still speak, for example, of "church elders"; but in practice we've often lost touch with what that means. An aging congregation may now be seen as more a liability than a resource. Here the Native American perspective provides a useful reminder. The clan mother, as elder, is seen as uniquely able to pass on the Longhouse laws and ceremonies. In the same way, we, too, can be spiritual mentors in life's second half. We can share what has been most meaningful to us—our religious beliefs, our spiritual methods, our personal experiences of God— with those who are active seekers.

Still we may feel frustrated. Perhaps we want to mentor, but have little contact with young relatives, colleagues, or spiritual seekers. We're all dressed up for a party with nowhere to go. What to do? Why not make that party happen? Somewhere there's a place where we're uniquely needed, and our heart can supply the address.

Maybe we feel moved to cuddle abandoned crack babies warehoused in a local hospital. This gift of love is a simple kind of mentoring. Perhaps we might teach a business class in a local penitentiary. The inmates may be desperate to acquire usable skills, not to mention some self-esteem. Or maybe we will decide to volunteer time assisting a young AIDS patient. In helping him work through his fear of death, we might begin to process our own.

In addition, creative programs in our community may exist

which bring together the generations. One example is the SAIL program (Senior Academy for Intergenerational Learning) affiliated with the University of North Carolina at Asheville. There, retired doctors mentor premedical students; older adults with international experience work with political science majors; research teams composed of elders, professors, and students together assist community agencies. Members of SAIL have even "adopted" a local sixth-grade class, acting as mentors, tutors, and friends up through the high school years.

So let's say, with Audrey Shenandoah, "One of my deepest concerns right now is about our youth." Let's not run away from the chance, and the duty, to reach across the generations.

✳ ✳ ✳

Who are the most important mentors you've had in your life? You might make a list of these, noting next to each name some ways they've influenced you. Have they changed any "tangibles"—for example, your place of schooling, area of study, career choice, hobbies, location of your home? How about the "intangibles"—your outlook on life, for example, or what you most enjoy?

✳

Are there individuals in your life now, or in the past, whom you mentored? Think a little on the gifts you were able to give them. And what did you receive back?

✳

Finally, ask yourself what gifts you would like to give away through future mentoring relationships. To use the computer analogy, what files do you want to be sure to "save" before your death? (Professional skills, spiritual experiences, special insights you've come to?)

Now let yourself imagine where you might pass on these gifts. See if particular people or settings come to mind.

✳

THE COSMOPOLITICIAN

The Eagle Clan Mother was committed to the welfare of all her people. Personal mentoring was a way to address this concern. But in addition to such one-on-one work, she also secured the common good through her political role. She selected a candidate for clan chief, and if his performance was not satisfactory, she was charged with replacing him, or "bringing him back to his feet."

In calling this role political, I draw on the word's derivation from the Greek *polis,* city-state. In ancient Greece the individual's welfare was seen as inextricably bound to that of the polis. For example, though Socrates challenged the Athenians, he also realized that this challenge would have been impossible without the education and freedoms Athens provided. As such he saw himself as *politikos*—a citizen with the duty to contribute back to his city.

It is well to remember the duties of citizenship in life's second half. Whatever wisdom we have gained can be put in service to our community. And especially in these days of multinationals, linked economies, instantaneous communications, and global environmental disturbances, our community is the world as a whole. The Hellenistic Greeks had a term for a person who so views their home: *kosmopolites.* The term "cosmopolitan" now calls up images of a rich sophisticate, but it once meant something deeper: the person who was a citizen not just of one city-state but of the cosmos as a whole.

The Eagle Clan Mother is a true cosmopolitan. The clan leader she helps choose serves in the council of the Onondaga nation, which in turn participates in the League of the Iroquois Nations, which interfaces with the outer world. Ultimately, as Audrey Shenandoah says, she teaches respect for the whole earth and every living thing on it. She does not refer only to its present inhabitants. She guards the seasonal and agricultural ceremonies that stretch back to times immemorial. And it is a Native American tradition to consider the effects of all decisions "unto the seventh generation" of those yet unborn. The cosmopolitan vision expands outward in space and time.

This role is one we, too, can adopt as we age. I call it being a *cosmopolitician*. Such a person doesn't act as a conventional politician, serving narrow interests and seeking partisan gain. On the contrary, the cosmopolitician seeks the welfare of the *cosmos*—"the world considered as a harmonious whole."

Just what do we do as cosmopoliticians? Here, no generalization holds water. Though concerned with the whole, we can only do our small part. As with mentoring, our heart will guide us to the proper service. Do we feel called to remedy a local problem or to involve ourselves with national or international issues? To effect some piece of legislation or to help shift our cultural mindset? To do these things through talking, voting, contributing money, writing letters, prayer, or volunteering our time? Concerning what—poverty, justice, the environment? Each of us is called to contribute in a different way.

However, there may be certain issues in which older individuals have a very special role to play. A first is to address the role of elders themselves. In our society they are often provided with neither honor, dignity, nor basic social supports. As elders or elders-in-training, we can help to redress this wrong. The very way we approach our aging can subtly influence others to shift their views. We can also fight for protections against age discrimination and assurance of an adequate social safety net. We can teach businesses the value of mature workers and the need for innovative programs to take advantage of this resource. We can seek the reform of dehumanized environments where the sick elderly are warehoused. We can also directly assist those in need. One model is the Shepherd's Center movement, begun in 1972 by Dr. Elbert Cole in Kansas City. There are now about one hundred Shepherd's Centers across the country, run "by, with, and for" older adults. There, seniors volunteer to help meet the needs of other seniors, providing chore services, meals on wheels, and the like. Each center chooses its own priorities; the process empowers everyone involved.

Interestingly enough, though, assistance to other elders is not Audrey Shenandoah's main focus. Her deepest concern is for the youth. The true cosmopolitician, we see, seeks the welfare of all generations. All too often our age-based organizations, like the American Association of Retired Persons (AARP), act as advocates simply for programs serving the aged. There's nothing wrong with defending Medicare and Social Security. But if we restrict ourselves to partisan politics, we can prompt a divisive mindset and generational warfare. How much better to think as cosmopoliticians! Can we imagine a new AARP (with its over thirty million members!) that acts this way, also advocating for the needs of the young—public education, enlightened family leave policies, maternal and infant nutrition programs, quality day care? Wouldn't this be an organization of clan mothers?

One example of such thinking happened in Brookline, Massachusetts. Through an innovative program, elders were enlisted by the school system to help tutor and share their life experience with children. By the end, Brookline's elders had become strong supporters of a bond issue to provide tax increases for the local schools. The mentor role led naturally to political action—cosmopolitical action, that is.

Finally, cosmopolitics lead us not only beyond the division between old and young, but even that between the merely human and non-human. When the Eagle Clan Mother speaks of "respect for the earth" and for every "living thing," she draws on the Native American cosmology that views all natural beings as ensouled and interconnected. We live in community with other animals, and with plants, rivers, and mountains, all of which embody their own special power.

Brooke Medicine Eagle, an intertribal teacher raised on a Crow reservation, writes of elder women:

> No longer is their attention consumed with the creation and rearing of their own children. . . . Thus their attention turns to the children of All Our Relations; not just their own children, or the children of their friends, their clan or tribe, but the children of all the hoops; the Two-Legged ones, the Four-Leggeds, the Wingeds, the Finned, the Green-Growing Ones, and all others.[3]

As clan mothers and fathers, we can fight for all these children. We might do so with the ferocity of a mother bear guarding her young or the gentleness of a dove brooding over her eggs. We can act on the most local or the most global level. We might pick up trash as we stroll; recycle our paper and cans; help clean up a local stream; join a community board to oppose heedless development; contribute to ecologically minded organizations; write in support of antipollution laws; the list goes on and on. As elders we are meant to think of the impact of choices unto the seventh generation. And there may not be a seventh generation unless we safeguard the earth.

In the previous discussions I've emphasized the use of existing political routes. We can also imagine new ones that combine traditional wisdom with innovative technologies. For example, Rabbi Schacter-Shalomi's vision draws on the Native American model, whereby tribal affairs are often brought before a council of elders for wise discussion and decision making. In a contemporary version, elder councils could form to advise governmental bodies, religious congregations, and educational institutions. Shachter-Shalomi even envisions a worldwide council of elders linked by an electronic communications network. Though without direct political power, such a council could still exert influence on world leaders. Faced with a troublesome issue—the eradication of the rain forests, for example—the council could consider the interests of all concerned, and effects unto the seventh generation, before proposing creative solutions. Like the clan mother, such a council could help to bring our chiefs "back to their feet." Through such a council, in Shachter-Shalomi's words, "the seers of the planet [would] 'hold the field' for social and political action based on the contemplative insight of its wisest citizens."[4]

An outlandish vision? Sure, but why not?! In modern times, we've often assumed that new visions are the province of youth. Not so in the Native American tradition. It is the elder, in touch with sacred traditions and long life experience, who best guides a vision quest. And surely the world is in need of a vision.

✳   ✳   ✳

Imagine yourself a cosmopolitician charged with concern for the world. Where does your unique contribution lie? What issues bring out your passion or **compassion***? Are you already contributing in these areas, or have you in the past? Can you imagine new forms your service might take in the future?*

If you listed areas of possible involvement, do you feel inspired to act on any? If so, a few phone calls might guide you to a place of rich involvement. (Andrew Carroll's book, **Golden Opportunities***—see Appendix A—can also be a valuable resource for some.)*

✳

THE GUARDIAN OF RITUAL

Talk of elder councils and vision quests suggests another role of the clan mother. Along with being a designated "faith keeper," she is a guardian and transmitter of sacred ceremonies. The Great Law she teaches is not just a set of rules. It is a whole way of life in which ritual provides a central grounding. The Onondagas celebrate important festivals, including a three-week-long winter solstice ceremony, a spring planting dance, a six-day green corn dance, a running of the sap ceremony, a June strawberry ceremony, and a summer bean dance. Each celebrates the intertwining of the individual and the community, and this community with nature, and nature with the divine. Life is made whole by such ritual.

This use of ritual is largely missing from our culture. Even *holy days* like Christmas have become mere *holidays*—time off from work to exchange pricey gifts. We often end up exhausted rather than renewed. And for certain important passages of life—puberty, divorce, job changes, retirement—we simply have no developed rituals. Sometimes we seem as primitive in this regard as so-called primitive cultures are vis-à-vis our science and technology.

We can take a lesson here from the clan mother, preserver of ritual, but within our culture we must do more; we also have to be *inventors* of ritual, restoring this sacred dimension to life.

There are books that can help guide our imagination. Kathleen Wall's and Gary Ferguson's *Lights of Passage* teaches us how to design rites of passage suited to the modern world.[5] Robin Lysne's *Dancing up the Moon* is a woman's guide to creating ceremonies that hallow the ordinary.[6] Such books lay down some general guidelines. For example, ritual best unfolds in a time and space that are set apart. It can draw on universal symbols, such as the planting of a seed to symbolize new life; but it can also incorporate symbols personal to us. If, for example, we loved balloons as a child, we might release them in the air as part of a rite of self-renewal. While a one-time ceremony can be powerful, it's also important to "root" our ritual through follow-up prayer, journaling, reenactment—whatever deepens its presence in our lives.

Rather than deal with this subject in the abstract, I'll give some examples of invented ritual. I'll focus on rites that might help us through the aging process, using Native American rituals as an inspiration. Our culture does have its ceremonies of early life—first communion, Bar Mitzvah, and the like—but there is little to help us spiritualize the passages of midlife and beyond. I offer these four imaginary examples not to serve as a blueprint but as a stimulus for your own thought.

1. The vision quest

One Native American practice, central to the life of the Plains people, is the vision quest I've already mentioned. Sometimes also called the guardian spirit quest or prayer-fast, this ritualized retreat was to be embarked on one or more times by every man and woman. Joseph Epes Brown, a noted author on Native American ceremonies, describes it as follows:

> After rigorous preparations, which always include the rites of the purifying sweat lodge and instructions by a qualified elder, the candidate goes to a high and remote place with the resolve to fast and pray continually and so suffer through acts of sacrifice and exposure to the elements for a specified number of days. The ordeal is highly ritualized and may involve the establishing of an altar. . . . Prayers may be addressed to the powers of the four directions. . . . One may also remain silent, for it has been said that "silence *is* the voice of *Wakan Tanka,* the *Great Mysterious.*" Often the sacred experience comes in the mysterious appearance of an animal or winged being, or perhaps in one of the powers of nature. A special message is often communicated to the seeker, and this will serve as a guide and reminder through the person's life. . . . [Afterward] the candidate will explain the vision or dream which will be interpreted by the guiding elder, who will then give instructions as to what should now be accomplished in order to insure the continuity of the participation of the spiritual throughout the person's life.[7]

Vivian has decided to embark on an inner journey, loosely modelled on such a vision quest. The occasion? She's about to undergo a career shift. For decades she has served as a sales representative, and then an executive, for a manufacturing firm. Now in her early fifties and financially stable, she has decided to cut back. While she will still do consulting work with the company, as well as help out with her daughter's small business, she also wants more time for herself. But what exactly will she do with it? Travel, volunteer work, new friendships? Her ship is setting out from port but in need of a rudder and compass.

In the month leading up to her retreat Vivian keeps a journal about some of her feelings. She's sad, scared, joyful all at once. She chooses to share her experience with Judy, an older friend and mentor who's already sailed through a similar transition. That doesn't mean Judy can answer her questions, but maybe she can help clarify what the questions *are*.

The questions are three in number, Judy and Vivian realize in their conversations. First, "What am I to *do* in this new phase of life?" Second, "Who am I to *be*"? And third (this Judy suggested), "What gifts are present, within and without me, to see me through this process?" Vivian resolves to take a three-day retreat at a spiritual center located amid nearby rolling hills. Each day there she focuses on one of the three questions, walking, praying, and journaling it through.

Afterward she discusses with Judy some of the messages she received. What to do? She caught an image of herself and her daughter building a new relationship. Through the vehicle of working together on the business, the old hurts and power struggles might give way to something different. Equality. A spirit of cooperation. Maybe even a true friendship. Vivian realized she wished for this healing above all else.

Who to be? This answer was clear and simple: Herself! Not the company executive, or the mom who fixes everything. She was to grow into becoming just who she really was. And who was that? Here Vivian wasn't so clear. She sensed that more would be revealed over time.

What gifts would see her through all these changes? As she'd walked the hills, she felt strength surging in her muscles and in her own character. This joyful hardness would see her through. She also imaged, like a waterfall cascading, the love and support of all her friends, and of a loving God.

Wow! Listening to all this, Judy did little more than nod. But then she reminded Vivian of the need to root these insights more deeply through action steps. They resolved to talk each month about Vivian's new life and how it was progressing. And Vivian decided that every three months, at the season's change, she'd return to the retreat center to extend this vision quest.

2. The potlatch

Another Native American ceremony, particularly associated with the northern Pacific Coast tribes, is the Potlatch. Sandy Johnson writes:

> Potlatch celebrations, lasting for days, are held for initiations, births, marriages, mourning, and installing a new chief. The host family gives away blankets, clothing, artifacts, canoes—it takes years of preparation and can cost the family everything they own. However, what they lose in material wealth, they gain in respect.[8]

Seymour and Josie Hyde have decided to hold a ceremony inspired by the Potlatch (though also quite different). The occasion is their decision to give up their house. Now that the kids have moved away, the old homestead yawns as empty as an open mouth. Time to move on. The Hydes have purchased a smaller place in a nearby community. They like the fellowship and amenities, but they know they'll have to make do with a lot less room. It hurts to give up not only the old place but all the treasured possessions that will no longer fit.

They've decided to make a virtue of necessity. They'll come together as a family both to mourn and celebrate the change. On a lovely Sunday morning, their three kids and their families gather around the kitchen table. After a breakfast of bagels and fresh-squeezed orange juice (itself a time-honored family ritual), the ceremony begins.

One by one, Seymour and Josie gift away their things. One child gets the living-room sofa; another the painting of a seaside village; another the multivolume encyclopedia. Seymour and Josie are no fools—they've consulted in advance to find out what each family member really wants. Sometimes the motive was purely practical (our school-age kid can use the encyclopedia); sometimes more sentimental (I remember the vacation when we bought that painting!). In any case, the presentation of almost every gift is accompanied by the telling of its story. The Hydes are not celebrating a pile of objects, but their family's shared life.

Next it's time to adjourn to the den, where a number of other items have been gathered ready for pickup by a local charity. Josie and Seymour speak briefly about the organization they've selected. They voice a wish that their gifts bring blessing to the needy. Then it's out to the porch to honor another pile—box after box of trash destined for the junkheap. Mother raises her orange-juice glass in a toast: "God bless father for finally going at the basement!"

Now it's time to make the rounds of this lovely old home. Each room evokes a slew of memories. The kids tell of pancake batter on the kitchen walls; hide-and-seek games around the living room furniture; late nights reading in the bedroom with a hidden light. "Hey, I never knew about that," Seymour growls. He and Josie reminisce about tired but romantic dinners after the kids were asleep, and stargazing from the porch swing while sipping good red wine.

Finally, it's time to say goodbye. Josie, Seymour, and their kids say a prayer they've written together: "Bless this fine house and all that it's given us. We give it back to the bountiful universe. May this house always bless whoever comes within its walls, and may it always have a place in our hearts."

The ceremony is concluded.

3. Entering the grandmother lodge

In Native American cultures, postmenopausal women are often considered spiritual grandmothers to the whole tribe and to the world. Brooke Medicine Eagle writes:

> The Grandmother Lodge is the lodge of the white-haired (wisdom) women—those who have gone beyond the time of giving away the power of their blood, and now hold it for energy to uphold the Law. . . . Our relationship with this great circle of Life is ultimately in their hands.[9]

In this context, the passage through menopause is worthy of special honor and celebration. This is also true in the Goddess traditions, where menopause signals a transition to the archetype of the crone—the wise and powerful elder woman. Drawing on such inspirations, Eleanor Piazza each year holds a communal ceremony for "Women of the Fourteenth Moon"—those who have passed more than a year (thirteen moons) without bleeding.[10] Brooke Medicine Eagle also leads individuals through rites of menopause. The following ceremony is inspired by the work of these and other farsighted women.

Suzanne has decided to hold a ceremony celebrating her menopause. She has struggled with hot flashes, emotional ups and downs, and her own fears of growing old. Now it's time to affirm the positive. She has invited three women to join her at sunset by the banks of a river: Nicole, her teenage niece; Joanne, her thirty-four-year-old buddy; and Beatrice, an older friend and mentor now in her mid-sixties. Why these three women? They are some of Suzanne's closest confidantes. They're just kinky enough to get into the spirit of the event. Their range of ages also speaks to Suzanne of the three goddess archetypes found in world religions: the young maiden, the mother, and the wise crone. In a way, these are the stages of Suzanne's own life.

Beatrice, as the presiding elder, initiates the ceremony just as the sun sets over the river. She begins with a small prayer of gratitude. Suzanne then shares her concerns. Before embracing a new stage of life, she has to complete the previous one. She reads aloud to the other women from two lists. The first recounts some of her frustrations and disappointments over the last ten years. A job she really wanted and didn't get. A painful miscarriage. Deep hurt on both sides within her marriage. She tells it all, her voice choking at times. Then she goes on to her second list—the joys she most wishes to celebrate. An exciting promotion. Seeing her son grow up into a delightful young man. A family trip to the Southwest that was astounding.

When done, she ties these two lists each to a rock. With a joyful shout she heaves them into the river—out with the old, on to the new!

That is, the new business of embracing elderhood. Suzanne now receives from each of the three women a special gift symbolizing this passage. Nicole has selected, and reads aloud, Jenny Joseph's poem "Warning." She explains that in the old woman wearing purple she hears what she most loves about Suzanne—her independence and her outrageousness; for example, daring to hold this ritual. Joanne gives Suzanne a ring inscribed with their initials. It symbolizes their close bond, which the passage of time can't erode. Finally, Beatrice whips out a pair of clogging shoes. Clogging shoes? For years she and Suzanne have talked about learning to clog, a type of square dancing with wooden tap shoes, both wild and disciplined. "Hey, we've got no more excuses. Let's make it happen!"

After accepting the gifts with laughter and a few tears, Suzanne prepares for the ceremony's completion. She removes her red jacket, symbol of her menses, to reveal underneath a beautiful white dress. This is her wisdom garb. She embraces Beatrice, who graciously accepts her into the Grandmother Lodge. After a closing prayer of thanks, the women adjourn to a nearby Chinese restaurant for a feast of dumplings and beers. What does this symbolize? Nothing. But Suzanne loves Chinese food.

4. The elder council

In one form or another, a council of elders plays a central role in many Native American nations. Important tribal matters come before such a council; its considerations are guided by knowledge of tribal history and traditions, long personal experience, and sacred inspiration. Sitting in a circle, all are free to speak their piece. Ideally, the voice of wisdom becomes manifest through each individual and through the workings of the communal mind.

I've been privileged to participate in a number of ceremonies loosely modelled on the elder council and conducted by Rabbi Schacter-Shalomi, and others, through the Omega Institute in Rhinebeck, New York. The model I describe here is based closely on these gatherings. (See appendix B for further discussion of how to form a spiritual passages group, using this or other formats.)

John has decided to start something like an elder council. At some stage it might address the problems of his community, but first he envisions it as a tool to help its own participants. He's done some reading on spirituality and aging. He's excited about claiming a creative elderhood but is not sure he can do it alone. He wants to be part of a group of like-minded seekers who stimulate and support each other.

Not knowing of such a group, he decides to make it happen. Through friends, acquaintances from a workshop he attended, and a flyer posted at a local institute for learning in retirement, he's assembled a group of ten. All are forty-five or older, except for a thirty-something woman interested in the issue of aging. Her attitude is "Why not get ready now?"

The group has decided to meet every other week. They'll discuss readings on creative aging; share life experiences; formulate spiritual exercises to work at together. But the heart of the group process will be an elder council ceremony conducted once a month.

In this ceremony, participants form a circle, symbol of equality, harmony, and wholeness. In the middle sits a "talking stick." Inspired by Native American traditions, a member, Sylvia, has fashioned this stick from the branch of an old oak tree, decorating it with symbols of elderhood and wisdom. Tonight the question the group has decided to talk about is "What does aging have to do with compassion?" The ground rules are the same as always: when you feel moved to speak, go to the center and return to your seat with the talking stick. It entitles you to hold the floor. Begin your sharing on the topic with the word "and." You are adding to what others have said, not judging or arguing with an implicit "but." A fuller wisdom will emerge from the group mind than from any one individual. Each can help it emerge by sharing from the heart, not the mind. From experience, not book knowledge. Allow a greater Source to voice through you. When you are done, stop. Don't go on and on. Close your sharing with the words "I have spoken," returning the talking stick to the center. After a period of silence sufficient to absorb the message, another may reach for the talking stick. Your job then is to create a field of support and loving attention for the speaker.

That evening, as always (well, usually) the sharing runs deep. John speaks about growing in compassion for *himself* as he grows older. Sylvia talks about being better able to accept the compassion of her friends. Her age, and her bout with cancer, have worn away the pride that once kept others at a distance. At a distance . . . Frieda speaks of her compassion for the distant peoples in pain she sees reported on the nightly news. When younger it had meant little to her. Why the change? But Robert turns to a different change— he actually feels *less* compassion, less patience with those unwilling to take action to improve their lives. As a young man, he thought he had forever. Now he realizes there's limited time to waste.

Time to waste—what does that mean? At the evening's end, the group chooses this question as the topic of the next elder council. What is it to "waste time" or use it wisely? How has our maturing shifted our view of time? Linking arms, the members thank the spirit that has brought them together, and they disperse into the night.

———

Such rituals can help us turn the larger passages of life into genuinely spiritual passages. Yet we can also hallow the ordinary by building ritual into every day. Why not wake up each morning by proclaiming our health, with generous thanks to our body? Why not then take a brisk walk to greet the day or, putting on a favorite piece of music, engage in relaxing yoga stretches? At lunch time we can re-collect ourselves with a table blessing, a nice light meal, perhaps even followed by a refreshing rest. The difference between a mere habit and a ritual, Robin Lysne says, lies in our consciousness. When we pursue it with a spirit of attention and celebration, even lying down for a nap or brushing our teeth at day's end can become a healing ritual. After brushing our teeth, why not brush clean our mind? We can review the day before climbing into bed. What mistakes did we make that we need to learn from and amend? And where did Spirit shine through in the day's events—what do we have to give thanks for?

We can thus anchor each day in small rituals. And the more we learn to do this, the more we can teach others. This teaching is part of what we have to give as clan mothers and fathers. We are called to mentor the young; to act as cosmopoliticians; to serve as guardians of ritual. Ultimately, these roles are not separate. They are three intersecting ways to serve a world in need.

❊ ❊ ❊

Why not design your own ritual of passage? You don't have to actually perform it if you prefer not to. But at least imagine it through.

Choose a transition in your life that you are experiencing now or that you anticipate. It might involve a change in your job or home life, or some physical or spiritual transformation. Don't shy away from choosing something painful—ritual can help you work through that pain.

Now imagine a ritual with which you would process and hallow that change. Where might this ceremony happen and when? Would you be on your own or with others? Are there symbolic objects and actions you might incorporate into the event? Would it help to speak any prayers or read any passages aloud? Does the ritual acknowledge both sadness and loss (if appropriate) and celebrate new possibilities? Let your intuition run free as you seek the ritual meant for you.

Then, too, how might you ritualize your everyday life? Perhaps you already have some daily rituals—can you deepen your involvement with these? Or are there habits you might transform into rituals through bringing a new consciousness to them? Finally, are there any entirely new rituals you might adopt? It's often better to start small (for example, five minutes of meditation, or a short blessing before dinner, or one yoga stretch each morning). We're more apt to follow through, and then we can build on that success. This use of ritual can be a rewarding experience as well as a valuable tool in our spiritual journey.

❋ *Guided Meditation* ❋

THE EAGLE CLAN MOTHER

In the tradition of Native American shamanism, the healer can often take on the body of a bird or animal and make use of its powers. This meditation involves (literally) a flight of imagination. Allow yourself to enter into it as best you can.

Imagine that you are resting on a stone outcropping near a mountain peak. Arrayed before your gaze is the valley below. Allow yourself to see the fields that stretch beneath you, a checkerboard of green and tan. You notice a small house, as well, with white smoke curling from its chimney. In those fields you also see two very small figures—people, no doubt—with a herd of animals. They are so far below you that they all look like toy figures.

Now become aware of the fresh, cold mountain air. It smells of snow. And become aware of your own body—it is a human body no more. It is the body of an eagle. Your arms have become large, feathered wings. Your face is curved into a beak. You can make out the figures below because you have the powerful eyes of an eagle. You are perched near a mountaintop because you have the gift of flight.

And you begin to use it. Slowly, beating your powerful wings, you soar into the air. Any feeling of fear gives way to the feeling of freedom and exhilaration. Allow yourself to enjoy the sensation of flight. Your strong body is buoyed up by currents of air. Your body is attuned to them, and it shifts with each breeze.

As you fly, you gaze down at the valley beneath you. It is your home no less than the mountaintop. Beyond, in the distance, is a forest, mountains, another valley. You have, at some time, flown through it all. It is all your home. Your wings know no boundaries.

Now imagine that with your wings you could embrace the whole world. You feel surging in your heart a wish to protect it all. The mountains, the forests, the fields. The tiny human beings and animals so far below. You would shelter them all under the shadow of your great wings.

Finally, you alight back on your mountain perch. You rest for a moment. You notice beside you a nest of eggs. These are your children waiting to hatch. You wish to care for the whole world, but you can begin with these eggs—those nearest and dearest to your heart. Still you will never forget what you knew on the flight. It is the whole world that is your egg. The earth sits in your nest waiting to hatch. It needs your warmth and care.

7

The Use of the Useless:
The Taoist Tree

Carpenter Shih went to Ch'i and, when he got to Crooked Shaft, he saw a serrate oak standing by the village shrine. It was broad enough to shelter several thousand oxen and measured a hundred spans around, towering above the hills. The lowest branches were eighty feet from the ground, and a dozen or so of them could have been made into boats. There were so many sightseers that the place looked like a fair, but the carpenter didn't even glance around and went on his way without stopping. His apprentice stood staring for a long time and then ran after Carpenter Shih and said, "Since I first took up my ax and followed you, Master, I have never seen timber as beautiful as this. But you don't even bother to look, and go right on without stopping. Why is that?"

"Forget it—say no more!" said the carpenter. "It's a worthless tree! Make boats out of it and they'd sink; make coffins and they'd rot in no time. Use it for doors and it would sweat sap like pine; use it for posts and the worms would eat them up. It's not a timber tree—there's nothing it can be used for. That's how it got to be that old!"

After Carpenter Shih had returned home, the oak tree appeared to him in a dream and said, "What are you comparing me with? Are you comparing me with those useful trees? The cherry apple, the pear, the orange, the citron, the rest of those fructiferous trees and shrubs—as soon as their fruit is ripe, they are torn apart and subjected to abuse. Their big limbs are broken off, their little limbs are yanked around. Their utility makes life miserable for them, and so they don't get to finish out the years Heaven gave them, but are cut off in mid-journey. They bring it on themselves—the pulling and tearing of the common mob. And it's the same way with all other things.

"As for me, I've been trying a long time to be of no use, and now that I'm about to die, I've finally got it. This is of great use to me. If I had been of some use, would I ever have grown this large?" . . .

When Carpenter Shih woke up, he reported his dream. His apprentice said, "If it's so intent on being of no use, what's it doing there at the village shrine?"

"Shhh! Say no more! It's only *resting* there."

Chuang Tzu, Basic Writings, trans. Burton Watson

IT TAKES A DREAM to awaken Carpenter Shih to a larger vision of "worth." The oak tree scorned now comes to him in the form of a teacher and tutors him in the perceptual flip. He realizes that the tree's uselessness is also the source of great use. First, to the tree itself: rather than being torn apart by others, the oak can grow and flourish undisturbed. It comes to its natural fulfillment. This is a source of blessings to the wider world as well. The oak standing next to the village shrine provides serenity to the worshipper, beauty for the sightseer, needed shelter in a storm, soothing shade from the hot summer sun. Because the tree has remained whole, it can provide wholeness to the community, serving as a holy and healing presence.

This lesson is well worth remembering, especially if the passage of years leaves us feeling ever more useless. We may have children who grow up and move away. Perhaps we miss that sense of being needed. At work, the boss may favor young employees up on the latest trends and technologies, willing to toil long hours at a furious pace. We don't envy such laborers. Like fruit trees, they may be "torn apart and subjected to abuse" by a job that runs them ragged. However, even if "their utility makes life miserable for them," it yields sweet fruit to the company. The maturity and experience of the older worker are discounted.

When we do leave the job, whether in a forced or voluntary fashion, we may feel even more useless. Retirement is often experienced as the end of our fruitful days.

The wider culture reinforces this equation of age with uselessness. Media images feature the young and often target them as consumers. Clergy build programs for a congregation's youth but often seem less interested in its seniors. Pundits remind us of the potential drain on resources caused by the increasing numbers of elderly.

How to fight back? We've already seen one powerful response. As "clan mothers and fathers" we have a tremendous amount to contribute in life's second half. On the other hand, there's also a danger that we could fall right back into fruit-tree mode. We may feel guilty if we're not constantly mentoring the young, fighting political battles, cleaning up the environment, and organizing rituals on the side. Sounds exhausting just to think about.

We need the balance of another image and option. Here the Taoist tree comes to our rescue. Instead of a direct counterattack on the image of the useless elder, we can use a judo tactic: flow with the energy of the opponent and turn it to our advantage. Perhaps the biology of aging *will* render us less useful in certain ways. Perhaps social biases will exaggerate this trend. Still, the oak tree suggests we might celebrate all that. "I've been trying a long time to be of no use, and now that I'm about to die, I've finally got it. This is of great use to me."

Let's turn to some of the ways in which our "uselessness" can be of great use to us.

COMING TO WHOLENESS

The oak tree's first concern was preserving physical wholeness. If it had been a fruit tree ripped apart at harvest time, or a timber tree cut down for wood, it could not have lived out its natural life. Its uselessness was the secret of its longevity.

It can be so for us as well. To be "useful" in our society often takes quite a toll on our health. We are beset by multiple demands pulling at us like harvesters picking fruit. "Mommy, when are you coming home?" "I'd like that report on my desk by tomorrow noon." "You said you were going to stop at the grocery store after work." Pretty soon we're tearing our hair out, and this is not the only body part to suffer. We may develop high blood pressure from accumulated stress. Without the time for healthy eating and exercise, our cholesterol count and waistline grow larger. A chronic sleep shortage may leave us run-down, more susceptible to infections and accidents. When younger we were better able to cope with all this. We barely noticed the prices of a fast life. Not so as we age. We don't bounce back as quickly from acute illnesses or injuries. And over time the demands we place on ourselves may lead to chronic problems, either musculoskeletal in nature or involving wear and tear on our vital organs. Finally, our drivenness may even kill us. A classic example: the early heart attack of the overstressed professional. Such people, like the fruit trees, "don't get to finish out the years Heaven gave them, but are cut off in mid-journey." How sad. The very pressure to be of use may land us in an early grave, useless to ourselves and others.

So if age gives us the opportunity to relax, let's remember that it may be lifesaving. Perhaps the demands of work and family have lessened. Maybe there's also been an inner shift, leading us to claim more time for ourselves. In either case, we may realize health benefits. The word "health" comes from the same root as "whole" and "holy." It is a bodily expression of wholeness, intertwined with emotional and spiritual fulfillment.

How to claim this wholeness now, no matter what our age? For one thing, we might make time for more sleep. As biological psychologist Dr. David Dinges says, "I can't think of a single study that hasn't found people getting less sleep than they ought to."[1] One estimate, based on primate and human research, is that we should be getting nine to ten hours a night. Surveyed in 1910, students did indeed report sleeping an average of nine hours. But by 1988 a comparable survey showed students sleeping less than seven hours, a dramatic shift. Our increasingly fast-paced life robs us of sleep and all its restorative powers. As we age, why not reclaim this "useless" activity?

Furthermore, it is healing simply to slow down in general. We give our heart and other vital organs a much-needed break. We may also want to take more time for those activities that give us the most pleasure; studies have suggested that our immune system function depends partially on the emotions we feel. In addition, we can seek out the exercise we need to keep us strong and flexible. We should be careful, though, not to overdo it in driven fashion—this would be to relapse into an obsession with "useful" acts. We've done that goal-oriented fruit-tree thing. Now, it's time to be the long-lived oak. (I return to the issue of health and longevity in chapter 11.)

As we reach for wholeness of body, we also reach for wholeness of mind. In trying to be useful, our mind is often divided between multiple tasks and points of attention that all but pull us apart. We attempt to clean the kitchen while on a call to a needy friend, keeping half an eye on the baby. Spiritual teachers stress the virtue of one-pointed attention, but we can't see how that is possible, given our busy lives.

The aging process can help us to unify. Part of what pulls us apart is the focus on *having* and *doing* as much as we possibly can. This orientation is the fruit-tree aspect of young mind: How many plums can I produce or gather? In life's second half we move from having and doing toward an appreciation of just *being*. We don't have to make so many plums to prove ourselves worthy. Simply to be who we are, to appreciate the life we're given, turns out to be enough.

We might call this state "oak-tree mind." The oak tree is not seeking any particular goal. It need not justify its existence daily with tasty fruit. It simply *is,* and that is sufficient. Its roots reach deep into the soil. Its branches spread upward to embrace the sky. Here lies an image of our truest self—earthy, yet drawn to the divine.

An American psychoanalyst, Martin Grotjahn, provides an example of this mind-set in his essay, "The Day I Got Old":

> I don't work anymore. I don't walk anymore. Peculiarly enough, I feel well about it. . . . I sit in the sun watching the falling leaves slowly sail across the waters of the swimming pool. I think, I dream, I draw, I sit—I feel free of worry—almost free of this world of reality.
>
> If anyone had told me that I would be quietly happy just sitting here, reading a little, writing a little, and enjoying life in a quiet and modest way, I, of course, would not have believed.[2]

Perhaps we're reminded of the Aikido master who loved to sit in the garden and gaze on his persimmon tree. Freed of the compulsion to achieve, we can enjoy life's small pleasures. No longer seeking to do many things at once, we can focus our attention. As a result, even a mundane activity—thinking, drawing, watching leaves fall—begins to reveal new depths of meaning. We are fully present in the moment.

The Aikido master shared such moments with his wife. But Martin Grotjahn never mentions another person. We might wonder if he isn't lonely. For many of us the specter of growing old alone is one of our greatest fears. However, to be alone need not imply loneliness—a form of psychological distress. In fact, research suggests that elders experience much less loneliness per unit of time spent alone then do younger adults. Why? It's not clear. But we might speculate that it has to do with oak-tree mind: that ability to simply *be.* For someone who has mastered this art, the pain of loneliness may be largely supplanted by the pleasures of solitude. In solitude we can grow calm and unified, resting within the self. We may enter more deeply into our own thoughts, or lose ourselves more freely in the beauty of art and nature. And in solitude we may sense more clearly the presence of Spirit with us. Prayer and worship often flourish best in a garden of silence. Constant conversation all too often fills our day like weeds. It can choke off the contemplative flower.

Even the physical diminishments of age, in fact, can help weed the inner garden. How so? Imagine a Zen Buddhist attending to her practice. First, she stops moving every which way to sit down and unify her focus. Partially closing her eyes, she withdraws attention from the outer world. Though sounds still assail her ears, she concentrates her focus inward on her own repetitive breathing. She is no longer "doing" anything but simply allowing herself to be. Through sustained meditation her awareness gradually clears and deepens until she may achieve "satori"—an ecstatic breakthrough to enlightenment.

As Ram Dass points out, the biology of aging curiously mimics such practices. Perhaps a weakness or disability first slows us down. We need to stop more and sit. Then too, glaucoma or cataracts might dim our vision. And with time we may suffer a partial loss of hearing that makes casual conversation less inviting. We shouldn't minimize the suffering such conditions can cause. But the perceptual flip also shows the hidden grace. After all, isn't nature offering us what the meditator struggles to achieve? We are sitting more, with greater detachment from the senses, centered within the self. Instead of feeling torn apart by these losses, we can use them in our quest for wholeness.

Returning to Grotjahn's description, we can see another ingredient of wholeness. Just as the meditator suspends goal-oriented activity, so Grotjahn is not acting *for* any purpose. He's not watching leaves fall in order to publish a research study; he's not thinking in order to increase the profitability of his investments. His watching and thinking are *useless*; they have no end outside themselves. Precisely this uselessness opens up for him the experience of being wholly present.

I often begin my philosophy course with a little game that illustrates this point. I call it the Why game. (If you have a four-year-old you may be familiar with it.) "Why are you here in class?" I ask a hapless student.

"I need to be in order to graduate," the student replies.

"But why graduate?"

"I need the degree."

"But why get the degree?"

"So I can get a good job."

"But why do you want a good job?"

"So I'll make some decent money."

"But why go for the money?"

"So I can travel around the world."

"Why travel?"

"I just love to. It makes me happy."

Only here does the Why game terminate—when someone reaches the thing that is no longer a means to an end but holds intrinsic satisfaction. According to Aristotle, this quality is fundamental to happiness. Unlike intermediate goods, like wealth and power, that we pursue for the sake of what they can bring us, happiness we want in and for itself. This student equates travel with happiness. Maybe it's the sense of freedom, or learning, or the sheer excitement of new places. Whatever form it takes, this vision of happiness is what tugs him out of bed and plants him in my classroom.

Here we find a paradox. The student is doing what is useful (coming to class) in order to achieve his goal of happiness. But in so doing he has to engage in the opposite of what brings him joy. He loves freedom, but he must live out years of confinement to a classroom. Desiring excitement, he may have to put up with tedious (but well-paying) jobs. His quest for happiness thus takes him ever farther from that goal. As Chuang Tzu says of such people, "Their very concern for enjoyment makes them unhappy."[3]

"Wait a second," our sober side interrupts. "We can't always follow the whims of the moment. We must take the road that, in the long run, will lead us toward our aims." Well, there's some truth to this. However, there are also dangers. Always travelling toward some goal off in the future, we may never arrive at any resting place. Finally, we can't even remember what destination we were seeking.

Aging can bring us home to the present. As the years pass, we realize that happiness is *now or never*. We allow ourselves to do just what we wish; that is, to be useless. To pursue an activity, whether it is to travel, paint, read a book on medieval history, or laze away a summer afternoon watching leaves fall, simply *because we want to*.

There's a word for this in the English language—we call it *play*. The old woman wearing purple was an example of someone who knew how to play. It may be a dying art. In our world, increasingly focused on the useful, we have ever-diminishing opportunities for play. In a 1970s Harris poll, Americans reported working an average of forty-one hours a week, with twenty-six hours spent on leisure activities. By a 1990s poll, average work time had risen to forty-eight hours, and leisure time had shrunk to a measly sixteen, an almost 40 percent reduction in play time. Isn't it time to fight back?

Let's not be pushed by well-meaning friends, or our own inner drives, to feel we must be useful every minute. Instead, let's enjoy that holy uselessness that permits us to do as we wish. There's a place for service in later life: the Eagle Clan Mother teaches us about this. But we shouldn't feel pressured to do too much, or to take on work that we don't really want. "No" can be the most affirmative word in the English language; it creates a space to say "yes" to those things to which we're truly called.

Through preference or financial necessity, we may work well into our later years. Some suggest that the pattern of total retirement is becoming increasingly obsolete, replaced by more complex and nuanced options: part-time work and piecework, late-life second careers, volunteer jobs, and the like. We won't necessarily have or want unlimited time just for play.

What is play, though, after all? Isn't it more a spirit we bring to things, rather than a set of leisure activities? For example, the entire distinction between work and play has no meaning for my baby.

When Sarah "plays" with toys, she is intent on discovering their properties, extracting every ounce of learning she can. We might call it work, then, were it not for her playful spirit—spontaneous, joyful, alive. As she bangs a spoon on a pot and discovers its ringing sound, she'll break into sudden peals of laughter. She'll turn to me with a grin, as if to say, "Hey, wasn't that the greatest?!" Is this play or work? Perhaps it's both, *play-work,* the satisfaction intrinsic to the act.

Somewhere along the path we lose this experience. Work, we learn, is service rendered for payment; pleasure need not be intrinsic to it, but is something realized later in our "free time." Yet why not liberate the working hours too? For example, I'm doing my best to write this book playfully. It would be nice if it proves useful to its readers, and even to me. Sure, I wouldn't mind getting rich and famous! But I also know the disappointments that such a focus can bring. Better to focus instead on the pleasures of writing. Paradoxically, I think this playful spirit also makes for better work. When I am too driven and goal-oriented, my writing shrivels up. But a spontaneous mind is expansive, open to the creative spirit. I find my thoughts taking unexpected dips and turns like a bird intoxicated with the sheer joys of flight. I may be surprised at what emerges. We might call this the voice of the Muse speaking, or the subconscious, or God within. Chuang Tzu would no doubt refer to the Tao. The same creative spirit of nature that brings the oak tree to fruition can also guide our work. But first we must make ourselves "useless," empty. Only then can we be full-filled.

❋   ❋   ❋

*Think of certain times you have been alone and **lonely.** Now think of other times you've enjoyed **solitude.** What seems to be the difference between these two experiences? What determines which one you will have? See if you can find the inner attitudes that help you to have a rich and fulfilling experience of solitude.*

What things in your life do you do as **play***—that is, sheerly for themselves? What is it about these activities that unlocks your spirit?*

Now choose one "useful" activity that you do only because you have to. How might you bring the spirit of play to it? Is there a way to experience more enjoyment in the act? (For example, if you chose "cleaning the floors"—could you listen to music as you do so? Make it a prayer time? Really "get into" the cleaning? Reward yourself with a treat at the end?) Be creative in imagining options.

Paying Attention

Our "useless" life, the oak tree teaches us, is of great value to ourselves; but our uselessness can also bless the human, natural, and divine world that surrounds us.

In early and midlife many of our human relations are defined by mutual utility. At work, we interact with the boss, colleagues, and underlings. Our communication is often carefully circumscribed by our respective work roles. We are appropriately friendly or distant, never getting to know the other *past a certain point.* This limitation is even more the case with the multitude of people we interact with in passing. The waitress who brings us coffee; the bank teller who forks over cash; the store clerk who sells us merchandise; these are people we see for their use, so hardly see at all. It's vaguely irritating when our waiter says, "Hello, I'll be serving you today, my name is Bruce." What do I care what your name is? Just tell me the specials.

Even our relationships at home slip into this functional mode. We come through the door to a busy house and lots of useful talk. "Can you take Suzy to soccer practice? I'll pick up something at the store for dinner. Did you reach the baby-sitter yet? Remember to call your mom. And, oh yeah, how was your day today?" More meaningful conversation is set aside until the duties are sorted out and completed. But somehow they never quite are.

What could be more important than to spend *useless* time with one another? Time not to *do,* but simply to *be* together? The twentieth-century French mystic, Simone Weil, tells us that in the original legend of the Holy Grail, it "belongs to the first comer who asks the guardian of the vessel, a king three-quarters paralyzed by the most painful wound, 'What are you going through?' "[4] Useless time gives us the chance to ask such questions. "What's really happening? How are you feeling? What's it like to be you today? I'm in no rush. I'm all ears."

A curious expression that, being "all ears." The ears don't exactly do anything, unlike the busy hands; nor are they selective, like the eyes that seek out or turn away from what they wish. No, the ears just rest and receive. They create a space that allows the other's voice to enter.

More broadly, Simone Weil identifies this openness with the faculty of *attention.* "Attention consists of suspending our thought, leaving it detached, empty, and ready to be penetrated by the object."[5] According to her, the love of our neighbor is rooted in this capacity to pay attention. When we ask the other, "What are you going through?" unvoiced but present is another message: "You matter. You're worth my time. I'm ready to listen." Like a flower given good soil and water, the other is free to blossom.

I just returned from my twentieth college reunion. There were many old friends I was delighted to see, but my richest conversation was held with a man I'd barely known when we were schoolmates long ago. Back then he had seemed to me a bit of a jock. We moved in different circles, and I was fine with that. This reunion day we found ourselves stranded together at a picnic waiting for a bus to carry us back to campus. As the minutes dragged on I grew increasingly frustrated. Such a waste of time! But in that useless time, he and I fell to talking. It turned out we had much in common: we both lived in the same city, had young daughters, cared about great books. Back in college, he told me, he'd take seven courses a semester for the sheer love of learning. So much for being a dumb jock! Years of superficial judgments fell away. In their place a real person stood before me, rich and complex.

In Simone Weil's view, we thus resurrect one another through the practice of attention. This process is especially true when we make time for someone whose personhood has been robbed by illness, exile, or poverty. "Those who are unhappy have no need for anything in this world but people capable of giving them their attention."[6] The Aikido master we met in chapter 4 knew this lesson well. He alone pays attention to the laborer; in doing so, he helps this shattered man rediscover his own humanity.

How useful, then, are the useless moments we spend simply being together with one other! As we age, we may find ourselves with more time, more freedom, more wisdom, and more opportunities for such interactions. A familiar example is grandparenting. Often the relationship between parent and child is distorted by mutual using. Parents can become overinvested in their child's success because it reflects well on themselves. "Robert's such a whiz at school—*we* must have done something right!" Children, in turn, know how to use their parents to secure things they want. "Hey, I got straight As. Won't you buy me a car?" We circle one another like wary fighters locked in a struggle for advantage. As grandparents, we are not central players in this game. We've discussed how this situation can free us up to be mentors; it can also free us up to be delightfully useless. We can simply *be* together, talking, playing, paying attention to the world and to one another.

In such relationships we are like the Taoist oak tree that creates an inviting space to sit and contemplate. The result: "There were so many sightseers that the place looked like a fair." If we are oaks, whether with our grandchildren, other family and friends, or simply the person who serves us coffee in the diner, we need not grow lonely with age. People will naturally gather beneath our shade.

For Simone Weil, attention is not only the substance of human love; it is also the substance of prayer. Nothing can strangle prayer more effectively than endless chatter directed at God. Such reaching out may be a beginning. But we must also fall silent and listen. We must create an empty, attentive space in which Spirit can say something back. This practice, too, demands "useless" time, as is illustrated by the well-known Gospel tale wherein Jesus visits two sisters.

> He entered a village where a woman whose name was Martha welcomed him. She had a sister named Mary who sat beside the Lord at his feet listening to him speak. Martha, burdened with much serving came to him and said, "Lord do you not care that my sister has left me by myself to do the serving? Tell her to help me." The Lord said to her in reply, "Martha, Martha, you are anxious and worried about many things. There is need of only one thing. Mary has chosen the better part and it will not be taken from her." (Lk 10:38–42)

At first we may leap to Martha's defense. After all, while Mary just sits on her duff, Martha's busy getting stuff done! Moreover, she's doing it in service to her Lord. We often admire such people, those who demonstrate their faith through good works. In our needy world, time spent in a soup kitchen or homeless shelter seems so much more useful than time spent just sitting.

Jesus suggests otherwise. It's not that he despises Martha's efforts. We sense the affection ("Martha, Martha") as he offers her a healing lesson. But it is a lesson in the value of useless time. Martha is burdened not just physically but mentally. Her mind, we might surmise, is also working overtime and is pulled apart by a dozen worries. Moreover, this tension will probably infect those around her, adding to disharmony.

But in her "uselessness" Mary is unified. She knows "there is need of only *one* thing." This centering presence can be a healing force. Perhaps even Jesus reaps its benefits as he rests from his arduous trip.

At the same time, Mary's stillness allows her to *pay attention* to Jesus' guidance. She is able to receive messages the busy Martha will miss. Then, when Mary resumes her own activities, they can emanate from a deeper place, informed by Spirit and not self-will. Jesus himself spent some forty days in the desert before he began his public ministry. It is well to take such "useless" time—centering, checking our motives, seeking guidance—before we set out to save the world.

It's also interesting that this story focuses on two women. We might think that in our culture it is men, raised to be compulsive producers, who most need the lesson of stillness. This tale reminds us to question traditional women's roles as well. Martha, after all, is doing the expected thing—bustling about in service to a man. Though the text isn't specific, we might imagine her cleaning house, preparing the meal, setting the table, and on and on. Many women know all too well this experience of being "burdened with much serving." Jesus encourages Martha to rebel against this pattern. She is more than just a beast of burden. Time for contemplation and spiritual growth is her birthright, not just that of male disciples.

Beyond attending to the callings of Spirit, as well as to the people in our lives, the Taoist story leads us one step further to consider our relations with nature. The Tao is not just immaterial, or in the souls of people; it permeates the whole natural world. In this story, a tree is teacher to a man. Such a relationship seems unthinkable within our culture; we rule "dumb" nature through superior intellect. Yet this attitude has caused problems for our world, leaving us in need of the Taoist corrective.

We've long treated nature as simply an object for our use. We dam rivers for hydroelectric power. We pave over the moist earth. From its womb we extract metals for our tall buildings and fast cars. We raze its forests to clear more ground for the cattle we slaughter and eat on our hamburger buns.

We treat nature like the fruit trees in the Taoist parable: "As soon as their fruit is ripe, they are torn apart and subjected to abuse.

. . . Their utility makes life miserable for them, and so they don't get to finish out the years Heaven gave them." At the same time, we, the *users,* may also find ourselves torn apart. We do not, finally, stand outside of nature as all-powerful potentates. We are a part of it. When nature is abused, we too suffer. If it is killed off, we die with it. Soaring rates of heart disease and cancer, influenced by poor diet, stress, and polluted food, air, and water, are grim reminders of this interdependence.

What, then, can we do for nature and ourselves? Nothing! That is, we can do the nothing that lets things be. As the oak tree was allowed to come to its natural fruition, so we can give peace to the planet.

Let's then resist the producer and consumer models of a good old age. Let us remember instead Grotjahn's description of his later-life contentment with thinking, dreaming, watching leaves fall. He thereby adds not a cent to the gross national product. He neither makes nor purchases a blessed thing. But his peace is a blessing to the world.

This changed attitude is not simply the consequence of Grotjahn's incapacities; it also comes as we develop *new* capacities with age. Just as we can learn to pay attention to other people, and to the voice of Spirit, so, too, we can learn to observe the splendors of nature. Polly Francis, a fashion illustrator and photographer, who wrote a series of articles in her nineties, notes:

> A new set of faculties seems to be coming into operation. I seem to be awakening to a larger world of wonderment—to catch little glimpses of the immensity and diversity of creation. More than at any other time in my life, I seem to be aware of the beauties of our spinning planet and the sky above. And now I have the time to enjoy them. I feel that old age sharpens our awareness.[7]

As the years pass, we may attend better to these immensities of nature, and also to its small beauties—a goldfinch outside our win-

dow, a waterbug rippling the lake, the first crocuses of spring—
sights that when we were younger we rarely paused to see.

If we do attend, we may arrive at a paradox: our embracing of
uselessness leads us to forms of service not unlike those of the Eagle Clan Mother. By letting nature be, we act as *mentors* to the
young. Without even trying, we plant seeds of oak-tree mind in the
next generation. *Cosmopoliticians* in spirit, we serve and preserve
the earth. We may even feel drawn to honor its riches in *ritual* ob-
servance. As yin gives rise to yang, so the useless to the useful.

※　　※　　※

Note a few occasions when you have truly paid attention to:

 1. another person;

 2. the voice of Spirit;

 3. the wonders of nature.

*What did this process feel like? What kinds of experiences were opened up
when you paused to pay attention?*

※

*Today (and each day, if you wish) you might set aside a little time to con-
sciously* **pay attention** *in each of these three areas. (For example, you might
spend a few minutes today getting to know a coworker better; sitting in quiet
meditation to hear any messages from Spirit; going for a short walk and really
looking at the trees.)*

※

SABBATH TIME

The oak tree's lesson can also bring us to a new experience of time. The question of time, needless to say, is central to our aging. The Taoist tree teaches us that the vibrant life incorporates "useless" time. To elaborate on this idea, it may help to turn to a different religion—Judaism, with its Sabbath. In the words of W. Gunther Plaut:

> I view the Sabbath . . . as a "useless" day. We must once again understand that doing nothing, being silent and open to the world, letting things happen inside, can be as important as, and sometimes more important than, what we commonly call the useful.[8]

This practice is central to Jewish spirituality. As the twentieth-century philosopher and religious leader Abraham Joshua Heschel writes, "Judaism is a *religion of time* aiming at *the sanctification of time*. . . . The Sabbaths are our great cathedrals."[9] To walk into a cathedral is to enter a holy region set apart from the profane world. Similarly, in the Jewish tradition, one enters Sabbath time. Guarding its gates are a set of prohibitions defining forbidden activities. Most crucial is the requirement to do no work on the Sabbath. In Orthodox interpretations, this ban includes driving a car, operating machinery, carrying money, even turning lights on and off. Nor should one lapse into mental work. Heschel retells a traditional story of a man who, on the Sabbath, saw a hole in his fence and determined to repair it when the Sabbath had ended. Later, he decided otherwise. He would *never* repair it, since the thought of this work had occurred to him on the Sabbath.[10]

We might imagine that Sabbath time is thus set aside for spiritual endeavors. Indeed, it is traditional to attend synagogue and engage in Torah study. Significantly, however, we're told to refrain from overworking here also. We're not to exhaust ourselves on the Sabbath with spiritual labors any more than with mundane work.

Looking at the long list of forbidden activities, we may wonder what, after all, is the point. Is this an ascetic practice focused on renunciation? No. Experience of the Sabbath reveals quite the opposite. The prohibitions clear out a space for rest, joy, and celebration. There's time for ritual meals filled with special delicacies and accompanied by blessings. The family, often pulled apart during the busy week, regathers. Intimacy is built through shared ceremony, leisurely walks, and conversation. Neighbors may stop by for a friendly visit. Each person can take time to commune with the self, or simply to catch up on sleep. This is hardly a day for austerities. Rather, it's a feast of comfort and pleasures for body and soul alike.

The ancient Romans thought the Jews a lazy people. How else to account for this useless day where no work at all is done? Perhaps, we counter, the day off has its uses. We must, after all, refresh ourselves in preparation for the work week ahead. But this is not the point of Sabbath. As it's written in the *Zohar,* the medieval mystical text, "The Sabbath is not for the sake of the weekdays; the weekdays are for the sake of Sabbath."[11] This day of rest is the holy climax of life. It's nothing less than an image, within time, of the eternal world to come.

It also harkens back to the origins of the world. In the Genesis account, after creating heaven and earth in six days, God rested on the seventh. It's in remembrance of this day that the Jews are commanded to keep the Sabbath (Ex 31:16–17). From a utilitarian standpoint, that seventh day of Creation seems a useless affair. God just sat around. Nothing happened. But the Jewish perspective differs. The ancient rabbis comment on scripture, "What was created on the seventh day? *Tranquility, serenity, peace and repose.*"[12]

As the Sabbath recalls Creation, so it does the defining story of the Israelites: their exodus from Egypt. "Remember that you were a slave in the land of Egypt and the Lord your God freed you from there with a mighty hand and an outstretched arm; therefore the Lord your God has commanded you to observe the sabbath day" (Dt 5:15). The Jews were freed from Pharaoh's backbreaking toil and led to a promised land. We reexperience a taste of this liberty with each Sabbath rest.

What then is the message for life's second half? Simply this: that we can age into Sabbath time. In the lessening of our obligations, the maturation of our oak-tree mind, we may find an avenue to sacred repose. Of course, the culture, like the Romans, may simply view us as slackers. What do we add to the national coffers? We may also have well-meaning Pharaoh-friends who urge us to always keep busy. Most significant is the Pharaoh-voice within our own heads. "What have you accomplished today? Sitting, thinking, reading, praying, that's hardly enough. Better *do* something, better *get to work.*" All our lives we've measured our self-worth according to how much we've produced. It's a hard addiction to break.

Let's take a lesson from the Israelites who rebelled against the harsh Pharaoh. They demanded the right to worship Adonai instead, the Lord of the Sabbath. Sabbath rest is an image of the world newly born and still at peace; the freedom from bondage possible in this life; the serenity of the world yet to come.

How do we enter Sabbath time? In the Jewish tradition less is said about what to do on the Sabbath than what to refrain from. That in itself is a valuable lesson. We begin by simply clearing out space in our busy lives. Several years ago, I felt directed to observe the Sabbath (after a fashion), claiming one day each weekend free from professional work. I didn't know in advance what I would do with that time. I would simply listen for inner direction. One day I'd find myself engrossed in prayer and spiritual reading. On another, I'd mainly lounge in bed, my tired body desperate for a nap. Or I'd find myself settling into a long Russian novel; setting out on a brisk walk along tree-lined streets; loitering in a bookstore-cafe with my wife; or (less sabbathlike perhaps) catching up on the bills while watching basketball on TV. Whatever I did or did not do, this time was a newly claimed zone of freedom.

In addition to this sabbath, I felt directed to embark on a fuller retreat every seventh weekend. I haven't kept to this schedule; but, as needed, I have periodically visited a rural retreat center to be alone with my thoughts and seek God. Usually I go with a specific question in mind. "Why am I so filled with sadness and rage?" Or "What type of service am I meant to focus on next?" Often the answer comes clear with prayer. Just as often, I find God carrying me in a direction I hadn't anticipated, as if to say, "No, *this,* not that, is the real issue." As the day deepens into evening I pace the chapel in prayer; browse the spiritual library; wander the fields that surround the center; or rest in a quiet room with a single candle flickering—and the voice of Spirit grows near, with me, *within.* A special glow lights up those days and spills over into the rest of my life.

This light, I've found, can be rekindled even in small moments. Shut off the computer. Switch off the phone. Claim a sabbath break, be it an hour or minute. Let its restful spirit silence the clamors of work.

As we enter life's second half we can thus practice weaving sabbath threads into the tapestry of our lives. In our later years, this presence may become ever more central. Just as the Jewish Sabbath begins at a prescribed hour, so we may celebrate its advent in special anniversary years. Author Maria Harris focuses on the significance of turning fifty.[13] She draws on the biblical account of the ritual of the Jubilee year. As decreed in Leviticus, during the forty-ninth year (seven times seven), a Sabbath of Sabbaths is inaugurated. Throughout the fiftieth year sowing and harvesting cease, and everyone returns to home and family; a holy time-out-of-time reigns. Then "you shall proclaim liberty throughout the land to all its inhabitants" (Lv 25:10). Harris advocates using the passage into our fifties as a Jubilee time for personal and spiritual growth.

We might also do the same with our sixtieth birthday. As the Sabbath is the seventh day of the week, now we enter our seventh decade. In the first six decades we have labored hard. But even God rested on the seventh day; shall we not make time for such rest in our lives? We may hear this call more keenly at age sixty-five (our culturally defined transition to elderhood) or at seventy (again resonating with the seven of the Sabbath). Of course, we may dread such birthdays. They might seem not like milestones but *millstones* around our neck. But through a perceptual flip we see otherwise.

These can be for us jubilee years, occasions for wholeness and healing.

On the other hand, Sabbath time is not simply defined by the calendar. It is largely a time set apart from that of calendars, watches, day-at-a-glance schedules. In our modern world, such devices help us to manage *productive* time. "Time is money," we're reminded. The more rapidly and efficiently we can work, the more profits will expand. They will also expand if we can add hours to the day through diminished sleep and play or through the use of technologies. Electric lighting turns night into day. Central heating and air conditioning eradicate the seasons. Natural time is thus supplanted by clock time, each hour homogeneous and *useful*.

Returning to our Taoist story, we might call such time carpenter time. Carpenter Shih strides by the useless tree without even pausing. It's not worth a moment of his valuable time.

In a sense, the tree has lived its life outside of this time—"That's how it got to be that old!" The tree inhabits a wholly different temporality. We might call it oak-tree time, also the time of the Sabbath. It unfolds according to natural rhythms. The oak puts out leaves in the summer, turns inward in the cold, drinks deep of the rain and sun as each appears. Without trying to be productive, the tree thus flourishes. The oak "measured a hundred spans around."

My young daughter inhabits this oak-tree time, meeting each moment as it comes. When children wander by, it is time to play. When she grows hungry, bring on food, now! When she's tired, it's time for a nap. Without seeking to produce anything, she yet grows before my eyes. She's recently celebrated her first birthday, but didn't know or care. Her time is not about numbers.

She will enter, all too soon, the world of carpenter time. Natural cycles will give way to schedules—school classes rung by the bell, then jobs paying by the hour. She will learn to count minutes in the name of efficiency.

But here is the wonder of life's second half: we can rediscover oak-tree time. To awaken in the morning with nothing to do, but so much to *be*; to respond to the serendipity of the weather or the unexpected visitor at our doorstep; to follow the voice of the day as it speaks to our heart; such is a *good time* indeed.

✳   ✳   ✳

Think of a day spent in "carpenter time," where you use your minutes in a structured, efficient way. (Perhaps that is what your workday looks like.) Now think of another day that unfolded in "oak-tree time"—natural and unstructured. (Perhaps this was a vacation day? A lazy Sunday? A day spent with the kids?)

Which kind of time do you like? Are there things you like or dislike about carpenter time? About oak-tree time? Ideally, how much of a balance between the two do you like? Has this preference changed as you've gone through different life stages?

(This is an exercise in self-understanding. Don't judge your answers good or bad.)

✳

Do you regularly take a Sabbath? If not, you might try doing so this weekend, or sometime soon. Clear out a day, or a good part of one. Make time for activities that will bring rest, pleasure, and a spirit of celebration. Recoil even from thoughts about work, or thoughts of an anxious or negative nature. Let this be a day of healing for body and soul alike.

✳

❊ *Guided Meditation* ❊

THE RIVER OF BEING

Imagine you are sitting by the banks of a river. Beside you sits your elder guide. This person can look however you envision them—male or female, serious or humorous, of any race in the world. Take a moment to see them there with you. They embody the wisdom of someone who's lived long and well. They have come to help you find your vision.

The two of you sit and watch the river flow. Somehow you sense this is the river of your own life, flowing, like time, before you.

Finally the elder speaks. "As we sit here together, I have only three questions for you. First, what material things do you wish to *have* in your life?"

Allow the answer to formulate within. Be honest. What are a few of the things you most want? These may include things you already have, or things you long for in the future.

Now imagine these material things cast into the river. See them there, bouncing and turning in the water. Each one finally disappears from view, carried away by the current.

Only then does the elder speak again: "Here is my second question. What things do you wish to *do* in your life?" Allow your answer to surface. What activities or accomplishments have been most important to you, or do you most wish for in the future?

When you are clear on these, know that they too are cast in the river. Envision a symbol of each one floating away, until they've all disappeared from sight.

Now, in a soft voice, the elder speaks again. "Those things you *have* in your life, those things you *do*, all come and go. They are carried away on the river of life. But they are not the river itself. Now I ask you the important question. Who do you wish to *be* in your life? Who *are* you truly?"

Allow the answer to formulate in your mind and heart. It may come in words or images, or just as a feeling. But let it come until it fills you up. If you wish, you may speak of it to the elder. Or you may simply hold it inside.

Finally, the elder speaks one last time. "That which you *are* goes beyond anything you *have* or *do*. It is the river itself. And it is the skies that give it water, and the earth that supports it, for everything is a part of this river. Always remember you are this river—not just the things that float by."

※　※　※

Part IV

Looking
Backward
and
Forward

8

Completing the Past:

Scrooge's Ghosts

"Who, and what are you?" Scrooge demanded.

"I am the Ghost of Christmas Past."

"Long Past?" inquired Scrooge: observant of its dwarfish stature.

"No. Your past." . . .

[Scrooge] then made bold to inquire what business brought him there.

"Your welfare!" said the Ghost.

Scrooge expressed himself much obliged, but could not help thinking that a night of unbroken rest would have been more conducive to that end. The Spirit must have heard him thinking for it said immediately:

"Your reclamation, then. Take heed!"

It put out its strong hand as it spoke, and clasped him gently by the arm.

"Rise! and walk with me!" . . . As the words were spoken, they passed through the wall, and stood upon an open country road, with fields on either hand. . . . "Good Heaven!" said Scrooge, clasping his hands together, as he looked about him. "I was bred in this place. I was a boy here!" . . . They walked along the road; Scrooge recognising every gate, and post, and tree; until a little market-town appeared in the distance, with its bridge, its church, and winding river. Some shaggy ponies now were seen trotting towards them with boys upon their backs, who called to other boys in country gigs and carts, driven by farmers. All these boys were in great spirits, and shouted to each other, until the broad fields were so full of merry music, that the crisp air laughed to hear it. . . .

Why was he rejoiced beyond all bounds to see them! Why did his cold eye glisten, and his heart leap up as they went past! Why was he filled with gladness when he heard them give each other Merry Christmas, as they parted at cross-roads and bye-ways, for their several homes! What was merry Christmas to Scrooge? Out upon merry Christmas! What good had it ever done to him?

"The school is not quite deserted," said the Ghost. "A solitary child, neglected by his friends, is left there still."

Scrooge said he knew it. And he sobbed. . . . The Spirit touched him on the arm, and pointed to his younger self, intent upon his reading. Suddenly a man, in foreign garments: wonderfully real and distinct to look at: stood outside the window, with an axe stuck in his belt, and leading an ass laden with wood by the bridle.

"Why, it's Ali Baba!" Scrooge exclaimed in ecstasy. "It's dear old honest Ali Baba! Yes, yes, I know! One Christmas time, when yonder solitary child was left here all alone, he *did* come, for the first time, just like that. . . ."

Then, with a rapidity of transition very foreign to his usual character, he said, in pity for his former self, "Poor boy!" and cried again.

"I wish," Scrooge muttered, putting his hand in his pocket, and looking about him, after drying his eyes with his cuff: "but it's too late now."

"What is the matter?" asked the Spirit.

"Nothing," said Scrooge. "Nothing. There was a boy

singing a Christmas Carol at my door last night. I should like to have given him something: that's all."

"My time grows short," observed the Spirit. "Quick!"

This was not addressed to Scrooge, or to any one whom he could see, but it produced an immediate effect. For again Scrooge saw himself. He was older now; a man in the prime of life. His face had not the harsh and rigid lines of later years; but it had begun to wear the signs of care and avarice. There was an eager, greedy, restless motion in the eye, which showed the passion that had taken root, and where the shadow of the growing tree would fall.

He was not alone, but sat by the side of a fair young girl in a mourning-dress: in whose eyes there were tears, which sparkled in the light that shone out of the Ghost of Christmas Past.

"It matters little," she said, softly. "To you, very little. Another idol has displaced me; and if it can cheer and comfort you in time to come, as I would have tried to do, I have no just cause to grieve."

"What Idol has displaced you?" he rejoined.

"A golden one. . . . I have seen your nobler aspirations fall off one by one, until the master-passion, Gain, engrosses you. Have I not?"

"What then?" he retorted. "Even if I have grown so much wiser, what then? I am not changed towards you." . . .

"But if you were free to-day, to-morrow, yesterday, can even I believe that you would choose a dowerless girl. . . . I release you. With a full heart, for the love of him you once were." . . .

"Spirit!" said Scrooge, "show me no more! Conduct me home. Why do you delight to torture me?"

The Ghost [of Christmas Yet to Come] pointed downward to the grave by which it stood.

"Men's courses will foreshadow certain ends, to which, if persevered in, they must lead," said Scrooge. "But if the courses be departed from, the ends will change. Say it is thus with what you show me!"

The Spirit was as immovable as ever.

Scrooge crept towards it, trembling as he went; and following the finger, read upon the stone of the neglected grave his own name, EBENEZER SCROOGE. . . .

Holding up his hands in a last prayer to have his fate reversed, he saw an alteration in the Phantom's hood and dress. It shrunk, collapsed, and dwindled down into a bedpost . . . Yes! and the bedpost was his own. The bed was his own, the room was his own. Best and happiest of all, the Time before him was his own, to make amends in! . . .

"I don't know what to do!" cried Scrooge, laughing and crying in the same breath; and making a perfect Laocoön of himself with his stockings. "I am as light as a feather, I am as happy as an angel, I am as merry as a school-boy. I am as giddy as a drunken man. A merry Christmas to everybody! A happy New Year to all the world! Hallo here! Whoop! Hallo!"

Charles Dickens, *A Christmas Carol*

It's one thing to place ourselves in the position of the Buddha, a Taoist master, a Native American clan mother. In fact, it's rather flattering. But Scrooge? His very name has entered the language to signify the cold and miserly sort.

Yet if we look closer, Scrooge has much to teach us. In fact, his story includes within it all the other figures so far described. He has an awakening experience, not unlike Buddha's. As it does for the Hindu forest dweller and the Taoist sages, later life becomes for him a time for spiritual attainment. His ghostly journey, stripping away pride and prejudice, leaves him with the elder wisdom of the Aikido master. This wisdom also incorporates all the playfulness of the old woman in purple. Long a selfish man, he's now eager to be of service, not unlike the Eagle Clan Mother. This orientation is also the result of his oak-tree mind: he's let go of his focus on profits and productivity to embrace the "useless" spirit of Christmas.

Isn't such wholeness of heart what we wish for ourselves? In the last four chapters we've focused on some of the fruits of maturity: wisdom and playfulness; the ability to serve and just to be. But we may sense that, in our own lives, these fruits are still unripe. We wish to become more whole, but how? It's not enough just to pile up the years. We see too many examples of old curmudgeons, Scrooge himself being a prime example.

Yet Scrooge then went through spiritual passages. Hereafter we'll focus on certain passages which have the power to transform our consciousness. They have their dark aspect. We need to face mistakes in our past; come to terms with our future death; work with present suffering. The darkness of these passages, like that of a birth canal, is preliminary to new light and life.

THE LIFE REVIEW

Scrooge's move toward new life begins when he looks back on the old. The Ghost of Christmas Past, the first of three spirit visitors foretold by his ex-partner Jacob Marley, leads Scrooge to recall his past. This ghost can be seen as a metaphor for memory. Of course, memory is selective: certain scenes stand out from the undifferentiated background. For Scrooge, the memory of a childhood Christmas sums up a whole period of his life. The glad spirit of children in a rural town is counterpoised to his own youthful loneliness. He also remembers the breakup of his engagement, a moment that changed the course of his life—not for the better.

Ah, memory, what joys and sorrows it brings! Our present is always saturated with the past—the feelings, events, relationships, that made us who we are today. As we age, rather than growing away from our past, we often seem to grow toward it. In our earlier years we bounded impatiently toward the future; the focus was on climbing the mountain of adulthood, and we cast off the past like so much dead weight. In life's second half, we've achieved that ascent. We can rest a bit, look back on the journey. And how could we not? We feel both tired and strengthened by every step we have climbed.

It's a cliché that many older folks tend to "live in the past." This behavior has often been viewed as a bit pathetic, maybe pathological, even by professional gerontologists. That changed, however, with Robert Butler's ground-breaking article, "The Life Review: An Interpretation of Reminiscence in the Aged."[1] According to Butler, the confrontation with mortality as we age triggers a retrospective review. We are trying to discover the meaning of our life. To do so, we must go back to the past, even those parts we'd rather forget. Scattered memories begin to surface and coalesce. We recall conflicts, painful experiences, hard choices. It's not always a pleasant journey down memory lane. Indeed, Butler acknowledges that this life review can lead to anxiety, depression, and obsessive guilt. Like Scrooge, we might well prefer "a night of unbroken rest." But this process, if carried through, can also serve as a tool of deep healing and insight.

Through memory, truths are revealed. We trace, like a connect-the-dots puzzle, the hidden patterns in all that has befallen us, and gradually a coherence emerges. We can see who we were meant to be and who we've actually become. We can celebrate our triumphs and come to peace with our mistakes. As the philosopher Arthur Schopenhauer writes:

> the first forty years of life furnish the text, while the remaining thirty supply the commentary; and . . . without the commentary we are unable to understand aright the true sense and coherence of the text, together with the moral it contains and all the subtle application of which it admits.[2]

What Scrooge is engaged in is not idle wandering. What's at stake here, as the ghost says, is nothing less than "your welfare! . . . Your reclamation, then. Take heed!" In this chapter we take heed of the myriad tasks of memory.

The Joys of Nostalgia: Coming Home

Scrooge's first memory is a happy one. He recalls the boys from his hometown. "Why was he rejoiced beyond all bounds to see them?" Why, indeed, when Scrooge was himself a lonely child on the way to becoming a sour old man? And why does he feel such "ecstasy" when he remembers Ali Baba? Conjured up in a boy's imagination, this is only a storybook character.

We might chalk it up to an aging person's nostalgia. We know what a form of self-delusion that can be. Wearing rose-colored glasses, we remember just what we wish. The harsh glare of what life was really like, with all its griefs and irritations, is conveniently filtered out by the mind.

However, that's not what is happening here. The Ghost of Christmas Past is leading Scrooge not into illusion but toward the truth. Years of staring at the brightness of his golden idol has blinded him to what has most worth. Only memory can restore his sight, help him sort out the real gold from the dross.

Here his heart serves as an instrument of discernment. If it leaps at certain remembered scenes, it is because they are of true and lasting value. The quiet order of a little market town anchored by bridge, church, and river. The aliveness of broad fields and laughing, crisp air. The joy of young boys cavorting on Christmas morning. The entrancements of a storybook, from which Ali Baba mystically appears—ah, the powers of the human imagination! These are the real values of life, places where the sacred shines through the veil of the everyday. Growing older has not been Scrooge's path to elder wisdom; it has only carried him ever farther from these truths. But, in recollection, he has a chance to *re-collect* himself. He can gather his life back together, remembering those things that have given it meaning.

If Scrooge feels joy, then, it is not false nostalgia. He's regaining contact with the real. We see this implicit in the term "nostalgia" itself. It's derived from the Greek word *nostos,* "returning home." Nostalgia is, first, a kind of coming home. It's not just his hometown that Scrooge recollects, but his spiritual home. It's always Christmas there, with its connotations of joy, love, imagination, and rebirth, all rooted in the sacred.

So our memory can help guide us home. But how? We will, of course, have many memories as we age. Some will come unbidden, some will be purposefully sought out. What are we to do with them?

Scrooge's nostalgia suggests a first answer. Let's *celebrate* our joyful memories; let's use these glad moments to re-collect our true self. One person may think back on a week spent bicycling through glorious countryside with a friend. The memory still glows. Another recalls a young love, the first throes of delighted passion. A third person remembers time spent alone in the woods. Another calls to mind a startling experience of God that summoned her to a new way of life.

We might also think of times when we rose to life's challenges and exhibited the best of who we are. Perhaps we faced a perilous crisis with courage. Or someone needed help, and we reached out with sensitivity. Maybe we stood up for what we believed in at a time when it was hard.

All such fulfilling memories are like signposts for a lost traveller. They remind us not only where we have come from, but, more important, of the path that leads us home. For such recollections speak of love, creation, freedom, virtue—each a way that Spirit has shone forth in our life.

Yet "nostalgia" is not just about the joys of home; it also contains the root *algia,* "pain." We are pained by our distance from home. Scrooge feels this pain keenly as he recalls the innocent joys of childhood. He begins to realize all he has lost in his relentless search for gain.

So, too, when we think back to our youthful dreams, or that first love, or that special time of solitude or adventure, we may feel sadness for all that has passed. It's important to let in this grieving. That these things are gone is a very real death. If we insist on not feeling sadness, we can't experience life's joy. Our heart, like Scrooge's, will grow cold with the years.

As we feel the pain inherent in our nostalgia, let us remember that it, too, plays a part in our healing. The sadness of the separation gives us an impetus to search for home. This home is not simply in the past, unreachable. We couldn't even remember an experience unless it were still alive in our soul. Be it innocence, joy, strength, or wholeness, it can be reclaimed—this is what Scrooge discovers. When he first thinks of his happy hometown boys, their spirit seems so far away. But by the story's end, he is "merry as a school-boy" himself; his soul-work has brought him back home.

※　※　※

Think back to your past life. Let a few of your happiest memories come to mind. Allow yourself to experience some of the joy these memories hold for you, and any sadness that accompanies them. This joy and sadness are more precious than Scrooge's gold.

※

Now ask yourself, what makes these moments so valuable, so lasting, for you? How did Spirit shine forth in them? (For example, are they about beauty? love? creativity? freedom? truth? courage?) Recognize the particular grace embodied in each memory. Think of these memories as signposts guiding you home to your truest self.

※

Painful Memories: Compassion for the Self

As far back as Scrooge's mind ranges, he also finds bitterness and loss. He was, after all, "a solitary child, neglected by his friends." As time progressed, he withdrew even more. He sought a substitute for human society, first in the pleasures of reading, then in the accumulation of gold. For the latter he pays a heavy price: his face "had begun to wear the signs of care and avarice." It was this change that led to the painful breakup of his engagement. In the words of his fiancée: "I have seen the nobler aspirations fall off one by one, until the master-passion, Gain, engrosses you." Across the distance of time, Scrooge knows her words are true. Memory reveals that on life's journey he took a very wrong turn.

As we age, we are sure to recall painful episodes in our past. We missed opportunities. We made mistakes. We suffered grievous losses. It will be tempting to stuff such memories down into the dark recesses of the subconscious. With Scrooge we may call out, "Spirit! Show me no more. Conduct me home. Why do you delight to torture me?"

However, the purpose of such memories is not simply to torture us. They offer an opportunity to heal the wound left by original events. Through remembering, we can continue to work through the trauma. We can assimilate the lessons we need to learn and let go of lasting hurts. If we do so, the painful memories, no less than the joyous, can help to guide us home. When Scrooge says "conduct me home" to the ghost, he doesn't realize that it is doing just that. The route runs through painful truths.

Working with such memories is a tricky thing. Thinking back over a painful incident, we may say, "How could I have been such a fool?" It's O.K. to do that once or twice, but it's not good to engage in obsessive remorse. The word "remorse" is from the Latin roots *mordere*, "to bite," and *re,* "again." As if the first laceration weren't enough, we bite ourselves again and again in memory. Thoughts of humiliations, lost opportunities, and wrong choices can tear into us like sharp teeth.

Here Scrooge has something to teach us. Remembering his solitary childhood, "With a rapidity of transition very foreign to his usual character, he said, in pity for his former self, 'Poor boy!' and cried again." He doesn't thunder, "It was my own damned fault. I was a sickly, cowardly lad!" Instead of condemnation, he has compassion for himself.

Here's a valuable lesson concerning our journey home: we need to exercise self-forgiveness. If we made mistakes, we might not have known better at the time. We were operating according to the truth as we then saw it, though subsequent experience may have proved us wrong. Such is the human condition. We see through a glass darkly.

It may also help to recognize that our greatest flaws often go hand in hand with our strengths. Carl Jung wrote when he was in his eighties:

> Much might have been different if I myself had been different. But it was as it had to be; for all came about because I am as I am. . . . I regret many follies that sprang from my obstinacy; but without that trait I would not have reached my goal.[3]

We see this intertwining of weakness and strength in Scrooge's own character. He's a solitary boy, and we know the sad consequences for the adult he later became. Yet his solitude also led to his vivid imagination. In the long lonely hours he learned to see Ali Baba. Maybe, even as an aged man, this self-same power is what saves him. His strong memory and imagination (symbolized by the ghostly spirits) set him on the path to redemption.

Dickens may also be speaking of himself. As described in a friend's biography, Dickens "was a very little and very sickly boy, subject to attacks of violent spasm which disabled him from any active exertion." However, "he had always the belief that this early sickness had brought to himself one inestimable advantage . . . having strongly inclined him to reading."[4] Would Dickens have become the great author he was without his disability?

As we look at our own lives, we may find equivalents. Were there strengths intertwined with our weaknesses? Maybe we had a raging ego. It led to many a downfall, but it gave us the confidence to accomplish great things. Maybe we had a driven need to be "helpful" that people took advantage of. Didn't some good come from this helpfulness, both for self and others? Maybe in the face of certain tragedies we lost the capacity to feel. Yes, but that numbness may have assisted us to survive those very hard times.

Such realizations foster self-acceptance, yet we may still be plagued by a particularly painful failure, or a sense that our whole life went wrong. Clearly Scrooge wrestles with such feelings, and he triumphs nonetheless. He neither clings to denial nor sinks into morbid reflection about what cannot be changed. How did he manage it?

One answer: Scrooge received spiritual help. The ghostly powers who visit him not only represent his own memory and imagination; they also signal powers beyond the self. Through this divine assistance he is shown what he needs to see. He's also enabled to assimilate it in a way that will be healing and not destructive to the self.

We, too, can ask for such assistance. If we are the praying sort, we might say something like, "Dear God, help me to see myself not as I do, but as you see me. I need to be honest about my flaws and mistakes. But I also need to see them in the light of your compassion. Help me to forgive myself."

We may be surprised by the results. In the parable of the prodigal son, a young man, quite aware of his sinful past, is reluctant to return home. When he does so, his loving father rushes to meet him. "This son of mine was dead, and has come to life again; he was lost, and has been found" (Lk 15:24). The father has not forgotten the past; but the child's errors are washed clean by his love. We do well to remember such forgiveness as we survey our past mistakes. Better to attempt such painful work wrapped in the loving arms of Spirit.

If we're not the praying sort, we can still access this sense of forgiveness from within. One powerful method is provided by the Buddhist practice of *metta*.[5] In this practice we send thoughts of loving kindness to the self. "May I be happy. May I be free from mental torment. May I dwell in peace. May I experience all the joy and fulfillment I seek." The precise words we choose might vary from person to person, and over time. As we repeat such phrases during daily meditation, the practice can unlock compassion for the self.

Sometimes our weaknesses and strengths come from the same root. Can you see this phenomenon in your life? Think of two or three examples of how your "character flaws" have been intertwined with your virtues and successes. Does this awareness help you with self-acceptance?

Scrooge said "poor boy" as he looked back on his former self. Think back to yourself as a child, calling up your flaws and vulnerabilities. Were you prone to moodiness, or anxiety, or loneliness? Were you a bit of a bully? Did you suffer certain losses?

Whatever you remember, try to view your childhood self through loving eyes. Can you say "poor boy" or "poor girl" to this young person? Can you exercise understanding and compassion?

In seeking this self-love, you might use prayer or the metta practice. Even if it doesn't come easily, stay with it over time.

Painful Memories: Forgiveness for Others

When Scrooge saw the "poor boy" that he was, not only did he not condemn himself, he didn't condemn others for his condition. Given his acid character, we might have expected a vituperative outburst. "Those damned boys who would never play with me! Curse their cruelty!" But we hear nothing of the sort.

We must take this lesson to heart. Blaming others, as much as self-blame, can sidetrack our journey home. As we survey past wrongs, angry emotions surface. "I can't believe my own friend did that to me!" "I gave the best years of my life to the company, and then they threw me over the side." Or even "How could God have abandoned me just then?" Scenes of victimization and betrayal insistently come to mind. How can we deal with them constructively?

A first route to forgiving others is the work of self-forgiveness just discussed. When Scrooge thinks compassionately of the poor boy he was, his heart softens toward others. "There was a boy singing a Christmas Carol at my door last night. I should have liked to have given him something."

This connection is confirmed by the world's religions. As we've seen, the Buddhist metta practice begins with sending love to ourselves; it continues with sending love, through similar phrases, to our friends, neighbors, and even our "enemies." The circle of compassion expands from the center. This principle is implicit also in Jesus' injunction to "love thy neighbor as thyself." How can we do so without self-love?

The reverse is true as well. Kindness to others empowers us to be kind to the self. Jesus says to pray, "Forgive us our trespasses as we forgive those who trespass against us." Is he really implying that God won't forgive us otherwise? Not likely. God's love is not bound by human weakness. But this prayer speaks to a psychological truth: only to the extent that we forgive those who have harmed us can we *experience* God's forgiveness flowing in.

Therefore, as we think back to painful scenes, it can help to embrace both the self and the other together. For example: "I still feel hurt by the way Joanne left. I don't fully understand, even after all these years. But I forgive any wrongs that she did me. I totally release her from blame. I know that she was in her own pain and confusion. And I, too, made mistakes. I was arrogant and judgmental. I was no saint. But I also offer myself forgiveness, total forgiveness. I hereby let go of all the hurts we did to each other. May our souls be free to advance into the light."

The exact words we use are not crucial, but the spirit is. Just as Jacob Marley's ghost drags a heavy chain behind him, we too have been chained to the past by resentments. How much lighter we feel when we let them go!

Some chains can be very hard to cast off. Thinking back, we may find ourselves still bound by anger. So-and-so, we are sure, did us grievous wrong. We just can't seem to forgive and forget. What to do?

Here, a personal example might help. Over time I've had to do a lot of memory work concerning my mother. She died over twenty years ago, but that didn't mean my resentment passed away. I felt she had seriously harmed my life, and those around me, with her controlling ways. Shortly after her death from cancer, my father and brother had both died of suicide. In this tragic affair I pegged her for the villain. Hadn't she dragged us all down with her blame, her fears, her relentless demands? The love she gave—wasn't it always conditional, dependent on fulfilling her wishes? My whole family dead and gone, I was left alone with my bitterness.

Through the help of therapy and Twelve Step work, I have achieved much resolution. It hasn't come easily. Yet over the years, self-examination and prayer have brought about a shift in my view of the past. This work has not been a matter of putting on rose-colored glasses. Quite the opposite. Forgiveness has only emerged as the result of a search for truth not unlike Scrooge's.

My own "ghosts" of memory and understanding took me through a three-dimensional journey. The first dimension: I had to learn to see *her*. Not "my mother," but the person she was within herself. Yes, she was a very controlling person. But who wouldn't have been, given her past? Her father had left home when she was a young girl, never to return. She had witnessed her first husband's death in a diving accident. Is it any wonder she was overprotective about us kids? What's more, she had breast cancer, which, after a long period of remission, finally did her in. She lived for many years under its shadow of death, without spiritual resources to console her. If she was prone to mood swings, anxiety, controllingness, who could blame her?

Broader factors were also at play. She was a smart, ambitious woman who lived at a time when women were supposed to stay home. Without a direct outlet, all this energy ended up directed toward the kids. It was understandable that there'd be some sparks along the way. Besides, no matter what the circumstances, it's never easy to be a parent. Now that I am one myself, I understand the pressures and anxieties better. The more I comprehended my mother's struggles, the more I could forgive. She wasn't the villain I imagined. She was a person, like any other, trying to get by, and in need of kindness and understanding.

Had I given these to her? The question opened up the second dimension of my work. I needed to look at *myself*. I saw that for all my mental criticism of her, I, too, was far from perfect. As I entered my teen years I had withdrawn emotionally—cut her off cold. I wasn't really there for her as she fought her fatal illness. Even after her death, I continued to nurse my anger. It's not that I'm a terrible person. Again, I had to look at myself with compassion. At the same time, I needed to see honestly where I was at fault and stop pointing the finger at her.

The third dimension of my truth journey involved perceiving not simply the truth about her and about me, but about *our relationship* to one another. I had been focussing exclusively on the harm she did me, and that was far from the whole story. One day, praying in a synagogue, I thought of the biblical injunction to honor thy father and mother. What would it mean to honor my mother, who I felt had done me such damage? Suddenly, thoughts came rushing in of all the things she had given me: the confidence to believe in myself; a love of books and learning; an ambitious personality that could make things happen; a lively sense of humor; an ethic of hard work; wonderful travel experiences; a sense of being loved and cherished. The list went on and on. My mind had denied all that I'd gained from her and had focussed on the negative. Of course, I'd rather claim credit myself for the good that was within me. It's humbling to have to admit debts. But in honoring my mother I began to pay these debts back with greater acknowledgement and gratitude.

Doing so does not deny the grievous errors she made. That's part of the truth as well. It does not honor her or anyone else to falsify history. But my bitterness was based on a falsity, too. The more truth I saw—about her, about me, about our relationship—the more forgiveness could enter my heart.

It's one thing to recall a mother's love, but what about a boss who screwed us over, an anonymous mugger, a treacherous schoolmate? It seems that certain people did us *only* harm. With time and work, it is still possible to offer them forgiveness. Furthermore, in many cases we also discover, on reflection, hidden benefits of their actions. Rabbi Zalman Schacter-Shalomi gives an example of a man who forced him, for no good reason, out of a much-valued rabbinical position. Yet the upshot was that Zalman found an even better job—in fact, he was catapulted into a series of life-expanding experiences that wouldn't have happened without this man's "help." Rabbi Zalman suggests that we recognize such people as our "severe teachers" in life. Their harshness may have done us as much good (though perhaps unintended) as those who sought our welfare. In this spirit, he offers a visualization entitled "A Testimonial Dinner for the Severe Teachers."[6] Here, meditating on the surprising graces received, we offer thanks and blessings to our severe teachers, releasing them from blame and ourselves from resentment.

There may still be situations in which we find it impossible to forgive. Perhaps we were subject to violence and incest as a child, or we lost family in the Holocaust. We feel no benefit from the severe teachers who caused these grievous injuries, nor forgiveness for them in our hearts. At least we can begin by offering ourselves understanding and forgiveness. These bitter feelings are natural. To let go of them might require supernatural healing.

Our anger can make it hard to open to such healing. It may seem like God collaborated in the evil, or callously permitted it to happen. As someone who lost his whole family at an early age, I can relate to such feelings. Anger wells up not only toward a person but also toward a supreme being who seems so harsh and uncaring.

When we encounter such feelings on our memory trip, what are we to do? The usual strategy is probably the worst: to stuff them back down. We may believe certain thoughts are impious. We may even fear punishment for what we feel. Maybe the Cosmic Tyrant will take revenge if a lowly subject rebels!

Spiritual traditions suggest the opposite. The Hebrew Bible is filled with heroes—such as Abraham, Job, Moses—who dare to talk back to the divine. Jacob goes one step further; he wrestles with a divine angel. And in the New Testament, Jesus hanging on the cross was not meekly submissive and consoled. "Why have you forsaken me?" he cries out to the heavens.

Jesus' words are not a closed-minded pronouncement of betrayal. They are a *question* directed toward God. As such, they open up a channel of communication. Jesus' challenge is part of his discovery and affirmation of God's ever-present love. Scrooge also questions and talks back to the Christmas spirit as he proceeds on his journey to redemption.

As we survey the losses of the past, we also do well to question God, argue with God, even rail in anger against God (or whatever name you use for universal forces). In his book entitled *May I Hate God?*[7] Pierre Wolf answers with a resounding "Yes!" Through honestly expressing our issues and feelings, we can deepen our spiritual life.

Like Jacob wrestling with an angel (Gn 32), we may find ourselves wrestling with God. "Why was my only child taken from me by a drunken driver? It still hurts, still seems senseless. Where were you? What's the point?" It would be facile to predict what answer we'll arrive at. No one-size-fits-all response can ease our pain, nor can pat doctrines from theology. We have to find answers deep in the soul. One person might see all the good that came from tragedy: a renewed closeness with family, a reminder of the preciousness of life. A second realizes that God does not prevent loss, but gives us the strength to deal with it. A third discovers that the God she was angry at is angry too. God doesn't want drunken drivers killing people but also can't tamper with free will. Another arrives at a strong faith that his child has gone to a better place. Death is not simply an end. Another finds the answer to be that there simply is no answer: God's ways are beyond our comprehension, but we can accept a life bathed in mystery.

Whatever the results, such struggles deepen our spiritual quest. Like Scrooge, we are laboring toward the light, with divine helpers by our side.

✳   ✳   ✳

Think back to a time when you felt hurt, abandoned, or betrayed by God (or whatever term you use for spiritual forces). Take a moment to allow yourself to feel the anguish, and whatever question(s) it provokes. (Perhaps "Why?" or "Why me?" or "Where were you?" or "How can you be trusted?")

Do not just drop the question(s) or give a facile response. Stay with the question. Let it deepen in your heart. See your question as precious, an avenue of communication with the divine. Now bring it into thought, meditation, prayer—however you can best wrestle it through.

Over time, allow answers to come to you. They may unfold within your heart, not only your head. Don't worry if others might disagree with them, or if your own rational mind is not totally persuaded. Listen for the answers that resonate best in your soul.

✖ ✖ ✖

Think of a difficult relationship. It might be with a family member, or perhaps with a teacher, boss, old friend, or schoolmate. Choose a relationship for which you feel residual anger, whether or not the person is still in your life. Now ask yourself a series of questions, noting down the responses.

1. *If the person did you harm, what might have been motivating them? (Try to imagine how things looked from their perspective. What might they have been thinking or feeling? What might have affected them from their own past or present?) Does this reflection help you go beyond judgment to understanding?*

2. *Now look at yourself. How might you also have contributed to the conflict? (Did you have fears or self-centered wishes that helped create a struggle? Did you behave, think, or speak in some negative ways? Have you held onto your grudge over the years?)*

3. *Finally, seek to look anew at this person's treatment of you. Are there ways they were helpful or caring? Did you learn any valuable things from them? For the moment, try to honor the good in the relationship instead of dwelling on the bad.*

Even if the person mainly did you wrong, can you see some positive things that came out of it? Did their harsh treatment lead to unintended gifts? Were they a severe teacher in Rabbi Zalman's sense? If so, acknowledge them for this teaching and give them thanks.

✖

MAKING AMENDS

In Scrooge's life review, what most grips his focus are not the wrongs of others, or of God, but those he has perpetrated himself. The dissolution of his engagement is a symbol of his errors. He placed the love of money ahead of the love of people. He worshipped a golden idol instead of the Christmas spirit. Surely he has harmed himself through his wrong choices: they've made him into a bitter and solitary man. But his actions have harmed others just as much, both in the past and present. He treats those around him rudely. He lords it over Bob Cratchit in a tyrannical way. Scrooge pays him a pitiful salary, causing hardship for his family. And Scrooge's sins are not only ones of commission, but of omission. He might have offered Christmas cheer; charity for the poor; kindness to passersby; consideration to his workers. His life is a story of missed opportunities.

Yet the story's also far from over. His life review offers the possibility of reclaiming possibilities, righting past wrongs. " 'Spirit!' he cried, tight clutching at its robe, 'hear me! I am not the man I was. I will not be the man I must have been but for this intercourse. . . . Assure me that I yet may change these shadows you have shown me, by an altered life!' " He finds that it is possible to do so, and his joy knows no bounds. "Best and happiest of all, the Time before him was his own, to make amends in!"

To make such amends for conduct that has hurt others is part of our spiritual passage work as we age. Earlier I discussed self-forgiveness for the past. We're no help to anyone (including ourselves) if we slip into morbid self-loathing. But self-forgiveness by itself is not enough. It's also important to learn from past mistakes and to correct whatever we can. Without this, guilt remains unresolved.

We may recall a spouse or lover we mistreated. We may think back to something we wish we could undo in our parenting—perhaps we were too harsh or controlling with a child. We may have pilfered from a business or cheated a friend. We all have such skeletons in our closet.

How to go about making amends? Happy as we'd be to clear that closet out, it's surely a daunting task. Scrooge wasn't willing to go at it until haunted by spirits and a confrontation with death.

The Twelve Steps, originated in Alcoholics Anonymous, offer an amends process for those similarly haunted by compulsive problems. The later steps speak of making "a list of all persons we had harmed" and "making direct amends to such people wherever possible, except when to do so would injure them or others."[8] In this spiritual program, such actions come only after a life review similar to Scrooge's. Recoverees survey their fears, resentments, sexual wrongdoings, and character defects, exposing them to another person. After asking God to remove these defects, an amends list is compiled. My own list included an old girlfriend I had been cruel to; those to whom I owed money; a family member I had not contacted for years; and many other individuals I had mistreated in ways that still stung my conscience. Even I, myself, was on the list. Through self-hate and self-destructive behavior I had done myself serious wrongs.

The next step was to think and pray on what would be an appropriate amends. This step usually involves a direct apology to the person, but by itself an apology often isn't enough. After all, if I owe someone money I need to do more than simply say "I'm sorry." The amends surely involves paying them back. I was told to think of how I could best "pay people back." I'd been harsh to an old friend, tearing down her self-esteem, but I could build her self-esteem back up, in some small way, by telling her the things I most admired about her. I'd left another person feeling uncared for; now I might show him some tangible signs of caring, such as a call, a visit, a gift. I could also be resolutely kind to myself to make up for past cruelties. Even to people who were now dead and gone, I could seek to make "spiritual amends." I visited my family's grave site. In my mind and heart I spoke to them of all they had given me in life. I offered my own apology and understanding, and I could feel their presence with me.

Needless to say, I was scared to make some of these amends. I didn't relish the idea of admitting that I was wrong, especially to people who were eager to agree with me on this point. However, for the most part, people received me graciously. As the process unfolded, I felt a healing take place. Sometimes years of distance and hurt were cleared up in a couple of hours. I sensed my own ancient guilts resolving and dead relationships being revived. As much as I dreaded the amends step, it was filled with joy and grace.

Although Scrooge did not go through a systematic amends process, his spirit led him through something similar. Before his story ends he has spread Christmas cheer instead of sullenness; visited his nephew, whom he had once scorned; raised Crachit's salary and assisted his family; and given to charity, with "a great many back-payments . . . included." Clearly, his amends bring great help to others. But no one benefits more than Scrooge. "I am as light as a feather, as happy as an angel, I am as merry as a schoolboy." He has taken another giant step home.

※   ✳   ※

Make a list of certain people you feel you have harmed in your life, past and/or present. Now, in a second column, you might write down the harms you think you have done them. (Been cold and unfriendly? Too blaming? Taken something of theirs? Hurt their reputation with others?) Try to be specific. (You might consider discussing what you have uncovered with a trusted and sympathetic person in your life.)

In a third column, you might then write down amends that would seem to best undo any harms you've uncovered. (You don't have to commit to doing such amends now—this is an exercise in self-reflection.) Do you owe an apology to someone? Is there a kindness you might do them, or another way to heal and renew the relationship? Even if the person is dead, is there some "spiritual amends" that might bring healing? Remember to be open to divine inspiration, not just your rational mind, as you think about these amends.

✳

Now ask yourself if you're willing to follow through on them. Allow yourself to explore the fears and resistance that may surface. Are there particular amends you feel most reluctant about? Even if you don't sense yourself ready, be open to the possibility of returning to these amends in the future. Mean-while, embrace any healing amends you feel yourself ready for now.

✖

LIFE COMPLETION

The Ghost of Christmas Past, or memory, gives Scrooge the tools for self-transformation. But that is not all that facilitates his change. The Ghost of Christmas Present shows him the neighbors with whom he dwells. Through the Ghost of Christmas Yet To Come, he comes face to face with his own mortality.

As Robert Butler says, the awareness of mortality helps trigger our life review. But it does more than that: it beckons us to consider our future.

Imagine we're reading a gripping novel. The first half is filled with interesting characters and turns of plot. But we know the real significance of the story will only emerge in the second half. We count on the author, mindful of the end, to draw together the diverse strands and bring the book to a satisfactory conclusion. What will that be? It remains to be seen. Will the fallen hero be redeemed? Can a badly damaged relationship survive? Will hope or despair triumph for the central character? So much depends on the final chapters.

The most significant story we'll ever encounter is the one we're writing each day—the story of our life. The chapters we pen in life's second half help determine the meaning of all that came before. Will ours be a story of redemption and fulfillment or "a tale told by an idiot, full of sound and fury, signifying nothing"?[9]

When Scrooge has a vision of his mortality, it is not death per se he dreads, but the end of an incomplete life. He witnesses his neglected grave, his unmourned corpse, all that's left of his mis-spent days. But these revelations lead him to alter his future. They do not necessarily prolong his life but allow him to act to round out that life with fullness.

Cleaning up past wrongs, I have suggested, is a key action step toward our fulfillment. The thought of death reminds us not to put off this work indefinitely. Shortly before he died, Hasidic master Rabbi Eliezer was approached by his students for one last teaching. "You should repent one day before you die!" he said. His students asked, "How can we know just when that day comes?" His answer: "Thus you should repent every day."[10] We never know how much time we have left, so now's the time to seek redemption.

Furthermore, it's never too soon to think about the legacy we wish to leave. On the most mundane level, it's a good idea to prepare a will. This task need not be seen as gruesome. We are clarifying how we want our assets and keepsakes to be distributed, so it's a time to reflect on the family and friends we love, the charities and causes we support. It's a grace that we can do them good even in the sadness of our passing.

In pondering life completion, we may also choose to prepare a "living will," which can state what forms of life support we do or don't wish and who we want to be our surrogate decision maker should we become incapacitated. It's hard to think about, but worth the effort. So many of us now die in alienating environments. We are surrounded by machines rather than loved ones; filled with needles and tubes, rather than peace and acceptance. Having a living will may help us regain some mastery over our passage. We can seek to bring our life to the conclusion we wish, not one determined by strangers.

In Judaism there's also a tradition of writing an "ethical will." If we're concerned with leaving others our money—that being perhaps the least of what we have to give—we might also like to pass on the values and insights that have guided us through the years. In our ethical will we set these down on paper. Perhaps we wish our children courage in the face of censure, the ability to laugh, appreciation of nature's small beauties. Maybe there are family stories we want to record for posterity, as well as the tale of our own life and spiritual journey.

Such a document might be opened, like a legal will, after we're gone, but why not gift it to our loved ones while we're still alive? In such a ceremony we can sanctify our closeness across the generations.

Scrooge himself left a precious legacy. "It was always said of him," Dickens writes, "that he knew how to keep Christmas well." But he came perilously close to having nothing to leave. Before he could pass on the richness of life, he had to claim it for himself.

So, too, for us. As we survey our past, we may discover what Rabbi Schacter-Shalomi calls "unlived life."[11] So many unfulfilled dreams and desires. Why did I never make that trip across the country? Why, when it gave me such satisfaction, did I stop singing in the choir? I always wanted to take nature photographs; why is that camera still gathering dust in the closet? If we don't address our unlived life, our death will always seem premature, even if we live to be a hundred.

At the close of *A Christmas Carol*, Scrooge is a delighted man. He has faced and exorcised his demons. He finds compassion for himself and others in his past. Where he's done wrong, he's sought to make amends. All the unlived life he neglected he's now addressing with joyful abandon. Bountiful gifts, socializing, laughter, and play have replaced his sullen, solitary existence. So much has been gained from his ghostly visitors!

We, too, may be visited by ghosts as we age. But let us remember what business brings them there: "Your welfare . . . your reclamation, then. Take heed." Let us, indeed, take heed and speedily welcome our visitors. They come to us, like Christmas Magi, bearing precious gifts.

❋   ❋   ❋

Ask yourself if you have pockets of "unlived life." Make a list of whatever comes to mind: experiences, adventures, talents unembraced. Are there ways you might still live these things through (either now or in the future)? What action steps might this process entail?

❋

Ask yourself: "What kind of legacy do I wish to leave others?" Imagine yourself writing an ethical will, in which you gift to your descendants the best of who you are. What virtues, insights, stories, would you like to pass on to them?

You might make some notes on this page about what would go into this will, or even write it out in full. If so, put thought and care in the style, the format, the physical materials you choose, and to whom and when you would gift it. This will is a most precious thing.

❋

❊ *Guided Meditation* ❊

THE GHOST OF DAYS LONG PAST

(Note: This visualization draws on previous exercises in this chapter, but it can help you go deeper in experience and understanding. Don't prejudge what will come to you.)

Imagine that, like Scrooge, you are visited by an unearthly ghost. This spirit has come to help you re-collect yourself by viewing key scenes from your past life. Take a moment to image him or her coming toward you. Let this spirit take whatever form you are comfortable with. Now imagine yourself agreeing to this journey. You know that it will help to make you whole.

The spirit takes you through time and space to witness a first scene. You see a time in your own past when you were very happy. Perhaps you are remembering a specific event, a special day, or a good period in your life. Let the scene swim into view. See yourself within it. What do you look like, what are you doing, who are you with? As you watch the scene unfold, allow yourself to experience some of this remembered joy.

Now the spirit bids you say goodbye. There's another scene you must view. The spirit now guides you to a time when you were sad. Maybe you had suffered a specific loss or disappointment, or were in a period in which nothing went well. Again, allow yourself to watch this scene unfold. Image yourself within it. View your former self with compassion. You'd like to reach out and give yourself comfort.

When the time seems right, let the spirit guide you on again. Now you are witnessing a scene you feel bad about. Perhaps you took some action that was wrong. Perhaps there was something you should have done and didn't. Let the scene come to mind, though it may be painful. The spirit reminds you that this review is part of your redemption. You must look honestly even at your shadow side.

Finally, the spirit wishes to show you one last scene. This is a time when you rose to your best. Perhaps you were expressing some talent; or your compassion; or some other virtue of character. Let the particular scene gather in your mind. As you look on, feel proud of yourself. Allow yourself to enjoy the memory.

Finally, it is time to say goodbye. The spirit departs with a final message: "What you have witnessed is a great gift. You have seen yourself happy and sad. You have watched yourself at your worst and at your best. There is much to learn from these memories. Think about why these four scenes came to mind. What does each one tell you about yourself? What does each one say about what's important in life? And think, too, of how the scenes go together. In a hidden way they are all related, one to another. Try to connect the dots, find the coherence. Then the sense of your life may emerge."

Thank the spirit for providing these lessons.

※　※　※

9

Facing Death and the Deathless: *A Buddhist Mother*

Krisha Gautami had an only son, and he died. In her grief she carried the dead child to all her neighbors, asking them for medicine, and the people said: "She has lost her senses. The boy is dead."

At length Krisha Gautami met a man who replied to her request: "I cannot give you medicine for your child, but I know a physician who can."

And the girl said: "Pray tell me, sir; who is it?" And the man replied: "Go to Shakyamuni, the Buddha."

Krisha Gautami repaired to the Buddha and cried: "Lord and Master, give me the medicine that will cure my boy."

Buddha answered: "I want a handful of mustard-seed." And when the girl in her joy promised to procure it, Buddha added: "The mustard-seed must be taken from a house where no one has lost a child, husband, parent, or friend."

Poor Krisha Gautami now went from house to house, and the people pitied her and said: "Here is mustard-seed; take it!" But when she asked, "Did a son or daughter, a father or mother, die in your family?" They answered her: "Alas! the living are few, but the dead are many. Do not remind us of our deepest grief." And there was no house but some beloved one had died in it.

Krisha Gautami became weary and hopeless, and sat down at the wayside, watching the lights of the city, as they flickered up and were extinguished again. At last the darkness of the night reigned everywhere. And she considered the fate of men, that their lives flicker up and are extinguished. And she thought to herself: "How selfish am I in my grief! Death is common to all; yet in this valley of desolation there is a path that leads him who has surrendered all selfishness to immortality."

Putting away the selfishness of her affection for her child, Krisha Gautami had the dead body buried in the forest. Returning to Buddha, she took refuge in him and found comfort in the dharma, which is a balm that will soothe all the pains of our troubled hearts.

Buddha said:

The life of mortals in this world is troubled and brief and combined with pain. For there is not any means by which those that have been born can avoid dying; after reaching old age there is death; of such a nature are living beings. . . .

Not from weeping nor from grieving will any one obtain peace of mind; on the contrary, his pain will be the greater and his body will suffer. He will make himself sick and pale, yet the dead are not saved by his lamentation. . . .

He who seeks peace should draw out the arrow of lamentation, and complaint, and grief.

He who has drawn out the arrow and has become composed will obtain peace of mind; he who has overcome all sorrow will become free from sorrow, and be blessed.

Paul Carus, *The Gospel of Buddha*

DEALING WITH DEATH

Death first enters our life when we're young. One of our grandparents may die. Perhaps a treasured family pet is killed. We're not sure what to make of death yet (are we ever?), but it seems like an intruder who crashes in without knocking. He's made off with something of great value, which we learn will never be returned. It seems so unjust. Not only are we powerless before this force, but so are our parents, who had once seemed like gods.

As we grow toward adolescence we gain an intellectual understanding of death, but not necessarily a deeper acceptance. We are still wounded by the losses we experience. Maybe a buddy dies in a car accident. Another kid from school commits suicide. Each death tears a hole in life's fabric. St. Augustine describes the loss of a dear friend:

> My heart was darkened over with sorrow, and whatever I
> looked at was death. My own country was a torment to me, my
> own home was a strange unhappiness. All those things which
> we had done and said together became, now that he was gone,
> sheer torture to me. My eyes looked for him everywhere and
> could not find him. And as to the places where we used to
> meet I hated all of them for not containing him.[1]

In addition to such heart-rending losses, ordinary life brings a thousand "little deaths." When we leave the family home to go to college, part of who we were dies away. We can never be that little kid again. No sooner do we settle into college than that, too, is over. Classes end, everyone disperses, and another part of our life is gone. Maybe we fall in love, but finally it just doesn't work. Another death. A good friend moves a thousand miles away—it feels like a tender plant we had cultivated for years is suddenly torn from the soil. We murmur a lot about staying in touch, but inside we know it will never be the same. Death again in one of its thousand disguises. Coming to the end of a novel we have loved; seeing our sports team close the season with a loss; mourning the last day of summer vacation—there's that sadness again.

The truth that death and endings are an ingredient in all of life is especially clear in life's second half. Midway through the Bhagavad-Gita, Krishna, disguised as a charioteer, suddenly reveals himself as the Divine ground of the universe. But his words are hardly comforting. "I am time, the destroyer of all; I have come to consume the world."[2] His disciple, Arjuna, has a vision of all the kings and warriors rushing into Vishnu's jaws. And this is what things can seem like as we age. No longer seizing just ancient relatives, death homes in on our parents, and then our siblings and friends. Perhaps an older brother contracts cancer. A coworker has a heart attack. Then we hear of another, and another, and another loss. We feel as though we're on a battlefield watching comrades fall all around. How much longer before our own number comes up?

At the same time, we can sense our death approaching from within. Maybe we don't have the energy we once had. The body grows heavier, the stairs ever steeper. Or a doctor informs us that our trick knee will never fully heal. Never. We're starting to count not so much the years we have lived, as the years we have left. There are trips we'll never take, books we'll never read, career goals we'll never meet. Each day we awaken to brings death a little closer.

In the last chapter we spoke of confronting our past life. We must face, as well, the death that surrounds us now and waits, crouching, sometime in our future. As we mentioned, these tasks are intertwined. To complete life involves coming to terms with it all, including the presence of death.

What to do with death? We see Krisha Gautami's first response: "In her grief she carried the dead child to all her neighbors, asking them for medicine." She seeks a potion that will bring him back to life. Her neighbors know this is impossible: "She has lost her senses."

Don't most of us seek some such medicine? The emotions surrounding a loved one's death, our own anticipated death, and other painful endings hurt so much that we go to great lengths to self-medicate. Some turn to drugs or alcohol. There is also the frenetic pursuit of pleasure, work, or the habitual drug of TV. Anything to avoid the void. Along with the medicine of denial, we use magical thinking. We pursue the "perfect love" we imagine will make us whole and relieve all feelings of loss and aloneness. When that doesn't happen, we blame our partner. Maybe the next relationship will do the trick, so we seek out another lover. Or perhaps we think that if we just exercise enough, or eat right, or use positive visualizations, we will keep away all decay. While such measures can make for a healthier and longer life, they cannot finally stave off death. In truth, there is no medicine for death—at least not of the sort that Krisha, and we, would often like.

This realization provides the impetus that prepares us to receive Buddha's truer medicine. Buddha sends Krisha out to confront death at every turn. He knows she will bring back no mustard-seeds: no house remains untouched by death. But the quest that leaves her empty-handed is designed to fill her mind and heart. It teaches her that she's not alone in her pain; it is not an isolated tragedy but the lot of all humankind. Admittedly, the particulars may differ. Her only son has died—anyone with children can imagine the magnitude of this loss. But is it easier to lose a brother or sister? To be born in a time of war, like the children of Bosnia or Vietnam? To undergo a messy divorce? To be laid off in a company downsize after thirty years of devoted service? We all have deaths that seed our life; there's little point in ranking our sorrows. The truth is we're all in the same mess together, struggling with grief, disappointment, and a sense of exile and incompletion.

In sending Krisha on her search, Buddha does more than just clarify the problem; he also commences the process of healing. As Krisha goes from house to house, her awareness shifts. At first she just seeks help for her own loss, but the journey gradually awakens her to the suffering of others. "How selfish am I in my grief! Death is common to all." This experience of compassion (called *karuna* in Buddhism) is one part of Buddha's medicine. It helps give back what death has stolen—a sense of wholeness and connection. Grief is no longer something that isolates but a conduit for deep sharing. Before her pilgrimage, Krisha nursed a private pain, and so did her neighbors. As the doors were flung open, so were people's hearts. The community is knit together by its suffering.

This sharing is an important medicine to apply over the years. We will surely experience the deaths of loved ones, as well as our own diseases, diminishments, and losses. Suffering is unavoidable. Yet so much depends on how we handle it. Will we bar the door and sit alone with our grief? If so, we risk becoming lonely and embittered. Or will our own sorrow make us more sensitive to others, like Krisha's neighbors who "pitied her"? If so, heartache can give rise to precious charity. And will we have the courage to seek help for ourselves, like Krisha trudging from door to door? It's not easy to make ourselves so vulnerable, so humble. After all, someone might slam the door in our face. But more often we find the opposite. As we share our burden with others, they reciprocate, and, for all, the burden mysteriously lightens. (I discuss this process further in the next chapter on the passion of Jesus.)

❋ ❋ ❋

Imagine Krisha Gautami at your door, asking for a mustard-seed. You cannot give her one because your house has known death. Think of some of the deaths you have encountered already in your life. (You may wish to list these.) Include some of the physical deaths that have hit you the hardest—perhaps the passing of friends, family members, even public figures you have cared for. But also list some of the other losses you've experienced—for example, relationships broken up, geographical dislocations, jobs lost, dreams you left behind—the "little deaths" that have changed your life.

In dealing with the feelings surrounding death, what have been your preferred "medicines"? (Keeping busy? Exercising? Emotional denial? Black hu-

mor?) Are you willing, like Krisha Gautami, to expose and seek assistance with your pain?

�֍

And can you remember a time when someone came to your door, like Krisha Gautami, seeking solace for a loss? (Think of an example or two.) How did you treat that person? Did you invite them in, and give what you could? Did you share with them your own losses? What came of it? Is there some way you might have given more, or still could, to that person, or to someone else who needs help?

✷

THE REGION OF THE DEATHLESS:
RELIGIOUS PERSPECTIVES

The medicine of compassion is only part of what Buddha offers. When all is said and done, Krisha is still "weary and hopeless" after her journey. Her neighbors cry out, "Do not remind us of our deepest grief." Compassion alone simply isn't enough. The goal is a spirituality that can "draw out the arrow of lamentation, and complaint, and grief."

In a slightly different version of this story, Buddha ends up telling Krisha Gautami:

> *Though one should live a hundred years,*
> *Not seeing the Region of the Deathless,*
> *Better were it for one to live a single day,*
> *The Region of the Deathless seeing.*[3]

Cryptic as this message may sound to our Western ears, we can glean its essence. If death brings the arrow of suffering, only a realization of something deathless can extract it from our side. Buddhism, like other spiritual traditions, says the realm of the deathless is real and is accessible to the seeker. The Tibetan Buddhist Sogyal Rinpoche states:

> With continued contemplation and practice in letting go, we come to uncover in ourselves "something" we cannot name or describe or conceptualize, "something" that we begin to realize lies behind all the changes and deaths of the world. . . . It is as if all our lives we have been flying in an airplane through dark clouds and turbulence, when suddenly the plane soars above these into the clear, boundless sky. Inspired and exhilarated by this emergence into a new dimension of freedom, we come to uncover a depth of peace, joy, and confidence in ourselves that fills us with wonder, and breeds in us gradually a certainty that there is in us "something" that nothing destroys, that nothing alters, and that cannot die.[4]

The key to aging successfully may lie in this "Region of the Deathless." If death and loss are coming at us from every direction—both within and without—as the years pass, it's hard to accept change joyfully without a backdrop of transcendent meaning.

How do we find this Deathless Region? How do we gain the faith or knowledge to inhabit it with assurance? Many turn for help to the teachings of religion. Despite the modern world's skepticism of religion, one finds a treasure trove of wisdom there. The major faith traditions share several things in common: they all recount profound experiences of the sacred by the "realized beings" of their time; all capture the shared spirituality of a culture; all have undergone a process of testing and refinement over the centuries; finally, all have proven powerful enough to inspire the lives of millions. These are high recommendations, indeed. Not to say that all religious doctrines are true, or even helpful—we're well acquainted with the abuses perpetrated in the name of God. But if we use a discriminating eye, we can find in the world's religions both insight and inspiration.

For the most part, these religions agree with Buddha: there *is* a Region of the Deathless. Passing life arises out of and returns to something greater. Through "the valley of the shadow of death" we are ultimately heading home.

There are also serious disagreements concerning the details of our path and the home to which we return. Within major Western religions such as Christianity, Islam, and strains of Judaism, it's taught that we live but once on earth. Death does not render that life meaningless: on the contrary, it gives it special purpose. Since our time is so limited, each moment is precious. We're striving to express God's love, and to win our own and others' salvation. While death brings this earthly phase to an end, it may inaugurate our move to a better world. If we've lived well, death will bring our eternal self home to God.

Eastern religions such as Hinduism and Buddhism see things somewhat differently. The individual is undergoing an education on earth, and it can hardly be completed in one life. Our karmic transmission leads to rebirth again and again as we absorb the lessons that ready us for homecoming. Death is not life's end but the bridge to yet more life. It frees us to experience new identities and challenges. The ultimate goal is to awaken from this cycle of rebirth. When we've realized our identity with the all-encompassing, there's no need for further lessons. Our sense of separate self dissolves into the infinite like a drop of water returning to the sea.[5]

So far I've addressed the Deathless Region as if it were something other than this earth. What if it surrounds us here and now? Judaism, for example, focuses on the redemption of *this* world. In this context, how we spend our brief time has profound effects even after we're gone. Our life choices have impact on our children and their children, influencing the world for generations. We are like pebbles cast upon the waters, the ripples immeasurable.

Taoist, Native American, and animist traditions also remind us of our place in a more-than-human world. Our life cycle is simply a piece of the greater cycles of nature. As the death of a plant fertilizes the soil, so death and new life are intertwined. Perhaps the

Deathless Region is this never-ending dance. To die is to give back what we were so freely given. Our matter and life energy reenter the soil, the air, and the spirit of those to come.

Some pretty nifty visions. How can we believe any of them, though, when they disagree so with each other? In fact, the divergences of worldview are significant, but they may not be as central as they seem. In a well-known parable, a group of blind men describe an elephant. The one grasping the tail gives a very different account from the man holding a leg or the third man swinging from the trunk. But in truth they've got hold of the same beast. Aren't we in a similar position trying to understand death and the Deathless? We are struggling to describe only that part of an indescribable reality that our mind can perceive and bend into words.

We can listen for what reports from many enlightened people and traditions share in common. We may find there's a surprising amount. For example, the major religions (for the most part) agree on the following propositions:

1. There's an eternal Spirit pervading the universe.

2. We are a creation of that Spirit and participate in its essence.

3. The meaning of life lies in growing toward and expressing that divine nature.

4. Death plays its part in helping us to attain that goal. By the dissolving of the old we are released to grow.

5. What comes after death has much to do with what came before—with how well we travelled our spiritual passages.

Religions agree that death can be a time of transition and fulfillment—not simply a cosmic dead-end.

The Region of the Deathless:
Empirical Evidence?

Religious teachings may nonetheless fail to persuade many of us concerning the existence of a deathless region. After all, we live in a scientific age. Faith can seem the refuge of the dogmatist or the consolation of the romantic. Perhaps we want cold, hard facts before we'll believe in such spiritual matters.

Let's turn to evidence that, while not proving the existence of the Deathless, at least supplies some grounds for belief. I'll mention just three forms: evidence provided by past-life memories; near-death survivors; and our scientific view of the cosmos.

Dr. Ian Stevenson, the Carlson Professor of Psychiatry at the University of Virginia Medical School, has devoted much of the last twenty years to researching instances of apparent past-life memory. Beginning with *Twenty Cases Suggestive of Reincarnation* in 1974, his studies have been published in numerous volumes. Many of his cases share a similar pattern. A young child experiences spontaneous memories of a previous life; he or she may show specific personality traits, and sometimes complicated skills, consistent with that past identity. Upon investigation, the child's account fits an actual person who has died, often violently and within the last three years. The child, when tested, shows special knowledge of this person's life, with no explanation for how it could have been obtained from external sources. Usually the children lose access to these memories between ages five and eight.

The power of Dr. Stevenson's cases lies in their accumulated detail. I'll briefly summarize one case to give some sense of the phenomenon.[6] Parmod Sharma was born October 11, 1944. Between the ages of three and four he began to speak in some detail of his life in Moradabad, a town ninety miles away from where he lived. He claimed he had been one of the "Mohan Brothers," who had owned a biscuit and soda-water shop. According to his account, he had had four sons and a daughter. Though his parents never tried to explore his claims, word filtered to this other village and prompted contact from a family that fit the description well. The family's brothers had indeed operated just such a "Mohan Brothers" shop. One of the owners, Parmanand Mehra, had died in 1943 in ways consonant with some of young Parmod's "memories." He had, in fact, left behind four sons and a daughter. His family invited the child up for a visit.

When he arrived, Parmod correctly identified a series of Parmanand's family members, reacting to each in ways appropriate to his previous identity. He gave accurate directions for his driver to take him to the Mohan Brothers shop. There, he correctly noted a change in the shop's furniture. A complicated soda-water machine had been disconnected as a test; Parmod gave proper instructions on how to repair it. During a later visit he pointed out a man who had owed him (Parmanand) money. Only when he was promised that he wouldn't have to return it did the man confess that it was true.

Such details, as in dozens of others cases, continue at length. Are we convinced? Much depends on our assessment of such witnesses and of Dr. Stevenson's own methods. Out of thousands of cases, he focussed only on those that met certain standards of credibility. For example, there should be no evidence of ulterior motive or payment; no previous association between families, or mediators who might transmit information; generous recall of details; and, when possible, evidence of special skills or marks retained from the former life. The rigor of Dr. Stevenson's work has led to its being featured even in conservative professional journals—for example, the *Journal of Nervous and Mental Disease* and the *Journal of the American Medical Association*.[7] Dr. Stevenson also has his share of detractors, who question his methods and objectivity.[8] Even he does not claim he has proven reincarnation: there might be alternative explanations for these cases. However, his work, along with that of others, suggests that belief in rebirth need not be just a matter of wild faith. As a hypothesis, it's worthy of scientific investigation.

Even more striking to the public mind have been accounts of

so-called near-death experiences (NDEs). Whereas Dr. Stevenson draws on a few exceptional cases (spontaneous recall of a "past life" is rare), near-death experiences are a widespread phenomenon. A 1982 Gallup poll suggested that no fewer than eight million Americans had had such an episode. However, many refrained from discussing it in public, and until recently such experiences received little attention. Dr. Raymond Moody, trained in philosophy and medicine, has helped to change all that. He and other researchers have reviewed thousands of accounts of those who have been near death (and sometimes clinically dead) and have revived. Despite differences in individuals' religious beliefs, ages, and personalities, there are striking similarities in these NDEs. Survivors speak of undergoing one or more of a series of standard features, which in the full-blown NDE unfold in a progressive sequence.

First, the individual may realize they have left their body and are viewing it from another vantage point. Many then report travelling through a dark tunnel or valley, at the end of which they enter a region of light, associated with feelings of intense love and comfort. They're often welcomed by unknown "people of light" or friends and relatives who themselves have died.

Next, many speak of being guided through a comprehensive life review. Without judgment, they are shown, as in a sort of three-dimensional movie, the consequences of their prior actions.

Finally, they may experience a moment when they return to their body, either unexpectedly or as the result of a conscious decision or command. Often this journey back is undertaken reluctantly, with suffering on reentry.

As impressive as these experiences themselves are the lasting personality transformations they effect. Survivors of NDEs often show an increased sense of serenity and purpose. Their attention shifts from material ambitions to what they now see as the true goals of life: to give, love, and pursue knowledge and growth. Though their "death" was pleasurable, it doesn't reduce their zest for life. On the contrary, survivors often report an enhanced enjoyment, with no interest in suicide or premature death. At the same time, death anxiety disappears. One hears statements like the following:

> When I was a little boy I used to dread dying. . . . But since this experience, I don't fear death. Those feelings vanished. I don't feel bad at funerals anymore. I kind of rejoice at them, because I know what the dead person has been through.[9]

> After you've once had the experience that I had, you know in your heart that there's no such thing as death. You just graduate from one thing to another—like from grammar school to high school to college.[10]

Are these experiences real, or just hallucinations? Again, the verdict is undecided. Dr. Moody, like Dr. Stevenson, remains cautious in his claims. He argues that NDEs provide not definitive proof of an afterlife, merely reasonable evidence for this hypothesis. Readers intrigued by these NDEs can turn to many books that describe research on the phenomenon.[11]

So far I've focussed on accounts that seem to support some notion of personal survival. You might still find this idea implausible. The whole world view of scientific materialism seems stacked against it. If consciousness is merely a product of physical structures, it makes little sense to think the "I" can survive the body's death.

Yet twentieth-century science may provide some solace. It reminds us of the majesties of creation that encompass our little self. For example, the "Gaia hypothesis" suggests that the earth's biota has acted over time as a self-regulating homeostatic system. That is, life on earth has behaved like a unified organism. Despite a radically changing environment, it has sustained the conditions necessary for its own survival over millions of years. From this perspective, our own lives are but a tiny part of this greater being. And what science describes we may experience in our heart. A walk through the forest, a day by the sea, the panorama we witness from a high peak—all these can remind us of the vast splendors in which we are embedded.

To widen the horizon even further, gaze at the night sky. Scientists inform us that it contains some fifty billion galaxies, each composed of fifty to one hundred billion stars. By this calculation the total number of stars could be 5,000,000,000,000,000,000,000, or a thousand billion for each person on earth. Our individual life is dwarfed by such magnificence. Yet science also reminds us that we are an integral part of this whole. The carbon in our bodies was forged in the furnace of dying stars. When we look at the night sky we see our distant cousins. Let's face it, we're a miraculous thing— stardust gazing up at the stars.

Where each of us finds the Deathless Region is a highly individual thing. For some it lies in the eternal survival of the self. For others, this concept remains too small a vision: we arise out of and merge back into a universe that far outruns the tiny "me."

THE REGION OF THE DEATHLESS: A PERSONAL JOURNEY

Finally, neither the teachings of religion nor science may fully open to us the Deathless, for these are things we hear of from others. Death strikes at our very core; if we're to face it with clarity and confidence, we may need something that convinces from within.

In his last words before his own death, Buddha told his followers not to look to him for further enlightenment, or slavishly accept what they're told. "Those who . . . shall be a lamp unto themselves, relying upon themselves only and not relying upon any external help . . . shall reach the very topmost height!"[12] In seeking the Deathless Region we finally use our own lamp, light our own path home.

Since this journey is so individual, it's hard to lay out a general map. Perhaps it's best to simply provide an example. I'll draw from the life I'm most familiar with: my own. I speak of my path not to urge my methods or beliefs on anyone, but simply to help you reflect on yours, with its differing turns and signposts.

As I've mentioned, death became an issue early for me, with the loss of my whole family. Death came into my life wearing gruesome masks in a veritable Halloween dance of the macabre: my mother in agony from metastasized cancer; my brother choking on his own vomit; my father plunging from an eighth-story window. It was not until many years later that I faced up to it all, using a Twelve Step program, therapy, spiritual reading, and prayer. As I penetrated my own history, the question I faced became more universal. Not just how and why did Dad, and Mom, and Scott die—but why does *anyone* die? *What is death?*

Through my Twelve Step work I gained access to a loving God who was relieving my compulsive symptoms. The horizons of my life began to expand in all directions—a happy marriage, a wonderful job, a beautiful child—but the question of death remained. Life had vastly improved, but would death render it all a mockery?

My sense of a loving God answered, "No." After all, I felt a Power and a Presence carrying me: giving me guidance when I needed it; arranging outrageous "coincidences" for my benefit; showing me a tenderness I could not grant myself. Would this Presence abandon me at the grave? Surely not.

The stakes were clear to me; everything hung in the balance. If death eradicated the self, any notion of an all-loving God seemed a joke. Whether it's a single child dying of leukemia, or millions of Jews shepherded into the ovens, if death is final, then love and justice do not reign. The answer growing from within me said that they do. God is real—I can't deny my experiences. True, life is filled with suffering and loss. But these must be part of the soul's journey home.

To me, it made sense that this journey would involve reincarnation. I knew my soul was mastering certain spiritual lessons, but I was also aware of how slow my progress was. I couldn't imagine my schooling would be completed in one life. Nor did it make sense to me that this life would be a sufficient "testing ground" before the soul was plunged into infinite bliss or torment.

Without seeking such contacts, I met several people who had had NDEs. A woman I encountered on a retreat; a man who'd once been a low-life druggie before the NDE turned him radically around; then a good friend; then my wife's cousin; then even my mother-in-law! I felt myself surrounded by messengers.

Still, I wasn't satisfied. After all, I'd never had an NDE, or a past-life memory, that might convince me from within. I prayed for more illumination. "Raise my spiritual I.Q.," I would plead, "so I can understand better how it all works."

One answer arrived in the form of a visualization. I was about to teach a workshop on aging and needed a unifying theme. Late at night I received a series of images. I saw myself as a leaf on a tree. Autumn was approaching and would bring about my end. In the first part of the visualization, this thought was frightening. I saw no purpose, no solace, just the coming death. The second part presented the same scene, but from a different perspective. My leaf-self was part of a splendid tree. I served this tree both in life, capturing sunlight, and in death, as I returned to fertilize the soil. Autumn was not simply a time of loss. It freed me to explode in brilliant colors, and then to release myself beyond boundaries. I've since realized that this metaphor is used by many others, but I experienced it as a personal message from God. (This visualization is included at the end of this chapter.)

On another day, in response to prayer, a very different metaphor came flooding into my mind. When I was in high school my mother had worked with me for weeks in preparation for the college SATs. I did problem sets at the dining-room table. In my prayer-answer I was told that life is like working a problem set. If the questions are far too difficult, you're not really going to benefit; you won't either if the problems are too easy. You need to be challenged, make mistakes, and then learn from them. Life is a karmic curriculum geared at just the right level for the soul's advancement.

Furthermore, life experience by itself is incomplete. After all, even at the end of a problem set, you're not always sure what you got right or wrong. You finally need access to the answer key. Then, when you go over the test, your learning is maximized.

This activity, I thought, was the life review reported by people who had NDEs. The soul sees with vividness "how it did" and what would have worked better. Maybe that's why people after NDEs experience such an improved life—they got a peek at the answer sheet!

Some readers may find this image alien. Perhaps because I am a college teacher, it spoke to me. It also had a highly personal resonance. I'd always blamed my mother for the conditional nature of her love. Her SAT drills had seemed like a symbol of that—she was pressuring me to succeed. This prayer-image put it all in a new light. If God uses the problem sets of life to teach us, then my mother was expressing one form of God's love. I began to see more clearly the love in her efforts. It must have been tedious sitting there while I worked my tests, yet she loved me enough to do it. This realization was part of the forgiveness work I mentioned in the previous chapter.

I thought also about my father and brother. What did this metaphor have to tell me about suicide? A response came through strong and clear. Sometimes in working the problem set a child becomes frustrated. As wrong answers pile up, he might think the test is unfair or, even worse, feel like a failure. Finally, he becomes too frustrated to continue. The test is thrown down, and the child stalks away. That was what my father and brother did when they abruptly ended their lives.

What then? Well, a loving parent wouldn't rub a child's nose in failure. You'd do the opposite: give the kid a break, maybe take him out for ice cream. No blame. But sooner or later, when he is ready, he'll need to return to the table. The lessons remain to be learned, and the child, at heart, wants to learn them. Scott and Dad would still have that chance.

Over the years, it seems that God has reached out to me through an array of such images, as well as readings, "coincidental" meetings, and the like, geared just for me. Even the writing of this book I take as a series of lessons meant *for me* as much as for any reader. A friend once said, "We teach best what we most need to learn." Though I think I've come far, I also have much to learn about aging, and about accepting death. I still experience losses as excruciating. I don't feel ready yet to face the loss of more loved ones, or my own death, with equanimity. But I know my journey will continue.

We are each at a different place along the path. For some, like myself, like Krisha Gautami, it is inaugurated by a loved one's death. For some, the path then unfolds through a relationship with a spiritual figure—Buddha for Krisha, Jesus for many in the West. Our walk may be guided by religious and scientific reading, the answers to prayer, or insights that emerge from meditation. No matter what the particulars of our journey, we may arrive at a common destination. Buddha calls it the Region of the Deathless.

❋　　❋　　❋

Take a few moments to reflect on your own personal journey. Are there any teachings from within or without that have carried you toward the Region of the Deathless? (Being at the bedside when a friend died? Having a sense of someone visiting beyond the grave? Some special reading, conversation, religious teaching, that moved you?) You might make a list of these.

Alternatively, if you're visually oriented, you might actually draw a path, noting your milestones along the way. Draw them in at different places on the path. And note how you would image this path: Is it wide and straight? Does it have lots of twists and turns? Does it lead upward or downward? Is it a particular color? Where do you imagine the path finally leading?

❋

I have presented two images of life and death that came to me: the autumn leaf and the problem set. Is there a special image or metaphor to which you are drawn that helps you understand the meaning of life and death? The image might come from nature, poetry, some activity you love, a childhood game, et cetera. If you're a praying person, you might pray to have that image revealed. Or perhaps you want to meditate on it, or simply think about the question. If an image, metaphor, or story comes, write (or draw) it, and explore its many dimensions.

�֎

BEFRIENDING YOUR DEATH

If we are to fully extract the arrow of suffering, we must do more than gain a general belief in the Deathless. We must somehow become comfortable with *our own death*. To do so is one of the most important, if not *the* most important, spiritual tasks of life's second half. Without it we can't accept our own aging, since it inevitably leads toward the grave; nor can we fully embrace life's joy. C. G. Jung writes:

> That is why so many people get wooden in old age; they look back and cling to the past with a secret fear of death in their hearts. . . . From the middle of life onward, only he remains vitally alive who is ready to *die with life*. . . . not wanting to live is identical with not wanting to die.[13]

It doesn't work to simply not think about death. If we still have fear buried deep inside us, it weighs us down. Buddhists counsel an opposite strategy: to keep death ever before the mind, to prepare for its coming. In the words of twelfth-century master, Drakpa Gyaltsen, "Human beings spend all their lives preparing, preparing, preparing. . . . Only to meet the next life unprepared."[14]

Preparing for death is a time-honored notion even in the West, though now it is largely forgotten. We tend to think of the good death as being unexpected and instantaneous. To drop dead of a heart attack without warning—that seems like the way to go.

In medieval times, it was thought better to have ample time to ponder and prepare. Amends could be made, forgiveness sought, the soul cleansed, and the family gathered around the bedside. I have discussed such elements of life completion in the chapter on Scrooge.

The work of life completion also opens up a further possibility: that of actually *befriending* our death. Mozart wrote:

> As death, when we come to consider it closely, is the true goal of our existence, I have formed during the last few years such close relations with this best and truest friend of mankind, that his image is not only no longer terrifying to me, but is indeed very soothing and consoling![15]

The notion of our death may seem far from consoling. For many of us, our death is the stranger we most dread meeting. Afraid we'll be jumped in some dark alley, we run from it at every turn. What if we got to know it better? What if we looked our own death squarely in the face, engaged it in conversation? Might we convert a stranger, even an enemy, into our trusted companion?

Here too, the Buddha can give us some advice. Shortly before his own death, he said:

> *Of all footprints*
> *That of the elephant is supreme;*
> *Of all mindfulness meditations*
> *That on death is supreme.*[16]

Meditation on death is a longstanding Buddhist tradition. One may sit in a graveyard, or contemplate a human skull, and imagine the hour of one's own demise and the gradual decomposition of one's corpse. Such techniques are particularly developed in Tibetan Buddhism. In the "exoteric method" one visualizes one's death in vivid detail. The "esoteric method" for initiates goes further, involving the mental simulation of the five stages and the dissolution of twenty-five substances that, according to the Tibetan tradition, accompany dying.

Such meditations bring us face to face with death's "gruesome" features: regrets assailing the mind, slime forming on the teeth, and so on. In the West we begin with so much death-fear that such visualizations may only make things worse. We might do better to contemplate our death in a positive manner. Let's not wait until we're sick or in a morbid mood. We can meditate on death when we're feeling good, and seek images of consolation and meaning.

It's also a Buddhist belief that our manner of dying both sums up our past life and determines the nature of our next one. The death passage is thus a good time for spiritual advancement. We may not agree with this metaphysics, but we can still see our death as a fulfillment and transition. We can image the death we most wish for ourselves. For those interested in delving deeply into such practices there are a number of helpful guide books: for example, Stephen Levine's *Who Dies?*; Sogyal Rinpoche's *The Tibetan Book of Living and Dying*; John White's *A Practical Guide to Death and Dying*; and Anya Foos-Graber's *Deathing*. Even those who don't want to work extensively on this issue can explore their own vision of the good death. At a workshop I attended, anthropologist Joan Halifax asked participants how they would like to die. Here is the gist of some of their responses:

"I'd like to die in a setting like a womb, surrounded by spiritual symbols. I want music on so I can dance into the next world."

"I want to have my dog there, one or two friends. To finally feel accepted as a gay person."

"I want to have the experience of giving all back to God."

"I want to feel free of guilt, to release others so they don't have to feel guilt at my passing, just joy."

"I want to die while I'm meditating."

"I want children around me."

"I want to die with eagerness to see what comes next."

"I want to be surrounded by those I've loved, having talked through our issues and told them of the gifts they've given me."

"I want to die like my father did, reaching for some ice cream."

We're used to dreading our hour of death. Indeed, many go into it with such fear and resistance, or so drugged and intubated on a medical ward, that the death-scene can be a nightmare for all. These statements remind us that we can instead visualize the death we wish for ourselves and help prepare for its fulfillment.

That's not to say things will unfold just as we hope. It's one thing to rehearse in the mind, another to face the harsh realities. However, the more we mentally prepare for death, the greater our chance of meeting it on our terms. Furthermore, if we befriend our death, we'll find ourselves a better friend of life. "He who has drawn out the arrow and has become composed will obtain peace of mind . . . and be blessed."

*Ask yourself how **you** would most like to die. Allow the scene to come to you in words or images. What kind of environment would you be in? Who, if anyone, would be present? Are there certain actions, rituals, or emotions you'd wish to be part of your leave-taking? If you feel comfortable, allow yourself to enter into the imagined dying experience, and see how it feels "from the inside." Don't deny any unpleasant feelings that may come up—fear, anger, and the like. But also experience what is positive in your vision. See if you can befriend your death.*

If this thought-experiment or visualization works for you, it may be worth continuing to use. Return periodically to this scene wherein you welcome death. You might find that your definition of the "good death" shifts with changes in your life and understanding. As new images come to mind, allow them in.

�֎

Guided Meditations

THE CYCLE OF LIFE AND DEATH

(This first meditation is best done in silence. Allow yourself to enter into it emotionally, even if some of the images and feelings are unpleasant.)

Imagine you are a leaf. You are a leaf living on an upper branch of a big oak tree. During the spring you grew, and in the summer you absorbed the rays of the sun, but now it is fall. The air is growing colder. The sun's rays are growing dim. Your leaf edges are crisping. You feel the stem that attaches you to the tree, and feeds your life, growing brittle. The sap of life seems to be drying up. With each cold wind of autumn you become more and more afraid of breaking off. You curl up to fend off the bitter wind. You cling desperately to the tree, frightened of being blown off. But all the time you know that winter is approaching. You cannot hang on forever.

One by one you see your friends blown off in the wind. The tree is growing more bare. You are more and more alone, but you continue to cling to the tree. Finally, one night there is a winter gale, harsh and chilling. It grabs you and tugs on you; you fight back with all your might, but you know you are losing. Finally you feel your stem begin to break. You suddenly realize the end is upon you.

(After a suitable pause, now enter into this second meditation, which presents many of the same images, but with a different context. It may help to put on some quiet instrumental music for this visualization—music that you find peaceful and calming.)

Imagine again that you are a leaf. Again, you are a leaf living on an upper branch of a big oak tree. During the spring you grew, and in the summer you absorbed the rays of the sun, but now the days are growing shorter and the weather cooler. You are open to all this and breath it in. All summer long you labored in the hot sun making food for the tree. You do not regret your work, but you feel glad for some rest, for the slowing down. In summer, everything was busy and buzzing; now things are growing quiet.

Even the sunlight has a different quality. It is less harsh than the light of summer and is rich with new tones, new messages. You allow this autumn light in. Take a minute to ask yourself, what do you find in this light? What is it telling you, or calling you toward? (Pause, and open to whatever thoughts come.)

In response to this different light of autumn, you find yourself becoming different. The green chlorophyll that covered you in summer has gradually disappeared, but this process is permitting other colors to emerge. Allow yourself to see your colors—are there streaks of yellow, or orange, or bright red? All these colors are new parts of who you are, new possibilities you had not imagined in spring or summer. (Ask yourself—what are these new parts of yourself that are now emerging? Pause to see what thoughts come.)

You notice that along with your new colors there are other changes. Your edges are beginning to crack, your stem is growing brittle. (How is that happening in your life? Where do you feel the new cracks or brittleness?) You know that these changes are a harbinger of winter. You know some day a wind will come to release you. But this thought does not frighten you, for though you are a leaf, that is not all you are. You know you are also a part of the tree. The tree gave birth to you—it sent you forth to absorb the sunlight and help it grow. You are not just a leaf, but part of a magnificent oak tree. Soon your work will have been fulfilled. It will be time to make room for new leaves that will bud next spring. In letting go, you know you are not abandoned. When the time comes, you will float gently down to the ground. You will become part of the soil that feeds the tree. You will find yourself changed, and you will take on new form, but you will still be part of the tree of life.

Finally that day comes. A hard wind blows and whips you back and forth. You feel the cold in your face, but you reach out to it. Your stem begins to break, and you let it. You let go. Suddenly, it happens; the wind carries you upward, outward, in ecstasy. You swirl and dance in the breeze. Finally, you are free.

The first meditation tends to speak to feelings of fear and isolation in the face of aging and death. The second meditation shifts focus to the creativity, purpose, and joy available when these are viewed in the light of the Deathless.

Have you known anyone whose passing seemed to reflect the mood of the first meditation? Or who approached death in the spirit of the second? Which one better captures your own feelings about aging and dying? (Don't judge, just notice.) Or is it possible that each represents a different side of you?

❈   ❈   ❈

Part V   Suffering and Joy

10

Suffering as Gift:

The Passion of Jesus

During supper Jesus took bread, and having said the blessing he broke it and gave it to the disciples with the words: "Take this and eat; this is my body." Then he took a cup, and having offered thanks to God he gave it to them with the words: "Drink from it, all of you. For this is my blood, the blood of the covenant, shed for many for the forgiveness of sins."

Jesus then came with his disciples to a place called Gethsemane. He said to them, "Sit here while I go over there to pray." He took with him Peter and the two sons of Zebedee. Anguish and dismay came over him, and he said to them, "My heart is ready to break with grief. Stop here, and stay awake with me." He went on a little, fell on his face in prayer, and said, "My Father, if it is possible, let this cup pass me by. Yet not as I will, but as thou wilt."

He came to the disciples and found them asleep; and he said to Peter, "What! Could none of you stay awake with me one hour? Stay awake, and pray that you may be spared the test. The spirit is willing, but the flesh is weak."

Pilate's soldiers then took Jesus into the Governor's headquarters, where they collected the whole company round him. They stripped him and dressed him in a scarlet mantle; and plaiting a crown of thorns they placed it on his head, with a cane in his right hand. Falling on their knees before him they jeered at him: "Hail, King of the Jews!" They spat on him, and used the cane to beat him about the head. When they had finished their mockery, they took off the mantle and dressed him in his own clothes.

Then they led him away to be crucified.

From midday a darkness fell over the whole land, which lasted until three in the afternoon; and about three Jesus cried aloud, *"Eli, Eli, lema sabachthani?"* which means, "My God, my God, why hast thou forsaken me?"

The New English Bible: New Testament—The Gospel
According to Matthew 26–27.

The Young Old Man

In the last chapter we spoke of befriending our death, but it can be easier said than done. Not every death is easy. The death of Jesus is, of course, a prime example. Moreover, it is not only dying that we fear, but the pain that may accompany *living* through our later years. Age may bring with it suffering. How do we do more than just grin and bear it, or complain, if that's our style? How can we use the suffering as part of our spiritual curriculum? Jesus may seem an unlikely teacher concerning life's second half. After all, he died at thirty-three: by contemporary standards, a young man. Moreover, his "passion" (from the Latin *passio,* "to suffer") was, Christians would assert, a unique event in history. Whether or not we subscribe to this theology, his fate was certainly not the product of aging. He was martyred before his time by political opponents. His manner of death, particularly cruel, seems far removed from the modern world. Few of us will have to drink from such a cup of torture and persecution.

Yet this story resonates with a larger meaning. Jesus' passion contains reference to the myriad forms of human suffering, whether caused by nature or intentional cruelty. More to the point, it speaks particularly to the troubles of later life. In his final days, Jesus faces many of the same trials that we may go through in our final years. It's kind of like watching a film done with time-lapse photography. What ordinarily unfolds slowly—a flower opening to the sun, or clouds forming and shifting—is artificially speeded up. Similarly, Jesus' brief passion encapsulates much of the lengthier sufferings of age.

First, we see the pain of anticipated losses. In Gethsemane, Jesus is all but overcome by anguish, dismay, and grief. He already senses the pain he must face and would gladly avoid it. We may feel much the same way as we round the curve of midlife. We cannot see too far down the road, but we may already fear the loss of loved ones, of our health and independence, even of life itself. Who would not cry out with Jesus, "My Father, if it is possible, let this cup pass me by"?

Jesus' suffering in the garden is intensified by his isolation. He bids his disciples stay awake with him, but they fall asleep three times, leaving him alone in prayer.

We, too, may know loneliness. As the years pass away, so do many treasured companions—they move, turn to new pursuits, or die. Even in the midst of those who remain, we may feel isolated. Perhaps we wrestle with a chronic illness. Our friends and family, well-meaning as they are, cannot fully enter into our pain. It is unfolding within our body, not theirs. It whispers to us of our own mortality, which we must finally face alone. Even among his disciples Jesus must have felt isolated as he contemplated his fate; so may we as we face some of life's harsher tests.

At least, we hope, others will stay awake with us. Though they can't make it all better, they can be present to us when we suffer. What a consolation to hear a loved one say, "I'm there. I know what you're going though. Give me your hand. I'm staying up with you all night. You're not going to face this alone."

Such love is great to receive but difficult to give. After all, Jesus' disciples were committed to him, but they still went to sleep in Gethsemane. It's hard to stay awake to another's suffering. Why? For one thing, we know we might be next in line, and we hardly want to be reminded. Some of the disciples did, in fact, later meet with their own persecution. Similarly, to stay awake with an old or sick friend is to be reminded of what may await us. We might rather close our eyes and snooze.

It is not only our selfish side that wishes to escape. Our altruistic side is also threatened when we can't fix the other's problem. Kathleen Fischer writes:

> Sharing another's pain when we can do nothing about it is very costly. We feel sadness and helplessness. Sometimes we want to run away. Life can be unfair and cruel, and it is excruciating to stand by, unable to do anything. . . . our temptation is to try to rescue, give advice, or explain away the pain and frustration. It is much more difficult to acknowledge the helplessness.[1]

Maybe one reason the disciples went to sleep was that they didn't want to face their own helplessness. Perhaps we've done much the same ourselves. There may have been a sick or aging relative we were loath to visit; it was painful to watch the deterioration and be unable to do anything. This avoidance is not just some individual failing; it is typical of our culture. Our whole society closes its eyes to suffering, turning away from the poor, sick, and aged. Suffering is then compounded with loneliness.

Those in need are sometimes also subject to humiliation. Jesus was dressed in scarlet clothing and a crown of thorns, spat on, and ridiculed. We too may feel humiliated, if turned down for insurance because of chronic conditions; if wheeled around a hospital like a piece of meat; if overlooked for a promotion because we're "just too old." The mockery of Jesus went hand in hand with the soldiers stripping off his clothes. They were not simply seizing his possessions. Our clothes symbolize who we are inside, become part of our very identity; the soldiers were trying to strip away his personhood. We might find our own "clothing" stripped away by life. The job, family roles, income, even the body to which we're accustomed may be stripped away as we grow older. If we fall sick, we may end up in a hospital bed wearing the briefest of gowns that opens up in the back. We are virtually naked, side by side with Jesus.

As if all this isn't enough, the indignities of illness or age may be accompanied by physical pain. That crown of thorns *injured* Jesus; and he suffered the exhaustion of carrying the cross, the agony of nailed limbs and crucifixion. As we age, we may experience a crucifixion of sorts and, for sure, many a crown of thorns: the aches of arthritis; the weakened bladder; the heaviness of tired limbs; shortness of breath on exertion; the diminishment of hearing and eyesight. The litany goes on and on. And we cannot look forward to a speedy recovery, as we do in the illnesses of youth. These chronic problems often worsen rather than improve.

In the face of all these assaults, at least we can reach for spiritual solace. That, of course, is a central message of this book. However, let's acknowledge that we may face spiritual suffering as well. Even a "realized being" like Jesus cried out, "My God, my God, why hast thou forsaken me?" Can we assume we won't descend into this dark night of the soul? It's one thing to feel cared for by the universe when all is going well. But what if we do suffer through the loss of loved ones, a sense of loneliness and humiliation, all topped off by physical pain and the prospect of death? Our sense of a loving God, of a harmonious universe, can undergo a total collapse. We may stand amid the ruins and echo Jesus' cry, "Why hast thou forsaken me?"

So far, it all sounds grim; but the gospel account is not one of unrelieved suffering. "Gospel" literally means "good news." The good news is that Jesus' suffering is redemptive. It both brings his own mission to fulfillment and incalculably enriches the lives of those around him.

It can be so, too, in our own life. Of course, it would be hubris, if not insanity, to claim to be another Jesus. Nevertheless, Christians are meant to imitate his model. (The word "Christian," after all, means "Christlike.") And non-Christians may equally be inspired by, and learn from, this spiritual figure. It's important to remember that Jesus himself was not a Christian but a Jew named Yeshua. ("Jesus" is the Latinized version, as "Joshua" would be the English.)

So let's examine what Jesus, or Yeshua, or Joshua, has to teach us. He can show us the path, through life's suffering, to love.

✕   ✕   ✕

Thinking back over your life, come up with an experience that best matches each of these sufferings in Jesus' passion:

1. Feeling alone, as others "slept through" your suffering

2. Feeling stripped naked by others or by life

3. Feeling mocked by others, as if dressed in scarlet with a crown of thorns

4. Feeling and crying out, "My God, my God, why hast thou forsaken me?"

✕

STAYING AWAKE IN OUR SUFFERING

In Gethsemane, though others around him are sleeping, Jesus resolutely stays awake: probably no easy matter. Filled with anguish and grief, he may have been strongly tempted to run away or obliterate consciousness. Yet the story says he stayed up through the long night.

Here is our first lesson: stay awake to our sufferings, be they physical, emotional, or spiritual. These, as we saw through the first story of Buddha, can awaken us to greater life. How deep is the temptation to roll over and go back to sleep! One way is through denial: "Everything's fine! I've never felt so well in my life." Nothing wrong with such a positive attitude, but we have to make sure it's for real. Sometimes we're trying to avoid our fears and problems.

We can also escape by retreating from the world or exploding outward in a maelstrom of activity. The productive model of aging may encourage us to keep constantly busy. Great, if that brings us deep satisfaction. But we may also be running from thoughts and feelings that surface whenever we pause. Or, stimulated by the consumer model of aging, we may embark on exotic vacations or sink our savings into fun toys. We're so busy with externals that we don't have to be with ourselves. Those most unwilling to stay awake to suffering may even choose suicide. Older men, in particular, have a high suicide rate. It can seem like a tempting way to obliterate the pain: the Big Sleep.

Jesus' example is more about the Big Awake. He doesn't seek to obliterate his dark night but to see it through until morning. He goes through it all—anxiety, sadness, the grief of loss. And the way through proves to be the only way out. We see that in Gethsemane; by staying awake to his suffering, he is also present to prayer and grace. Not so his sleepy disciples.

How do we stay awake? We can start by acknowledging our feelings about loss, illness, and aging. There's often a fantasy that these feelings will overwhelm us if we let them come to the surface.

We might drown in fear, sadness, or anger. The truth is more the opposite: through allowing what we feel, we begin to heal.

✻　✻　✻

Ask yourself if there are forms of suffering that you are sleeping through, or trying to. A certain fear, perhaps? A painful loss from the past? A physical problem? An emotional struggle, or spiritual disappointment? See what comes to mind.

Choose one or more of these to focus on. Imagine that you are slowly and gradually **waking up** *to this pain. Let it come into your awareness. Let yourself experience it, as much as you feel safe doing. When you are done, you can put the pain away if you wish. But for the moment allow yourself to be in Gethsemane, awake to your suffering. Do this for however long it feels comfortable—one minute, one hour, one day. . . .*

✻

SACRIFICIAL LOVE

To unfold further the gospel message we must explore the root and purpose of Jesus' suffering. It is based in his sacrificial love. In his famous words, ever repeated in the Eucharistic ritual, he offers his body and blood for the redemption of others. He goes to a gruesome death out of love for those around him—not just the good citizens, but prostitutes and thieves; not just his supporters, but his enemies as well.

This passion was a gift not only to others but also to God. (In this and the next chapter I use the God-language of these spiritual traditions. If you are not comfortable with this term, feel free to substitute your own.) Struggling against his own misgivings, Jesus says, "Yet not as I will, but as thou wilt." He sacrifices his own life to carry out a divine mission. Such is a truer expression of love than any mere surge of feeling.

The notion of sacrificial love is central to a number of spiritual traditions. Mahayana Buddhism reveres the bodhisattvas, who, having achieved enlightenment, renounce personal nirvana to aid a suffering world. Hinduism recognizes as holy the path of karma yoga, wherein one labors selflessly for God and one's fellows no matter what the personal cost. Influenced by Jesus' Sermon on the Mount, as well as the Bhagavad-Gita, Gandhi is perhaps the greatest twentieth-century exemplar of this path.

What does sacrificial love have to do with our aging? Much age-related pain is involuntary, and seems to do no one any good. How can we emulate Jesus, the bodhisattvas, and Gandhi while dealing with hemorrhoids?

Well, maybe there's a way. On any spiritual path we must work with the stuff of daily life. Our challenge may not lie in world-changing accomplishments, but in hallowing the ordinary. Let's imagine an older woman dealing with hemorrhoids, and arthritis, and a weak heart, all restricting the compass of her world. Her husband died several years ago. She doesn't get out as much as she used to. One of her greatest joys is visits from her daughter who lives some eighty miles away. She'd gladly have her daughter over every weekend if she could. She's also aware that this daughter is newly married, absorbed in a demanding career, and an avid tennis player (when she gets the chance).

It's an act of sacrificial love for the mother to restrict her own demands. She knows well the guilt buttons she could push—"I have a bad heart, you know; I won't be around forever"—but she keeps her finger from pressing them. She'd love constant visits, but she limits her requests.

When her daughter does come to see her, the mother could unburden herself for hours. It's tempting to lapse into what Ram Dass calls the "organ recital." "Let me tell you about my arthritis. And I do worry about my heart," and so on. Joints, hearts, so many organs to recite! It can't be very pleasant, the mother knows, to be in the audience for such a concert, so she refuses to weigh her daughter down with the details of every symptom. Instead, she tries to make each visit enjoyable and to make conversation a genuine two-way street.

This behavior is sacrificial love. More visits and more self-centered complaint might feel good for the mother, but in consideration for her daughter she gives them up.

In the best scenario, the daughter reciprocates. Sure, she'd like to spend her Sundays playing tennis, but she also knows how much her visits mean to Mom. Despite her mother's protestations ("Go enjoy your own life!") the daughter sets aside the needed time, perhaps coming every third weekend. She tries to make each visit a special occasion for fun outings, shared memories, laughter, and tears.

What's the upshot of all this sacrificial love? In one sense, nothing. Timewise, the mother's and daughter's giving spirit might cancel each other out. They'll end up seeing each other just as much as if the mother had been more demanding, the daughter more resistant.

In another way, everything is changed. Each person is there on a mission of sacrificial love with concern for the other uppermost in mind. As a result the sharing is deeper, the joy and warmth that much greater.

This type of sacrificial love should not be confused with false martyrdom. Many of us (especially women who received the appropriate gender training), may go overboard in selling out the self. The mother who will not ask for *any* visits or the daughter who gives up tennis *entirely* may be going too far toward an unhealthy martyrdom. The difference is not just quantity but also motivation. We may martyr ourselves due to false guilt, or people-pleasing, or low self-esteem. Perhaps we feel worthless unless we are constantly in service. In such cases our motive is not genuine concern for the other; through "self-sacrifice" we're trying to fulfill our *own* psychic needs. It usually doesn't work, and then we grow burned out and resentful. "Here I've been coming every weekend for three months, and do you ever thank me? Don't you see all I do?!"

Real sacrificial love is a world apart. We're not seeking credit for ourselves, but to be genuinely helpful. Sometimes, as in the case of Jesus, we must give something up out of love for another. Only then is our self-denial a healthy thing. Only then does "sacrifice" take on its root meaning: to "make sacred." It is love that sanctifies suffering.

※   ※   ※

When have you acted in your life from sacrificial love? You might think of some occasions that stand out in memory. But look also at your current life. There may be numerous small ways in which you sacrifice for others, be it a child or grandchild, a spouse, a friend, a volunteer cause, whatever.

With each case, you might ask yourself: What is it that I give up, what "suffering" do I endure (however minor) in my act of love? You might then ask yourself a second question: What do I gain from the experience? Are there gifts of intimacy, growth, enhanced self-esteem, that flow back from my giving?

※

Think also, for a time, on the sacrificial love others have shown you over the years. What people, what experiences stand out in your mind? (You may think of the loving acts of parents, mentors, friends, colleagues, even helpful strangers.) What gifts has this love brought you? How have such people changed and enriched your life?

This question is quite something to meditate on. You might want to offer thanks in your heart to such people for the sacrificial love they have shown you.

※

DEDICATED SUFFERING

The notion of sacrificial love seems to work in the case of sacrifices freely chosen, like those of the mother and daughter just described. But can involuntary and seemingly useless sufferings also be transformed into sacrificial gifts? The surprising answer is yes. No matter what the cause, we can transform our pain into an offering to God and a needy world: we can *dedicate our suffering*.

Imagine an active man in his mid-forties who, while hiking through the mountain ridges of Kentucky, takes a serious fall that shatters his leg. His recuperation is slow and painful.

Before he can dedicate his suffering, first he must accept it. We might imagine him in prayer: "Lord, I sure didn't ask for this accident. I hate being laid up, and I've been fighting it all like crazy. But that's just making things harder. I'm becoming a crotchety pain in the ass, even to myself. So enough is enough. This is the cup I have to drink from, so let me do it right. I'll work with my strengths, if you'll help me through my weaknesses. I'll do my best and dedicate it to you."

Jesus had to carry his cross to Golgotha. Deciding to accept and carry our own cross can bring us into a deeper relationship with Spirit. Paradoxically, when we do so, we feel our burden lightened. It no longer seems alien or purposeless. Nor, we find, do we need to carry the weight alone. We may sense a Presence beside us at each step.

The Gospels also teach us to not be overly hasty in accepting our suffering and proclaiming it God's will. As Jesus' life demonstrated, we should be open to even miraculous healings of both a physical and emotional sort. Nor need we imagine that God wills our suffering as some sort of grim test or punishment. Jesus preached a loving Father (or, we may prefer, Mother) looking after his/her children.

Finally, some suffering may be the result not of the divine plan per se but of human failing. We may feel trapped in an unhealthy relationship, or we may be damaging our own body and soul with deleterious habits. To acquiesce prematurely to such pain would hardly be "God's will." We do best to remedy the source of suffering.

Nevertheless, there does seem to be an unavoidable residue of anguish in our lives. We may not fall from a ridge like the man just described, but surely we will meet with accidents and illnesses. We all suffer disappointments and losses. We will probably grow frailer as we age, and finally we will die. We might call such diminishments God's will—that is, part of the Universe, the Tao, the Way of things. In accepting our share graciously, we can open ourselves to grace. We can dedicate our own suffering to God and feel empowered and sustained.

Jesus' passion was dedicated not only to God but also to the welfare of other people. How do we transform our pain into such a gift? First, we can use the energy of our own *passion* to open up *compassion* ("suffering-with"). Let me give an immediate, if somewhat trivial, example. As I write this I am suffering from a cold: runny nose, cough, congested chest, standard stuff. First my wife had it, then our baby, now me. Something happened when I fell sick. Up to that point I'd been feeling a bit frustrated: Does my wife really have to keep me up at night with her coughing? Why is she dumping the baby on me? Why is little Sarah so darn grumpy? When I caught the virus, suddenly I had the answers. Aha! So this is how Janice feels—no wonder she can't sleep and is too exhausted to do much child care. Poor Sarah—now I see why she's so grumpy. Along with my sneezes, I felt a sudden rush of understanding and compassion. I could feel the others' plight resonating in my own tired body.

Two weeks ago a friend of mine lost her only brother in a freak plane crash. I'm no model of compassion, but immediately I could identify with her grief, having suffered through my own brother's death. I knew that emotional roller coaster of anger, guilt, numbness, joyful memories, sad regrets. I could listen to her and share my own experience. This was a space we could inhabit together. Compassion—suffering with.

Last week I listened to another friend's struggles. Her beloved sister had decided to move a thousand miles away. Again, I could sympathize. Just the week before, one of my own best friends had skipped town for a new job in California. My sense of loss was excruciating. Because of it, though, I could feel more deeply for my other friend's loss. Usually I'm a "fixer," but not on this occasion: "I'm not going to say 'Look on the bright side' or 'give it all to God,'" I told her. "The truth is, *it sucks!*" We laughed, and she replied, "Thank God you said that." At that moment, she just needed permission to feel her pain, and my own pain had taught me that knowledge.

In the words of Spanish philosopher, Miguel de Unamuno:

> Spiritual love is born of sorrow. . . . For men love one another with a spiritual love only when they have suffered the same sorrow together, when through long days they have ploughed the stony ground buried beneath the common yoke of a common grief. It is then that they know one another and feel one another and feel with one another in their common anguish, and so thus they pity one another and love one another.[2]

The freight of pain and loss that the years bring can open us to compassion—for the poor, the sick, the fearful, the lonely, throughout the world. In our youth we may have been callous, having suffered little. In age, let's hope that loss puts more than lines on our face; that it deepens the capacity of our heart to feel. Then when a Krisha Gautami comes to our door, we will graciously open it wide.

Yet so much depends on what we do with our sorrows. Rabbi Harold Kushner writes:

> Pain makes some people bitter and envious. It makes others sensitive and compassionate. It is the result, not the cause, of pain that makes some experiences of pain meaningful and others empty and destructive.[3]

In my earlier example, the widow with hemorrhoids, arthritis, and a heart condition might let life turn her into a bitter old woman. She could become so absorbed in private pain that she would have little concern left for others. Or she can seek the reverse. Refusing to wallow in self-pity, she can channel her pain into compassion. Perhaps the ache of arthritis becomes her reminder to visit a neighbor worse off than she—frailer, older, with no family around. In such ways, compassion leads us back to sacrificial love.

Another issue arises here: Is there a way our suffering itself can be used *directly* to help others? In the gospel story, Jesus dedicates his own passion to the relief and redemption of the world. In a small way, we might seek something similar. Here we are advancing into the farthest reaches of "dedicated suffering."

A gerontologist friend, Jane Thibault, relates a story told her by Carl Middletown, an ethicist and pastoral counselor working for the Sisters of Charity. He was summoned to the nursing-home room of a woman suffering from cancer. She had made everyone else suffer as well: she could be ill-tempered, downright nasty in fact, especially when she thought she hadn't received her pain medication on time. The staff had taken to avoiding her, which had done nothing to improve her disposition. Finally, Carl Middletown was summoned. He arrived somewhat at a loss for how to help, but then he hit on a novel idea. He knew of an unfortunate couple down the hall: the wife suffered from multiple sclerosis, the husband from Hodgkin's disease. Perhaps the woman he was visiting might help them with their plight. How? Middletown suggested she take the pain she experienced while waiting for her medication and offer it as prayer for the couple down the hall. She could dedicate her own suffering to their welfare.

At first, the woman responded skeptically. The idea sounded awfully Catholic, and she wasn't even of that religion. Reluctantly, she agreed to give it a try.

When Carl Middletown checked back in at the end of the day, he was surprised at what he found. The woman had cheered up a good deal—she was livelier and had needed less medication that day. It seemed that as she dedicated her pain to the others, the pain itself had diminished. So had her self-centeredness. When Carl

Middletown entered the room, the first thing she asked was: "How is that couple down the hall doing?"

Was the woman's pain really transformed into effective prayer? Did the other couple benefit from this spiritual intercession? Hard to say. Such are matters of personal belief. But it's clear that the woman herself benefited. In the words of Nietzsche, "If we possess our *why* of life we can put up with almost any *how*."[4] The woman had found a *why* for her suffering—it was no longer meaningless but could serve in the healing of others. With that why, the how became so much more bearable.

This notion of dedicating our suffering to others—as Jesus did, and the bodhisattvas—can prove to be an unlimited grace as we age. Above all else we may dread a loss of usefulness. What if we become immobilized, institutionalized, with nothing left to give? What meaning will our life have then? This practice provides an answer. With it, we can turn a sickbed into a monastic cell from which love-energy for the whole universe can emanate. Our disability need not stop us from giving. In fact, it can provide us with the compassion, the time, the mental focus, the sacrificial gift, to aid a suffering world.

And why wait until we're physically disabled? Life has already provided us with ample material. Like an alchemist, we can transform the leaden burden of pain into the precious gold of love.

Give a try to "dedicated suffering." Take one instance of suffering in your life—it might be a loss or injury from your past, or some pain you're feeling right now. Try imagining it as the sacrificial gift you have to offer up in prayer.

First, ask that it be used somehow to relieve the pain of others who have suffered similarly. (For example, if you've struggled through the death of a brother, ask that your pain be converted into love and aid for all others who have lost a sibling.) You may even image yourself holding a symbol of the pain in your hands (for example, a broken heart) and offering it up in prayer.

Now, expand your focus of compassion. Ask that this gift help relieve the sorrow of others who have felt related losses (for example, all those who have suffered through a loved one's death). And think if there are any other people you wish to include in your prayer. Dedicate your suffering to the benefit of them all.

When you are finished, spend a few minutes unwinding. This can be a moving and difficult exercise.

❋

Receiving as Giving

The sufferings of life can help us not only to give ourselves more deeply, but also to become better *receivers*. Another spiritual challenge: it's often harder to receive than to give. After all, the giver seems to be the one in the position of strength and virtue. It feels good to give, and we enjoy being praised for it. When receiving, on the other hand, we may feel demeaned by our "lesser" status, by being dependent, the one in need. We may also sense a pressure to reciprocate. We worry that receiving a gift places us under an obligation.

To some extent this discomfort with being the receiver may be shaped by gender training. As discussed, men, from the time they are little boys, are often taught to be strong and self-sufficient. Male movie heroes, be they cowboys, astronauts, or shoot-'em-up cops, are usually cut from this "rugged individualist" mold. In response to these lessons, males may come to feel that dependence on others is a sign of weakness and failure.

Women can find receiving difficult for different reasons. As discussed earlier, women are often taught to be caregivers for their children, husband, aging parents, clients, in fact, everyone around. While this role can involve a destructive self-denial, it also has its paybacks. Women gain the satisfaction of feeling needed and seeing positive effects of their actions in the world. It can prove uncomfortable to have the tables turned. When forced into the role of the receiver, some women may feel their self-worth plunge. Their identity invested in helping others, they are loath to become the ones needing help.

The truth is that aging may force us to become more financially, socially, and physically dependent on those around us, be they family members, friends, or government agencies. Many of us shudder at this prospect. Here, the story of Jesus again provides some help. At the Last Supper, Jesus is portrayed as washing his disciples' feet. Peter, one of those who fell asleep in Gethsemane, is shown here as reluctant to receive: "I will never let you wash my feet," he says. But his teacher is adamant: " 'If I do not wash you,' Jesus replied, 'you are not in fellowship with me' " (Jn 13: 8–9). Peter gives in to the call.

This passage is often interpreted as a lesson in giving. Indeed, Jesus says he's teaching his disciples to serve one another as he is doing. But we also see here a profound lesson in receiving. Until Peter agreed to have his feet washed, Jesus' act could not be fulfilled.

Receiving, no less than giving, is an expression of love. First, it is an act of love to the self. When we willingly receive, we proclaim ourselves worthy of being cared for. We accept the right to draw on the care and resources of the world. In my earlier example, if the ailing mother refused all visits from her daughter, it would be an act of self-abasement. That would be as mistaken as demanding a stream of constant visits. A happy solution lies in a harmonizing of needs that honors both participants. Isn't that what the spirit of love would will?

At the same time that receiving helps affirm our worth, it can polish down the self's rough edges. The mother's refusal of visits might be tinged with more than a bit of ego: "I'll never ask for help, not me!" Conversely, admitting her need may humble and soften her. She is no longer the superior matriarch.

Receiving can also be an act of love to others. How so? Ever try to give someone a present and have that person refuse? Maybe their

intentions are good—they don't want to be a bother, and they feel
we should keep our money, time, or efforts for ourselves. Nonetheless, we come away disappointed. We wanted to make a generous
gesture, but it can't be fulfilled without a receiver. We reached out
only to have our help rebuffed. On the other hand, the gracious receiver offers something valuable back. He or she says yes to the
other's caring and allows for intimate exchange.

We see such intimacy in a young woman's account of tending
to her sick father, sketched in the book *How Can I Help?* He suffers from debilitating cancer; at first visit, she barely recognizes
him. But she recalls Mother Teresa's description of the lepers she
worked with as "Christ in all his distressing disguises."

> I never had any real relation to Christ at all, and I can't say that
> I did at that moment. But what came through me was a feel-
> ing for my father's identity as . . . like a child of God. That was
> who he really was, behind the "distressing disguise." And it
> was my real identity too, I felt. I felt a great bond with him
> which wasn't anything like I'd felt as father and daughter. . . .
> For the remaining months of life we were totally at peace and
> comfortable together. No more self-consciousness. No unfin-
> ished business. I usually seemed to know just what was
> needed. I could feed him, shave him, bathe him, hold him up
> to fix the pillows—all these very intimate things that had been
> so hard for me earlier.
>
> In a way, this was my father's final gift to me: the chance to
> see him as something more than my father; the chance to see
> the common identity of spirit we both shared; the chance to
> see just how much that makes possible in the way of love and
> comfort. And I feel I can call on it now with anyone else.[5]

This phenomenon is not just a matter of parent-child relations.
We may experience this wonderful reciprocity with those friends
with whom we grow old. Carter Catlett Williams relates an experience of sharing with a friend of more than sixty years. This woman,
like the father described earlier, is suffering from cancer. Though

she has lost her appetite, she responds warmly when Williams suggests making her some custard.

> In that light I see that my friend and I were both givers and receivers—she the giver of a concrete thing that I in my great need could do for her, I the giver of the work of my hands—and surely of heart—in the time of her mortal sickness. I received in my giving; she gave in her receiving.[6]

And so the distinction between giver and receiver melts away. The two roles interpenetrate like yin and yang, each birthing the other, each opening to wholeness. Such is the circular nature of love.

❈   ❈   ❈

Ask yourself where in your life you have had to receive. You might think of at least one time in the past when you were plunged into the role of the receiver. Also think of some ways in the present that you receive and rely on other's gifts.

Ask yourself how you feel about these situations. Do they bring up any uncomfortable feelings: shame, guilt, a sense of obligation, perhaps? Or are you able to accept being in the position of the receiver? Can you see how it creates a sense of connection with others? Can you see how you become more whole yourself? Take a minute to honor not only those who give to you, but **your willingness to receive.**

And ask yourself, are there ways you can open yourself to receiving more—at home, at work, wherever?

❈

GOD'S WITH-US-NESS

What if there's no one close to us, with whom to enact this exchange? Studies have shown that feeling part of a social network is a crucial factor in whether we age well; but not everyone is so fortunate as to be surrounded by loved ones. We may be in need of help but have few present to aid us. Perhaps we're unmarried or widowed. Maybe our relatives and friends are scattered in distant places or have died. We long for the comfort of human love, but we find ourselves facing trials alone.

Here, again, the example of Jesus has something to teach us. He was in much the same position when he was hung on the cross. His disciples had fled, and passers-by hurled abuse. He had to face extreme physical and emotional pain without the comfort of friends.

However, he was not ultimately alone. In Matthew's account, his last words are directed to God. Admittedly, they are a cry of anguish: "My God, my God, why hast thou forsaken me?" Yet his words also express something opposite. Jesus, after all, does not call out to an empty universe. He speaks to God, and not just any God—"*my* God." Even in the midst of absence—paradoxically, *through* absence—Jesus remains aware of the Father's presence.

As we age, we, too, may face certain crosses. We, too, may be left without human aid. Perhaps our body aches, and there's no one to comfort us. Or we awaken in the dark to a fear of poverty, illness, or even death, and we lie alone through the interminable night. Like Jesus, we can let this loneliness guide us to cry out to Spirit. We need a source of solace and meaning beyond the self, beyond even the human realm. When we discover this need, we realize that no person could have filled it to begin with. We've got to find God— *my God*. Sometimes the seeds of consolation germinate best in the dark soil of desolation.

This truth is implicit in Jesus' last lament. His words are a quote from Psalm 22, a source that would have been well known to him, as well as to the gospel writers and readers. This psalm begins:

> *My God, my God, why have you forsaken me, far from my*
> *prayer, from the words of my cry?*
> *O my God, I cry out by day, and you answer not; by night,*
> *and there is no relief for me.*

Yet the Psalmist goes on to speak of God's loving response:

> *For he has not spurned nor disdained the wretched man in*
> *his misery,*
> *Nor did he turn his face away from him, but when he cried*
> *out to him, he heard him. . . .*
> *The lowly shall eat their fill; they who seek the Lord shall*
> *praise him: "May your hearts be ever merry!"*

By the end, Psalm 22 has turned into a celebration of God's saving grace.

In fact, this grace comes to be interpreted by Jesus' followers as the whole message of his life and death. His name, Yeshua, comes from the Hebrew words for "God saves." He was also called Emmanuel, "God is with us." The theology of Jesus as God incarnate is a way of proclaiming God's "with-us-ness." Depending on our personal beliefs, we may agree or disagree with this theology, take it literally or as metaphor. But a central meaning is clear and is expressed by other religions as well. God is not some distant being up in the sky. S/he is right here with us, among us, inside us. God does not regard human suffering from a lofty distance, like the Greek deities of Mount Olympus. When we suffer, *God suffers with us.* S/he knows what it's like from the inside. Jesus' passion speaks forth God's compassion.

When we suffer with age, can we imagine God suffering with us? I gave the example of a mother with hemorrhoids, arthritis, and a weak heart. It may seem downright blasphemous to image a hemorrhoidal God. But why not? We're conceiving of a Friend who knows just how we feel, somehow from within . . . who has limitless compassion for our struggles . . . who will gladly provide us with the saving strength that we need. This presence doesn't mean that all our pain will be removed. There's no promise of that in the gospel story. After all, without pain there's less growth. But we are promised the power, solace, and the meaning to better accept our cross.

Thus, as we age, the challenge is not just to receive from other people but also from the divine. And to do so, yet another step is needed: we must be willing to receive from *ourselves*. If we are self-hating, we will have trouble feeling God's love.

I can speak to this issue from personal experience. For years I had a harsh view of myself and conceived of a judgmental God. Not surprisingly, I found little solace. I was used to associating spirituality with a ruthless inventory of my sins. But with time, therapy, and Twelve Step work, my attitude toward myself softened. I began to open to the possibility that I wasn't such a bad guy after all; that just perhaps when I found myself in pain, I was deserving of help and not censure.

This shift of attitude helped me open to a new range of God messages. When I was suffering, I'd pray for assistance, half expecting to hear God's rebuke and demands. Instead an inner voice would say, "Take a hot bath." That's all. But I'd feel a sense of loving presence with me. I'd sink into the soothing waters, fragrant with scented bubbles, and soon I'd feel a whole lot better—refreshed, calmed, *taken care of*. God was showing me how to be with myself in the fashion s/he wished.

This lesson is also captured for me by another prayer message I now frequently receive. I reach out to God in a period of exhaustion or pain, and a snatch of an old song floats into my head. Through its lyrics, I'm admonished to button up my coat, take good care of myself, because I belong to God. As the chill winds of age blow, we will need to take good care of ourselves, and remember that to do so is carrying out God's loving will.

Strangely enough, it may not always be our own will. A sense may linger that we deserve suffering, and subconsciously we may will its continuance. What better time to say to God, "Not as I will, but as thou wilt"? Sometimes taking a hot bath, a rest, a nice meal, can be an act of spiritual obedience.

Why do we so often feel that our suffering is deserved? This psychological/theological move is common. Many of us believe in a covenantal relationship between Spirit and humans. In a crude form, it looks like this: if we do God's will, nothing bad will happen to us. We set out to be good boys and girls, expecting to win our reward. But it might not come. Bad stuff happens anyway. Perhaps our health takes a turn for the worse, or one of our children unexpectedly dies. We struggle to make sense of this reversal, and our universe threatens to collapse. One way to preserve meaning is to think we've done something wrong. Consciously or subconsciously, we seek out our defects. I wasn't kind enough to my child, and I never went to church—no wonder she was taken from me. I did smoke for a time, I have a type-A personality—of course I've fallen sick. Punishment for my sins. That, in fact, is what Job's friends tell him as he tries to fathom his sufferings. *Sucker, it's your own damn fault.* Alternatively, we may blame God for our suffering. Believing we haven't done anything wrong, or that our "punishment" is disproportionate, we grow angry at an arbitrary diety. This was Job's own reaction; it's not me, but God, who's acting unjustly.

In such ways, suffering often *seems* to signal a break in the divine-human covenant. Someone's at fault, whether it's our unworthy selves or God, that Cosmic Creep. Either way, this notion can make it harder to reach out to Spirit just at the times we most need to.

In the story of Job, neither interpretation proves valid. Though Job suffers, he has not abandoned God, nor God him. The tale ends with reconciliation. So, too, with the passion of Jesus. His misery does not signal that he has forsaken God, nor that God has truly forsaken him. The covenant is still operative even in the midst of suffering. In fact, suffering deepens the covenant, taking it to a new level of meaning. Jesus is called to greater gifts of sacrifice and acceptance, and he comes to a deeper relationship with God, who stands by with resurrecting power.

It is well to remember this truth if we suffer with the passage of years. We may have done things that undermined our health, relationships, or financial status, but that doesn't mean our pain is God's punishment. We may be in a position of frailty and dependence, but that doesn't mean we're abandoned or worth less in God's eyes. On the contrary, our anguish, like Jesus', may be a further stage of our journey home. As a child runs to the mother when in pain, so we best run to Spirit when we need to. As suffering can be a fire that burns away the inessential, so may we be purified by our trials. We need not view illness, aging, even death, as our life's failed end. In the gospel tale, crucifixion is followed by a rebirth into the loving arms of God.

This lesson is hard to hold onto in hard times. We may need strengthening, as Jesus did in Gethsemane. The Christian paleontologist and theologian, Teilhard de Chardin, leaves us with such a prayer:

> When the signs of age begin to mark my body (and still more when they touch my mind); when the ill that is to diminish me or carry me off strikes from without or is born within me; when the painful moment comes in which I suddenly awaken to the fact that I am ill or growing old; and above all at that last moment when I feel I am losing hold of myself and am absolutely passive within the hands of the great unknown forces that have formed me; in all those dark moments, O God, grant that I may understand that it is you (provided only my faith is strong enough) who are painfully parting the fibres of my being in order to penetrate to the very marrow of my substance and bear me away within yourself.[7]

✳   ✳   ✳

In order to experience the "with-us-ness" of God, we must learn to be with ourselves. Think back to certain times when you experienced hurt, bodily or emotional. Remember at least one time when you were physically sick or injured. Remember at least one time when you felt failure, rejection, disappointment, or shame.

Now ask whether you were able to be with yourself lovingly at such times. Did you give yourself support and consolation? If so, what forms did they take? (For example, did you take good care of yourself physically? Did you seek the help you needed from others? Did you choose positive, self-affirming thoughts?) Or, on the other hand, did you abandon yourself when in pain? If so, what forms did that take? (Thoughts like "It's your own damn fault"? Actions like not getting enough rest or eating poorly?)

Perhaps it's a mixed picture. Sometimes you were "with yourself" and other times not. If so, you might ask why. Are there, for example, particular forms of suffering that trigger your self-hate? (For example, having someone leave you; making a mistake; et cetera.) If so, you face a challenge. Are you willing to be with yourself even at such times?

✳

Guided Meditation

THE EXCHANGE OF GIFTS

Imagine that you are in a circle of elders. Around you stand older men and women, their beauty sculpted by time. See their flowing gray hair, their warm, wrinkled faces. You, too, stand with them. In the middle of your circle is a cluster of jewelled boxes.

Imagine that one person now walks to the center of the circle. In his hands he holds a box. Suddenly you realize his eyes are vacant. He is blind.

"What is in your box?" someone from the circle calls out. "What is your gift to us?" The man replies, "In the box is a symbol of my blindness. My blindness is my gift. In my old age I have lost my sight. But through this blindness I have been able to see more deeply into others. When I hear your voice I am not distracted by surface appearance. I see your soul in all its beauty. I also sense your pain and fear. And my blindness helps me to understand that as well." Slowly the blind man places his box in the center.

Then another standing in the circle calls out: "This is your gift to all of us. Now tell us, what do you need to receive?" The blind man replies, "I have need of a trusted companion in life. Someone sighted who can help me across a busy street. Someone to describe the sunset that I'll never see." Then you hear a voice respond, "This shall be supplied." An elder steps forward to hand the blind man a box that another person had left in the center. Inside is a symbol of a trusted companion—just what the blind man needs. With gladness he returns to the outer circle.

Now, one by one, you see others step forth. Each person comes bearing a box. Inside is a symbol of some suffering they have undergone—a broken heart, a disability, a painful loss. But each person describes why this suffering is their gift; how it has deepened their ability to help others. And each person describes also what they need back. Always, the voice responds, "This shall be supplied." Each person is handed the gift left by another in this mystical exchange.

Finally, it is your turn. Imagine yourself stepping to the center of the circle. You are surrounded by the wise and compassionate elders. You hear the question, "What is in your box?" Pause here, and let yourself know. What is the suffering that is your gift to others? Think about the many ways this source of pain has enabled you to give. How has it made you more understanding, compassionate, open, or skillful? Think of the many people your suffering has enabled you to help. Friends, family members, clients? Hear yourself speak of all this to the elders. Your words may be halting. That's O.K. Stay with it. When you are ready, place your box in the center.

Then open yourself to the next question: "And what is it you need to receive?" Your suffering has also left you broken. What is it that you need to make you whole—from other people, from yourself, from Spirit? Let your answer well up from your heart. Speak of it to the elders. Take your time. Don't be afraid to ask for all you need.

When you are ready, hear the response, "It shall be supplied." Imagine an elder stepping forward to hand you a box containing all that you need. Think on ways this support has already come true in your life. What are some gifts you've received from others—love, companionship, assistance—that have helped you in your suffering? When has God or Spirit been present to see you through? Also know that much in your box has yet to be revealed. But as you age, you will be taken care of. What you need shall be supplied.

When you are ready, you can emerge from this visualization. But know that you can return to it in the future. When you have suffering, you can imagine placing it in a box as a gift to others. And you can remember that other box that has within it all that you need. Don't be afraid to open it.

※   ※   ※

11

Rebirthing the Self:
Sarah's Laugh

And God said to Abraham, "As for your wife Sarai, you shall not call her Sarai, but her name shall be Sarah. I will bless her; indeed, I will give you a son by her. I will bless her so that she shall give rise to nations; rulers of peoples shall issue from her." Abraham threw himself on his face and laughed, as he said to himself, "Can a child be born to a man a hundred years old, or can Sarah bear a child at ninety?" . . .

The LORD appeared to [Abraham] by the tenebriths of Mamre; he was sitting at the entrance of the tent as the day grew hot. Looking up, he saw three men standing near him. . . . Then one said, "I will return to you when life is due, and your wife Sarah shall have a son!" Sarah was listening at the entrance of the tent, which was behind him. Now Abraham and Sarah were old, advanced in years; Sarah had stopped having the periods of women. And Sarah laughed to herself, saying, "Now that I am withered, am I to have enjoyment—with my husband so old?" Then the LORD said to Abraham, "Why did Sarah laugh, saying, 'Shall I in truth bear a child, old as I am?' Is anything too wondrous for the LORD? I will return to you at the time that life is due, and Sarah shall have a son." Sarah lied saying, "I did not laugh," for she was frightened. But He replied, "You did laugh." . . .

The LORD took note of Sarah as He had promised, and the LORD did for Sarah as He had spoken. Sarah conceived and bore a son to Abraham in his old age, at the set time of which God had spoken. Abraham gave his new-born son, whom Sarah had borne him, the name of Isaac. And when his son Isaac was eight days old, Abraham circumcised him, as God had commanded him. Now Abraham was a hundred years old when his son Isaac was born to him. Sarah said, "God has brought me laughter; everyone who hears will laugh with me."

The Torah: A Modern Commentary:
Genesis 17, 18, 21, ed. W. Gunther Plaut

AT FIRST WE might dismiss the story of Sarah's late-life pregnancy as a miracle tale—delightful, but hard to grant much credence. What can it teach us modern-day skeptics? Barring technological breakthroughs, we won't have a child at ninety like Sarah. Nor would we want to—it's tiring just to think about. (I'm exhausted enough as a new father at forty-one.)

However, when we probe more deeply into the story, it yields hidden treasure. We learned from the story of Krisha Gautami about facing up to death. Jesus' passion spoke to us of the sufferings of age. But we should not think that life's second half is simply a time of doom and gloom. God also shines forth through bright gifts. The name Isaac is supposedly derived from the Hebrew word *yitzchak,* "to laugh." He's a symbol of the laughter, joy, and generativity possible in later life. We can give birth, if not to a baby, then to a renewed self.

Our guide here, the story of Abraham and Sarah, is central within Judaism. Samson Raphael Hirsch writes:

The entire beginning of the Jewish people is laughable, its history, its expectations, its hopes. God waited with the foundation of this people until its forefather had reached a "ridiculous" high age; therefore He began the realization of His promise only after all human hopes had come to an end.[1]

So it may be for us. In life's second half we increasingly confront limits. Energy flags. Certain hopes and dreams of youth have been dashed. It may seem unthinkable that we're to start anew. But let's think again, this story suggests. If we stand at the entrance to our tent, welcome divine visitors, and respond to their messages—who knows what adventures await us?

CARING FOR THE BODY

The story of Sarah is a spiritual tale through and through. But it also concerns the body. An older womb is rejuvenated. A postmenopausal woman is enabled to have a child. This intertwining of spirit and body is deeply rooted in the Jewish tradition. Consider the Bible's first sentence: "In the beginning God created the heavens and earth." That is, the material world is fashioned from the spiritual. "And God saw that it was good." This goodness of creation, and of the human body, reflects the goodness of their Maker.

Many religions share this rich sense of the spirituality that permeates the physical world. However, we also find a school of thought that strongly contrasts spirit and flesh. The body is associated with temptations to sin—through lust, gluttony, greed—which must be subdued by the will. Then there's also the view, as in Hinduism, that the body is not sinful per se, but external to the true Self. As the soul progresses through its many incarnations it takes on and discards bodies like suit jackets. The more we think we *are* our body, the more we become trapped in suffering and illusion.

Such is not the view in Judaism. When God created humans, the breath of life gave rise to a unitary thing, *body-soul*, spirit incarnate. In fact, one Hebrew word for "soul," *ruah,* comes from the word for "breath." The soul is the body's breath of life. The body, and its actions, are the soul's expression in this world. Our goal, then, is to sanctify the physical. We do so when we offer shelter to a homeless person; stand and *davin* in prayer; partake of a joyful Sabbath feast; link arms together and dance. With God, we proclaim the goodness of creation and the body.

To do this can be hard as we age. In some ways we may feel increasingly distant from, even hostile toward, our body as youthful beauty fades and aches and pains set in. But never have we lived longer; we're part of a generation of Sarahs and Abrahams. So never has the care of the body been more important. In 1992, those who were sixty-five enjoyed an average life expectancy of another seventeen-and-a-half years. What if you knew you'd have to drive your present car for the next seventeen years? You'd probably take better care of it; change the oil more often, jump on needed repairs, maybe even use higher-octane fuel. How many of us give such attention to the body, which has to last us a lifetime?

The car metaphor can help provoke us to better habits, but imaging the body as a machine, external to the self, is not finally true to Judaism. In rejuvenating Sarah's body, God is not simply acting as an auto mechanic. He is also rejuvenating her spirit, her relation with the divine. Introspection reveals that for us, too, our body and soul are interwoven. If our muscles are tense and rigid, so will be our mind-set; if we are always physically tired, we'll be of less service to others; if we die prematurely of a heart attack, we'll miss out on the rich soul curriculum of later life.

Therefore, part of a holistic spirituality involves taking good care of our bodies—not in the spirit of tuning up a machine, but of hallowing creation. In seeking a rejuvenated Sarah-body, we can't rely on divine intervention. (Too bad!) Sensing that such care is God's will for us, we must take responsibility for making it happen. Just what do we do to enhance health and longevity?

There are many fine books on the subject; I'll summarize a few key findings.

First, stay away from the bad stuff: smoking, overuse of alcohol or drugs, a high-fat diet, consequent obesity, and the like. When young we might have gotten away with it, but as the years pass we pay a price in increased disease and disability, and diminished life expectancy. We may also truncate our soul's growth. Through intoxicants we are seeking to release our burdens; with food, to fill an inner void. These become ersatz substitutes for the real thing—the release and fulfillment given by Spirit.

Besides the "thou shalt nots," what of the "thou shalts"? A key one is regular exercise. A genuine Sarah-elixir, it has been shown to reverse ten of the most typical effects of aging, such as high blood pressure, excess body fat, and decreased muscle mass.[2] Of course, different sorts of exercise have different benefits. Movement and stretching that promote flexibility can help loosen up the stiffness that comes with age. Working out with weights can restore strength and function. In one study, frail nursing home residents in their late eighties or nineties worked out on exercise machines three times a week. After only a few weeks they could get around quicker, climb stairs better, sometimes even throw away their walkers.

It is not necessary to go on rigorous programs to experience significant benefits. In a massive study of some thirteen thousand people, those who walked at least thirty minutes a day cut their mortality rates in half compared to sedentary people. This rate was almost as low as those who ran thirty to forty miles a week.[3] There's hope for us slowpokes.

Along with exercise, other practices can keep us fit and healthy. They're the sort of things your mother may have told you when you were little, but who listens? Get good, regular sleep. Eat a healthy diet, avoiding lots of fat but including plenty of fiber. Above all, be sure to enjoy yourself. Studies have suggested that life satisfaction is good for your health, just as good health can help make you satisfied.

What are some key components of this life satisfaction, which predicts increased longevity? Having a happy marriage or long-term relationship; liking one's job (job satisfaction markedly decreases the risk of a heart attack); experiencing a sense of personal happiness; having regular daily and work routines, a factor shown as important in many longevity studies.[4] Over two hundred fifty studies have suggested also that the greater one's degree of religious involvement (however the researcher defined that), the better one's health. Clearly, spiritual rejuvenation didn't end back in Sarah's time.

It helps, too, to keep a youthful frame of mind. In one 1979 experiment Dr. Ellen Langer and her Harvard colleagues isolated subjects aged seventy-five or older at a week-long retreat, during which the "clock was turned back." Asked to pretend that it was twenty years previous, they spoke of their careers as in full swing and debated Eisenhower-era politics. The environment was controlled: all the music they listened to, photos they saw, and magazines they read were drawn from the earlier era. The result of this "time-machine" week? The participants were physically rejuvenated. They enjoyed measurable improvements in joint flexibility, muscle strength, posture, hearing, and vision.[5] How much our body's aging depends on our mind!

A caveat is in order. Rarely a month passes without a new book coming out that suggests we can defeat the aging process through some product, exercise, or mental technique. Much of this material merely expresses the feverish fantasies of an age-and-death-phobic culture. The stories of Krisha Gautami and Jesus have reminded us that life's darkness is unavoidable. We will grow old despite all our efforts, and we will die. This doesn't mean we have failed.

Nor does it mean we shouldn't do what we can to sustain a long and healthy life. While Sarah accepts the aging process with grace, she does not scorn God's rejuvenation. Bearing Isaac brings her joy to fulfillment and allows her to share it with others. We can safeguard our own health in this spirit. In the words of Dr. Dean Ornish, a leader in reversing heart disease through diet, "Changes need to be based not on fear of dying but on joy of living."[6] Let's do a motive check as we seek to take care of our bodies. Are we fighting a battle against the dreaded enemies of age and death? If so, sooner or later, we will lose. Or are we joyfully affirming life? If so, we are in partnership with God.

✳   ✳   ✳

Your body needs to last a lifetime. Imagine you are coming up with a life plan for how to keep it fit and healthy. Know that your plan will be individual—it might incorporate the sorts of exercise you enjoy, healthy foods you like to eat, things that lower your stress level and raise your joy, et cetera. Sketch out your plan here. Are there parts you've already put into effect? Other parts you could do more with?

✳

CELEBRATING SEX

Sarah's story does not just address the body in general but speaks, in particular, to the body's sexual powers. When told she'll have a son, she laughs cynically. "Now that I am withered, am I to have enjoyment—with my husband so old?" (When God repeats her response to Abraham, He reports her saying instead, "old as *I* am." One Talmudic interpretation: God was trying to spare Abraham's feelings and preserve domestic peace!)

God's answer to Sarah's question is clearly yes—she *is* to have sexual enjoyment. We may be surprised to hear the Supreme One address the issue. We're used to religion's distrust of sex. This urgent drive can be so intense we'll do anything to secure its fulfillment: abandon commitments, use and abuse others, forget about God entirely. Yet sexuality, Sarah's story reminds us, can also be a way we speak *with God*. By celebrating the body, we testify to the goodness of Creation. Through sex we can even act as cocreators: our body imagines and creates intimate gestures. And sex is one way we have of expressing love and connection. Isn't that what spirituality is about? So let's not be too quick to divorce flesh and spirit. The Hebrew God didn't.

As we age, we may share Sarah's skepticism. As we and our partners grow older, are we really to enjoy sex? Will we feel attractive, and be attracted to the other? Will we be able to perform sexually as we once did? Will sexuality really bring fulfillment, or just create a mess? Our culture does little to reassure us. The media portrays sexuality as the province of the young. Hard, lithe bodies, in their teens or twenties, are the ideal. Passionate older people are satirized as dirty old men or horny grannies to be laughed at and fled. All that reminds us of Sarah's first derisive laugh.

There are also physiological concerns. As someone who has "stopped having the periods of women," Sarah might be more susceptible to certain physical problems around sex. For post-menopausal women, dryness and thinning of the vaginal walls may cause discomfort with intercourse. The urethra and bladder are less protected, which can result in pain and inflammation. Meanwhile, Abraham may be experiencing his own bodily shifts. Older men usually need more stimulation before becoming erect, and this erection may not be as large or firm as earlier. With age, a combination of physical and psychological factors can lead to occasional impotence.

So Sarah's laugh may also be a nervous one, as if to say, "Is this really a good idea?" Again, God answers yes. And this is true for us. The physical problems of later-life sex are eminently treatable.[7] For example, vaginal dryness can be alleviated with a lubricant or the use of an estrogen cream. The natural changes in male physiology need not lead to dysfunction when they are understood and accepted. Beyond that, these bodily changes can actually bring liberation. As discussed earlier, menopause frees many women up from pregnancy concerns. The result can be a newly relaxed enjoyment of sex for its own sake. Men may be less able to "perform" at the snap of a finger, but that can also push them beyond the performance ethic. So many men learn when young to use sex as a tool to prove virility and power. Mature sex can be about something different: closeness, vulnerability, caring.

Noted gerontologist Robert Butler and his coauthor, psychotherapist Myrna Lewis, term this kind of connecting the second language of sex. For young people, sex tends to be urgent and explosive. It often focuses on physical pleasure, and sometimes the conception of children. Such expressions are the first language of sex. The second language develops more slowly throughout life, as sexuality becomes a means of experiencing and communicating emotion. It forms a sensitive language for expressing tenderness, humor, and passion, even sadness and longing. A kiss becomes a question. A caress smooths away a fear. A hand tousling the hair becomes a playful affirmation. A hug provides a shelter where two can dwell in peace. Butler and Lewis write:

> In its richest form, the second language becomes highly creative and imaginative, with bountiful possibilities for new emotional experiences. Yet it is a slow-developing art, acquired deliberately and painstakingly through years of experience in giving and receiving.[8]

In our maturity we may be masters of a body language that when we were younger we barely spoke. Sarah, skeptical as she is, may find that her later-life sex is *more* enjoyable than ever.

Another caveat is called for here. Just as we need to be wary of all the new programs to "defeat aging," so too of programs that pressure us to have sex. Couples doing-it-like-rabbits-well-into-their-nineties are held up as exemplary models. But what if no partner's available in a period of our life? Given demographics, older women especially face this problem. And what if we just don't feel like it anymore? What if we're just not that interested in sex? That's

O.K., too, and can be its own form of liberation. Gloria Steinem writes of being postmenopausal:

> When I was younger, there was a part of my brain back here that was always thinking about sex. . . . It's not there anymore! It's funny—it's like you have an entire part of your brain that's free for other things. . . . All I can tell you is: it's wonderful.[9]

One goal of religious celibacy (as in Hinduism or Christianity) is to experience this kind of freedom. Energies once bound up in sex can be turned to active service or contemplative prayer. God is there, too. Just as we can use sex as a vehicle of Spirit, so too can we use any diminishment of the sex drive.

In your current life, do you speak more the "first" or "second language" of sex? This question is not about judging yourself—just recognizing your mode of sexual expression. Have you seen the meaning of sex change for you over your life course? How so? What further changes might you like to see in life's second half?

ISAAC STORIES

The story of Sarah and Abraham is finally about not just later-life sex but its miraculous outcome: the conception of a child. Here we must part with a literal interpretation of the story. We're not expecting to be expecting at ninety. But the story also speaks to a deeper truth. No matter what our age, and stage of life, we can give birth to "Isaacs." That is, we can develop new talents, relationships, and forms of contribution. Ultimately we can give birth to a new self.

Such rebirths are far from unusual in life's second half, Gail Sheehy found; they are a recurring pattern. As we've spoken of a first and second language of sex, so Sheehy writes of a first and second adulthood. During first adulthood, lasting roughly from age thirty to forty-five, we are preoccupied with pleasing others and establishing ourselves in the world. Around forty-five we begin to confront the limits of this project. Sometimes what Sheehy calls a "mortality crisis" is the prompt.[10] An illness, or the loss of a loved one, brings us face to face with death. Or perhaps there's a disruption in our smooth life plan. A divorce, a job loss, a rebellious child, turns our existence upside down. And the biology of aging may force itself on our awareness. Sheehy found that menopause, for many women, represented the experienced break with first adulthood.[11] Don't we sometimes call it "the change of life"?

Much depends on how we handle the transition out of first adulthood. We can cling blindly to our ever-receding youth. We can stumble into later life unprepared. But this transition also offers us "an opportunity to *reinvent ourselves.*"[12]

Incorporated within what Sheehy calls the second adulthood, lasting from age forty-five through the rest of our life, are many hazards, but also an abundance of opportunities. We can develop parts of our character that were dormant earlier. We can embark on new career paths and build more satisfying relationships. We can clarify what it is we find most fulfilling and jettison the junk. In this process, we rebirth the self.

In the Hindu ideal, we eradicate the self; through renouncing our former identity we seek to strip away that which separates us from Brahman. The Jewish ideal affirms our unique personhood. Through this we both reflect, and connect with, God. As we age, we need not cast off our identity; instead, we are called to renew it.

This readiness to ever begin anew is a mark of life in the spirit. Christian mystic Meister Eckhart stated (as translated and adapted by Matthew Fox):

My soul is as young as the day it was created.
Yes, and much younger!
In fact, I am younger today than I was yesterday, and if I am
*   not younger tomorrow than I am today,*
I would be ashamed of myself.
People who dwell in God dwell in the eternal now.
There, people can never grow old.[13]

These words surely describe Sarah and Abraham. Advanced in years, they were residing contentedly in Haran surrounded by family and flock. Suddenly God spoke, saying, "Go forth from your native land and from your father's house to the land that I will show you" (Gn 12:1). A tall order when you're getting on in years! But they obeyed the summons, even in *later* life, to embrace a *new* life, which was their *true* life.

For it was through this calling that they came to fulfillment. Abram (as he was then named) accepted a covenant that altered the destiny of a people. God was said to have granted him and his progeny the Promised Land forever. In turn, the male offspring were to be circumcised, a fleshly register of a spiritual bond. Isaac was the first of these children, progenitor of the Hebrew race.

As important as these outer effects were, they went hand in hand with an inner renewal. Abram and Sarai acted in trust, so their relationship with God deepened and changed. They were born into a new spiritual identity, signalled by a change of name. Abram was henceforth to be known as Abraham, and Sarai as Sarah.

Not to say that these new selves bear no relation to the old. The shift from Abram to Abraham, Sarai to Sarah, is a subtle one. Much remains amid the changes. Much of us will remain, too, as our identity shifts. If we always loathed sports, we won't suddenly, at fifty, become a rabid fan. If we're an accountant through and through, we probably won't transform into a later-life Byron or Keats. On the contrary, we may just become more of who we are—

who we *really* are. That true self, all too often, has been kept fetal by fear, convention, and pragmatic concerns.

In our second adulthood we can bring that self to fuller gestation. We can deliver a newborn Isaac. Here are a few fictionalized examples of this process, representative of the hundreds of stories told in such books as Sheehy's *New Passages*, Betty Friedan's *The Fountain of Age*, and Connie Goldman and Richard Mahler's *Secrets of Becoming a Late Bloomer* (see appendix A). You may have a few tales of your own to add, drawn from your own life or the lives of people you have known.

Robert M. has spent his life as a corporate lawyer. He's found his work mentally stimulating and financially quite lucrative. But socially redeeming? There, he's not so sure. Now that he's getting off the fast track, he'd like to use his skills for something he can feel proud of. After much consideration, he chooses environmental policy as "his issue," and works pro bono for a community organization fighting to preserve local wetlands.

Rhonda P. and Jeanne T. are the best of friends. In some ways, their lives are pretty well set: they've each got families, steady jobs, and other commitments that tie them down. Yet they share an urge to do something wild—not Thelma-and-Louise-style, exactly—something more like an inner journey. Rhonda, having read a book on the subject, suggests they study Tibetan Buddhist meditation together at a local spiritual center. Visualizing mandalas each morning, chanting together twice a week—their husbands think they're nuts. So what?

Samuel M. is stopped short by a heart attack at age fifty-seven. His doctor delivers the dire news: better make some changes, or else. Backed against the wall, Sam decides to make a virtue of necessity. He's thought about becoming a vegetarian for moral and health reasons, but he never could summon up the willpower. Now's the time. Soon, he finds he's lost all interest in meat, and he enjoys impressing his friends with creative dishes. Under his doctor's direction, he also takes up jogging. Nothing like hitting the open road at daybreak, with not a car around to break his reverie or mar the beauty of the sunrise.

Laura B., on retiring from her management position, decides to start an independent consulting firm. She's sick to death of having a boss, of her talents being underutilized, of being tied to a desk fifty hours a week. It's time to go for the flexibility and balance she truly wants in her life. Can she make it on her own? Only one way to find out.

Gary A., a semiretired plumber, throws himself into grandfathering two rambunctious kids. His own children grew up so fast while he was busy paying off the bills; it seems like he turned around and then they were gone. Now he has a second chance, and without some of the hassles and aggravation of parenthood. Not all, though. He's so good at it that his daughter starts dropping off the kids (aged two and four) three mornings a week. Minding them makes draining a clogged pipe look easy.

Now retired, Shirley H. feels called to offer her later years in service to needy kids. She remembers being one herself. Soon she finds herself organizing a toys-for-tots drive. Under her direction, literally thousands of presents are donated and distributed. The way she feels at the end seems like the biggest present of all.

Harry R. is faced with a reduced income in his later years. No way around it. When he's rummaging in a bookstore, a volume on "voluntary simplicity" catches his eye. Well, it sounds a lot better than "poverty." The recommendations are things he'd have to consider anyway: moving to a smaller house, clearing out a lot of possessions, cutting down on new purchases, cancelling cable TV and call-waiting. Even as his life "shrinks" in these ways, he experiences it growing more spacious. There's more inner and outer peace.

Sarah L., after the death of her husband, finds herself lonely in the big, old house they always shared. She can sit in the dim light and grow depressed, or she can do something radical. When an opportunity arises, she grabs it. She decides to move into an intergenerational house with two friends, along with an elderly pensioner they can help care for, and a young nephew working his way through college. She feels like she's back at college herself— uneasy and excited about new housemates. Will I like them? Will they like me? Can I make the adjustments? She'll give it the old college try.

Keith H. grew up a secular Jew—a lot of bagels but no Torah. Now in his later years, he feels drawn back to the roots of his tradition. It's never too late to learn. So what if he's the only fifty-eight-year-old studying Hebrew in the Bar Mitzvah class? Want to make something of it?

Though diverse, these stories share a common thread. Each individual faces the challenges of second adulthood. There is a confrontation with limits, and often with loss. This encounter, instead of leading down a path toward death, triggers a process of rebirth. A new experiment or lifestyle or relationship is born—ultimately a new self. From Abram we become Abraham, from Sarai we become Sarah.

Of course, it doesn't hurt to be realistic about our limits. We may not have the financial resources to explore certain possibilities and projects. Nor do we have limitless psychological resources— such as courage, energy, and imagination. For the most part, we're ordinary folks.

Here, again, Sarah's story gives us solace. She, like other figures in the Bible, is hardly a classical hero. She turned on Hagar, her Egyptian slave, treating her quite harshly. Moses spoke with an impediment. Jacob tricked his father to get the blessing meant for Esau. These are not models of virtue, wealth, and beauty, but flawed people like ourselves. How, then, did they accomplish great things? Not through their own power, but through that of God; God led them beyond themselves.

So much depends on how we seek renewal. We can try to be the self-sufficient hero, refashioning our lives, but this approach does not give rise to an *Isaac* story where God carries us joyfully past our limits.

Here, inspiration and guidance may come from within. We listen for what makes us most enthusiastic (from the Greek *theos*, "god"). Or guidance may come in a more outward garb. Perhaps a cluster of "coincidental" meetings, opportunities, or conversations all seem to speak of a new direction. They are like the divine messengers who arrive at Abraham's tent.

Dare we offer them a hearty welcome? If so, they may speak of our Isaacs. For me, trained in medicine and philosophy, this book is one example. The theme of spiritual passages seemed far from my professional work. Over dinner with colleagues from a medical ethics research center, an idea popped into my head. Why not, using the Hindu life-stage model, open up spiritual centers for older adults? I was intrigued by the idea, but like Sarah I laughed it away. Aging and spirituality? That just isn't my field. The thought kept returning, though, as much as I tried to abandon it. Then a coincidence happened—that self-same research center started up a new fellowship on "the meaning of aging." Why not apply? To my surprise, I was selected. That fellowship, in turn, led to a series of meetings that fired my enthusiasm, firmed up the ideas in this book, and introduced me to the people who encouraged me to write it. So much fell into place so easily. It almost makes me laugh.

There's someone else who makes me laugh each day—that little girl of mine. For years my wife and I, getting on in years, were unable to conceive. It was a dark time. Prayers seemed to float away unanswered as month after month brought hope, then bitter disappointment. Finally we had to let go of that dream to embrace a new one. We went halfway around the world to China and were given a child meant just for us. The way her face lights up like neon in a nose-crinkling smile; the delight she takes in draping noodles on her head; the evenings she grows tired and cuddles close, climbing up into our arms— what a joy she has been, rejuvenating our days even while exhausting our aging bodies! On adoption, what name did we give her? That was easy: Sarah. (Who ever heard of a little girl named Isaac?)

Of course, my dark passages haven't always led straight to happy endings, nor will yours. In seeking to follow "God's leadings," I've sometimes experienced confusion, struggles with others, and unexpected setbacks, and so might you. You might start a new business with great gusto only to see it fall on its face. You may summon up the courage for a long-desired trip and then have to cancel it due to illness. You may set out to be more genuinely loving and end up crankier than ever.

Abortions? Stillbirths? Not necessarily. With persistence you may still arrive at what you seek. If not, maybe your very struggles and disappointments are the labor pains of a new self. Here, Jesus' sufferings again provide a teaching. It might have seemed to him and his followers that his mission had proved a failure. Frustration, dismay, abandonment. Yet all of it became part of an Isaac story. In the gospel tale, crucifixion led to resurrection; doubt gave way to renewed faith; death gave birth to new life.

Isaac stories can come at any time. They may be born from the blood and sweat of your darker days, or from lighter moments when you're joyful and inspired. They may result from a protracted labor, or a surprisingly easy one. They may involve you in new relationships, or set you happily apart.

Does this birthing ever end? Florida Scott-Maxwell writes:

> Age puzzles me. I thought it was a quiet time. My seventies were interesting, and fairly serene, but my eighties are passionate. I grow more intense as I age.[14]

Sarah, remember, was in her nineties. Maybe that's why things got so hot.

�֍ �֍ ✖

Have you already experienced some Isaac stories in your life? Take a moment to think or write on these experiences, and to laugh or feel gratitude. Do you ever share these experiences with others, so that "everyone who hears will laugh with me"?

✖

What if you could write your own Isaac story? What elements might it have? What new births could you imagine in your future life? Don't be pragmatic: let yourself fantasize. Jot down any of the ideas that come to you. (The following visualization may also help you go deeper.)

✖

�֍ *Guided Meditation* ✷

THE DIVINE MESSENGERS

Imagine that you are sitting at the entrance to your tent. There is a hot sun overhead, and a bare, flat landscape surrounding you. Suddenly you become aware of another's presence. Looking up, you realize that three men are standing near you. You sense that these are not ordinary men. These are the three divine messengers who came to Abraham and Sarah. They announced God's will—that Sarah would bear a son.

Now they have come with a special message for you. It is a message of love. They will speak of things that Spirit intends to help bring your life to fulfillment. Like Sarah, you may laugh at their message. It might seem improbable that such things will come to be. Yet your laugh may also be one of joy, as you hear of God's good plans for your future.

Now listen within. That is where the messengers dwell. What do you hear them saying? Let their message come in words, or images, or feelings. Don't struggle; take it easy.

If and when you feel you have received a message, allow yourself to sit with it. Is it a surprise to you, or was it expected? Does it require some action on your part, or merely patience? Does it reflect a yearning of your own heart? Is it your Isaac, waiting to be born?

✷   ✷   ✷

12

Coda:

The Dance of the Sages

IMAGINE: YOU SEE a high hill decorated with wildflowers. Clear fresh breezes blow, leaving the air clean and cool. Above, a late afternoon sun shines through passing clouds, dappling the hillside with light. It's a shifting kaleidoscope of colors and textures, delighting all the senses.

Look closer. Now you see gathered on the hill a circle of men and women. Their hands are linked. They are dancing together as the circle turns round and round. This dance is performed to a stately rhythm. Looking closer still, you realize many of the dancers are no spring chickens: they're getting on in years. Yet a playful lilt enlivens their steps, and there's a hint of a smile on their lips.

Now it's all coming into focus. You recognize who the dancers are; they are figures you've met before. There's Buddha, arm in arm with the Hindu forest dweller. Next to them, cutting a humorous figure, is a crookedy Taoist sage. The Aikido master stands directly across the circle from the old woman in purple. The Eagle Clan Mother gazes at her counterpart—a talking tree. Jesus holds the hand of Krisha Gautami; each knows loss all too well. Opposite them Sarah and Scrooge kick up their heels. Not bad for a couple of old codgers!

You realize what you are witnessing: the *dance of the sages*. In this circle, archetypes of elder spirit have gathered from all over the world. But something's still missing. Counting the dancers, you realize there are eleven in all—an incomplete number. There must be a twelfth to round out the symmetry, to make the circle whole. But who is to be that person? Who's left? As the dancers turn around and gaze at you, you realize it is *yourself*.

You hesitate. How dare you dance in such esteemed company? Why, you'd be as clumsy as an oaf! You're always tripping over your own feet. Besides, you're not even fully an elder. Come on, come on, they beckon, none of us is perfect. You don't have to be perfect to become whole. You don't have to be old to become wise.

Hands reach out to clasp yours. Tentatively, you join the dance. Hey, this isn't so bad, you think. It's even kind of fun. Little by little, your body begins to move more freely, expressing feelings long locked inside—the pain of all your losses, then the joyfulness of a child. Still, you fear you will stumble. What if you lose your footing? But the hands hold firmly onto yours. You can let go, because they will not. Their touch, while gentle, will support you through everything. You are part of the healing circle.

Finally, this image dissolves, and you are back wherever you are sitting and reading this book. However, this vision can assist you to work with this book even after you put it away. You've been introduced to some wonderful sages. They've already taught you much. If you simply let them, they can be your companions as you dance through life's second half.

You will face difficult passages. Perhaps, for example, you'll leave a long-standing job. Simply ask then: Who do I most need now as my dance partner? Who stands next to me, holding my hand? Is it the Taoist tree, guiding me to embrace the useless? Suffering Jesus, assisting me through loss? The Hindu elder bidding me retreat to my forest? Or the Eagle Clan Mother summoning me to serve the world in larger ways than I've hitherto imagined?

Your heart will tell you which helper you most need. Using visualization, reading, and journaling, you can keep that person, and the example of their life, present in your thoughts. Of course, days or weeks later your needs might shift. For example, you might first have to go through the dark night of grief, where Jesus stays awake with you. When that is done, you might sense your grief transforming into the labor pains of new birth; Sarah steps forward to offer herself as a skilled midwife. You work with her story. But what, or who, is being delivered? The old woman in purple now speaks out: it's *you*, in all your wild freedom. In such ways we can keep dancing with our spiritual companions.

At the same time, we need companions of this earth. We need the help and support of other people like ourselves. Spiritual passages are difficult to negotiate; they are even harder when we try to do it alone. How do we locate these companions? How do we find the community of fellow dancers we crave? Three resources follow.

First, Appendix A suggests some further readings on the spiritual passages of life's second half. The sources quoted throughout my book can lead you to many wonderful texts geared to the particular topics being discussed. But in Appendix A I highlight *general* works written by contemporary authors. They're men and women of our own time dealing with our own issues. We may never meet them face to face, but as they share their inspiration and personal stories, they, too, can become dance partners.

In Appendix B, I suggest how you might form a "spiritual passages group," gathering with like-minded seekers in your community. There are others, like yourself, who are interested in using the aging process as a spiritual curriculum. You may already know such people among your friends. If not, there are ways to locate them. Coming together in a group will enable you to share readings, life experience, support, and inspiration. You may find you are all at similar stages of the journey or are quite diverse in age, gender, and outlook. Either way can work. There's mutual empowerment both in our differences and in all that we share together.

Finally, appendix C shifts us into visionary modes. I've spoken much of the individual's path through spiritual passages; we also need to build a *social context* to better assist this process. The sociomedical model of aging has its Medicare and nursing homes. The consumerist model has generated retirement communities and elder vacation plans galore. What institutions support the spiritual model of aging? We have to build them in our hearts, and then in reality.

I suggest one such place, which I call an ElderSpirit Center. Imagine a retreat house you could enter for prayer and meditation at crucial later-life junctures: when leaving a job, perhaps, or losing a loved one. A learning center where you could absorb the world's spiritual wisdom as it bears on life's second half. A home where you might even reside. Not like a nursing home, or a conventional retirement community, this would be a community for those who wish to use the later years to deepen their spiritual quest. What spaces of blessed silence we might find there. What prayer, what laughter might resound in its halls as we dance our dance together!

But whether with others or alone; with earthly companions or spiritual guides; in our outer lives or inner hearts; by all means, *let us dance.*

Appendix

A

Suggested Readings

Bianchi, Eugene C. *Elder Wisdom: Crafting Your Own Elderhood* (New York: Crossroad, 1994).

A bit scholarly, but filled with rich material based on interviews with one hundred impressive elders.

Carroll, Andrew. *Golden Opportunities: A Volunteer Guide for Americans over Fifty* (Princeton: Peterson's, 1994).

Just what it says: a useful listing and explanation of service opportunities.

Chinen, Allan B. *Once upon a Midlife: Classic Stories and Mythic Tales to Illuminate the Middle Years* (New York: Jeremy P. Tarcher/ Putnam, 1992).

Excellent book by a Jungian-influenced psychiatrist, exploring traditional tales that can help adults negotiate the psychospiritual tasks of midlife.

———. *In the Ever After: Fairy Tales and the Second Half of Life* (Wilmette, Ill.: Chiron Publications, 1989).

Using fairy tales to explore psychospiritual wholeness in later life; both of Chinen's books would work well for a spiritual passages group.

Cole, Thomas R., and Mary G. Winkler. *The Oxford Book of Aging* (New York: Oxford University Press, 1994).

An excellent resource book, including over two hundred excerpts on aging from poets, philosophers, novelists, and essayists the world over.

Fischer, Kathleen. *Autumn Gospel: Women in the Second Half of Life* (Mahwah, N.J.: Paulist Press, 1995).

An intelligent book on the psychospiritual journey of women, including suggested prayers, exercises, and rituals.

Fowler, Margaret, and Priscilla McCutcheon, eds. *Songs of Experience: An Anthology of Literature of Growing Old* (New York: Ballantine Books, 1991).

A collection of poems, essays, and short fiction, organized by themes.

Friedan, Betty. *The Fountain of Age* (New York: Simon and Schuster, 1993).

Not spiritually oriented, but filled with useful information and inspiring "Isaac stories" concerning the creative possibilities of later life.

Goldman, Connie, and Richard Mahler. *Secrets of Becoming a Late Bloomer* (Walpole, N.H.: Stillpoint, 1995).

Based on interviews with "extraordinary ordinary people on the art of staying creative, alive and aware in mid-life and beyond."

Harris, Maria. *Jubilee Time: Celebrating Women, Spirit, and the Advent of Age* (New York: Bantam Books, 1995).

Based on biblical teachings concerning the Jubilee year ("hallow the fiftieth year"), this book provides illuminating teachings and exercises for women entering life's second half.

Levine, Stephen. *Who Dies? An Investigation of Conscious Living and Conscious Dying* (New York: Anchor Press/Doubleday, 1982).

A manual for the spiritual approach to death (and life), including powerful stories, exercises, and meditations.

Mannheimer, Ronald J. *The Second Middle Age: Looking Differently at Life beyond Fifty* (Detroit: Visible Ink Press, 1995).

Not spiritually oriented, but an excellent guide, written by distinguished contributors, on a wide range of issues concerning life's second half.

Rinpoche, Sogyal. *The Tibetan Book of Living and Dying* (San Francisco: HarperSanFrancisco, 1993).

An excellent guide to spiritual issues surrounding death and dying. You don't have to be Tibetan to find it helpful.

Rountree, Cathleen. *On Women Turning Fifty* (San Francisco: HarperSanFrancisco, 1993).

A set of illuminating interviews with women, some well known, others "ordinary folk," on negotiating this life passage.

Schacter-Shalomi, Zalman, and Ronald S. Miller. *From Age-ing to Sage-ing* (New York: Warner Books, 1995).

An informative and inspiring book by one of the founders of the conscious aging movement in America—a must read.

Sheehy, Gail. *New Passages* (New York: Random House, 1995).

Based on extensive research, but a breezy read, this book examines the psychosocial passages of middle and later life.

A Spiritual
Passages Group

A S WE EMBARK on the journey outlined in this book it's a good idea to find fellow voyagers, who will provide sustenance and inspiration for the trip ahead. Here are a few suggestions on how to locate such people and how to work with them so that we empower one another. These ideas are hardly a fixed roadmap; the leadings of the spirit may lead you to unanticipated places.

A Spiritual Passages Group (you might also call it an "elder circle," or any name you please) gathers those who wish to work consciously with the aging process, using it as a curriculum for spiritual growth. Perhaps you have friends or acquaintances who might be interested. They, in turn, may suggest others to invite. You might also be able to network through your place of worship, a learning institute you've attended, or other such settings. If you are feeling adventurous, you could post flyers or place a notice in an appropriate newspaper announcing the formation of your group.

In shaping a group, it's important to consider the criteria for joining. Do you want a particular gender composition? Do you have a certain age in mind for participants—say, over forty-five? This focussing may lead to a certain commonality of experience as you grapple with spiritual passages. On the other hand, it can also be exciting to open to, even seek out, younger members. After all, they're aging, too, and may wish to get a jump on preparing for elderhood.

Once your group has gathered, you probably want to clarify objectives. Are you primarily seeking to foster each other's spiritual development? Or will there be more emphasis on intellectual and emotional growth? Do you want to focus on the personal challenges of aging? Or on a way to contribute, as elders, to the outer world?

There are also some structural issues to iron out. How long, how often, and where will you meet? Will you have a leader at each session, and should this responsibility rotate? What kind of format will best serve the group's ends? I'll mention a few possibilities.

The elder council was discussed in chapter 6. Here, a formal ritual involving a "talking stick" grounds the sharing of elder wisdom. You might want to review that section if this structure appeals to you.

Another format involves shared readings and discussion. You might begin with books about the creative and spiritual possibilities of life's second half. I've provided a number of suggestions in appendix A, and members may have their own recommendations. Whatever texts you use, you'll probably want to go beyond purely intellectual exchange. Readings can provide a taking-off point for members to reflect deeply on personal experience. The questions and exercises in this book are a good example for how you might structure such a discussion. At a certain point you might even leave books behind to explore a particular life issue in depth.

Another sort of spiritual passages group focuses on a shared practice. Perhaps you have friends at a church or synagogue you attend. You may want to form a prayer group to sustain each other's spiritual journeys; or you might join with like-minded "elders" for meditation, nature walks, or poetry writing, processing life material as you go. You might also focus your group on service. Visioning yourself as wise clan mothers and fathers, you can gather to address needs in your community.

Of course, these models can be mixed and matched. You might have a reading-and-discussion group that hosts an elder council once a month. From that elder council, a group sentiment might emerge to organize a certain service project. In such ways the winds of Spirit can shift direction, and the sensitive group follows.

Somewhere along the line, problems will probably arise. Perhaps member attendance and preparation are sporadic. Talkers grow to dominate the more quiet folks. Personality clashes flash forth like lightning. Or the group as a whole begins to stagnate.

If not dealt with, such issues may undermine your group. But if you work them through successfully, these "problems" may prove to be your greatest teachers. Through the crucible of conflict, much elder wisdom is forged. A few simple principles help, such as: being honest with one another; hearing from all participants; seeking a "win-win" outcome rather than simply "getting your own way"; and listening for the voice of Spirit, which provides creative solutions.

I've focussed on building a formal group structure. But you may sense that your spiritual passages group never is so named, yet is there, in a close friendship sustained over the years, or a workshop with others you'll never see again. Spirit may place in your path, in a timely fashion, just the people you need. Let us honor these teachers and companions. Let us revere all the gifts we exchange.

The ElderSpirit

Center

IT'S NOT ENOUGH to just internalize the spiritual model of aging; we also need cultural institutions that will help support us on this path. What might they look like? I discussed one ancient Hindu response: the socially sanctioned forest retreat. For most of us today, it would be impractical. Furthermore, it might only intensify the loneliness that sometimes comes with age. Many would realize divine presence better through participation in a caring community. (Even in India the spiritually minded elder nowadays is more likely to join an ashram, or spiritual community, than go off to the forest alone.)

A spiritual passages group (see appendix B) can provide some sense of community. There also are many wonderful centers that gather those seeking personal growth in life's second half. For example, the Omega Institute in Rhinebeck, New York, has run several conscious aging conferences, and hosts a plethora of spiritually based workshops. There are similar "holistic" centers in other parts of the country. There is also a burgeoning network of adult education institutes and Elderhostel programs affiliated with college campuses.

I would also propose a more far-reaching model, deepening the possibilities for involvement: that of a center set aside exclusively for older adults who wish to use the later years for spiritual growth. Let's call this an ElderSpirit Center. I have described this model elsewhere in more detail—here I'll provide a brief sketch.[1]

You could join an ElderSpirit Center either as full-time *resident* or as an independent *affiliate*. As a residence, the center might provide many of the same services as a conventional retirement home. However, it would be distinguished from such a place by its spiritual mission, drawing on the tradition of the monastery and retreat house. Affiliates would continue to live independently while drawing on the center's resources. The center could house a library of spiritual literature and audiotapes. In addition, it could offer spiritual formation groups, classes, and one-on-one spiritual direction, focussed on the issues of life's second half. Special retreats would be run for those going through particular passages, such as retirement or the death of a loved one. The physical environment would be conducive to this inner work. For example, the center might include a chapel, rooms for prayer and meditation, communal gathering places, a cloistered garden, and paths that lead out into nature.

What would be the spiritual mission of such a place? Would it be designed for monastic contemplation? Activist engagement with the world? Solitude? Community? Ideally, my answer would be yes to all. Some might come to the center on an introspective quest; they would find there a place for peaceful retreat. Others who prefer a more activist spirituality could remain deeply involved with family, friends, and work, while using the center as a base of operations. The center could also foster holistic mind/body practices, such as exercise, yoga, and healthy eating. It could experiment, as well, with the sort of later-life rituals discussed earlier in this book.

In this way, many paths can be available in one place. This would enable the center not only to serve more people but also to meet the changing needs of individuals as they go through spiritual passages. On the other hand, if a number of centers spring up, each might have its distinctive tone. One might be more rural and contemplative, another more an urban learning center.

Who would run these centers? Better for each one's participants and their hirees to do so than an external bureaucracy. We don't need yet another disempowering old-folks home. Capable residents might assist those who need help with tasks of daily living. This mutual caring builds community. Just as in a monastic setting, one person might work in the kitchen and another in the garden, with the understanding that each task is part of the person's spiritual discipline, so jobs would be tailored to the needs and capacities of each person. The center might also sponsor outreach service projects. Imagine a day care center on the premises, or a mentoring program for high school kids. Such projects could help assure that the fruits of elder wisdom (and youth energy) are shared across the generations.

The question arises of the relationship between such a spiritual community and religious institutions. There's much to be said for an independent center open to all forms of belief. We've seen how the world's sacred traditions each has its unique insights to contribute. On the other hand, a particular religious denomination might also sponsor a center. This orientation could help focus liturgy, classes, and spiritual direction, while leaving room for diversity of belief.

In an intermediate model, a center might build loose ties with a number of religious congregations in its area. It might also invite the involvement of elderly religious from different orders. Some of these people have been "put out to pasture," their wisdom and talent going to waste. They might give life to the ElderSpirit community and find new life, themselves, in the process.

The ElderSpirit model can also inspire changes in existing institutions. For example, nursing homes, adult day care, and senior centers could offer more in the way of spiritual programming. A conventional retirement community could support a spiritually oriented "subcommunity" within its walls, including many of the features just described.

The ElderSpirit model itself can be modified in a number of directions. One colleague of mine wishes to set up small-scale congregate housing for elders with a strong spiritual orientation. Why not live with like-minded seekers? At the other extreme, another colleague envisions a nationally known center that would host workshops, retreats, conferences, even a cable TV station, all oriented toward later-life spirituality. Rabbi Schacter-Shalomi's *Spiritual Eldering Institute* has already taken first steps in this direction.[2] Other acquaintances, builders of senior housing, are now scouting sites for a holistically oriented retirement community.

Such experiments are at various stages of development. But together they suggest that the ElderSpirit Center, or something like it, is not just a utopian dream. I think it's a highly practical alternative for the not-so-distant future.

Notes

CHAPTER 1—AWAKENINGS: THE STORY OF BUDDHA

1. C. G. Jung, *Modern Man in Search of a Soul* (New York: Harcourt, Brace, 1933), pp. 95–114.
2. Kahlil Gibran, *The Prophet* (New York: Alfred A. Knopf, 1965), p. 17.
3. Leo Tolstoy, *The Death of Ivan Ilych and Other Stories* (New York: New American Library, 1960), pp. 131–32.
4. Martin Heidegger, *Being and Time,* trans. John Macquarrie and Edward Robinson (New York: Harper and Row, 1962), pp. 304–11.
5. Carlos Castaneda, *Journey to Ixtlan: The Lessons of Don Juan* (New York: Simon and Schuster, 1972), pp. 46–57.

CHAPTER 2—LOSS AS LIBERATION: THE HINDU LIFE STAGES

1. Henri J. M. Nouwen and Walter J. Gaffney, *Aging* (New York: Image Books, 1976), p. 86.
2. Christian Feldman and Jack Kornfield, eds., *Stories of the Spirit, Stories of the Heart* (San Francisco: HarperSanFrancisco, 1991), pp. 28–30. Reprinted from "As a Physician," by Rachel Naomi Remen.
3. Ernest Kurtz and Katherine Ketcham, *The Spirituality of Imperfection* (New

York: Bantam Books, 1992), p. 42.

4. Betty Friedan, *The Fountain of Age* (New York: Simon and Schuster, 1993), p. 548.

CHAPTER 3—EMBRACING CHANGE: THE YIN AND YANG

1. Ram Dass and Paul Gorman, *How Can I Help?* (New York: Alfred A. Knopf, 1985), pp. 90–91. From an unattributed account collected by the authors.
2. R. L. Wing, *The Illustrated I Ching* (Garden City, N.Y.: Doubleday, 1982), no. 12.
3. C. G. Jung, *Modern Man in Search of a Soul* (New York: Harcourt, Brace, 1933), p. 109.
4. Lao Tsu, *Tao Te Ching*, trans. Gia-Fu Feng and Jane English (New York: Vintage Books, 1972), p. 31 (no. 29).
5. Jung, *Modern Man in Search of a Soul*, p. 107.
6. Gail Sheehy, *New Passages* (New York: Random House, 1995), p. 319.

CHAPTER 4—THE WISDOM OF AGE: AN AIKIDO MASTER

1. See Eugene C. Bianchi, *Elder Wisdom* (New York: Crossroad, 1994).
2. William Gleason, *The Spiritual Foundations of Aikido* (Rochester, Vt.: Destiny Books, 1995), p. 6.
3. Gleason, *Spiritual Foundations of Aikido*, p. 6.
4. Lao Tzu, *Tao Te Ching*, trans. Stephen Mitchell (New York: HarperPerennial, 1988), no. 2.
5. Barbara G. Walker, *The Crone* (San Francisco: HarperSanFrancisco, 1985), p. 49.
6. Betty Friedan, *The Fountain of Age* (New York: Simon and Schuster, 1993), p. 107.
7. Cited in Allan B. Chinen, *In the Ever After* (Wilmette, Ill.: Chiron Publications, 1989), p. 36. Quoted in J. McLeish, *The Ulyssean Adult: Creativity in the Middle and Later Years* (New York: McGraw Hill Ryerson, 1976), p. 126.
8. Lao Tzu, *Tao Te Ching*, trans. Stephen Mitchell, no. 48.
9. Christian Feldman and Jack Kornfield, eds., *Stories of the Spirit, Stories of the Heart* (San Francisco: HarperSanFrancisco, 1991), p. 212.
10. Shunryu Suzuki, *Zen Mind, Beginner's Mind* (New York: John Weatherhill, 1970), pp. 21–22.

CHAPTER 5—THE FREEDOM OF THE FOOL: AN OLD WOMAN IN PURPLE

1. Adolf Guggenbühl-Craig, *The Old Fool and the Corruption of Myth*, trans. Dorothea Wilson (Dallas: Spring Publications, 1991), p. 110.

2. Martin Buber, *Tales of the Hasidim: Early Masters* (New York: Schocken Books, 1947), p. 251.

3. Cathleen Rountree, *On Women Turning Fifty* (San Francisco: HarperSanFrancisco, 1993), p. 139.

4. Rountree, *On Women Turning Fifty,* p. 3.

5. Gail Sheehy, *New Passages* (New York: Random House, 1995), p. 180.

6. Glen A. Mazis, *The Trickster, Magician and Grieving Man* (Santa Fe: Bear, 1993), p. 15.

7. Sheehy, *New Passages,* p. 245.

8. Sheehy, Ibid., pp. 248–49.

9. Walter Kaiser, *Praisers of Folly* (Cambridge: Harvard University Press, 1963), p. 6.

10. Kaiser, Ibid., p. 8.

11. Norman Cousins, *Anatomy of an Illness As Perceived by the Patient* (New York: W. W. Norton, 1979), pp. 27–48.

12. Wes "Scoop" Nisker, *Crazy Wisdom* (Berkeley: Ten Speed Press, 1990), p. 52.

CHAPTER 6—CARING FOR OUR WORLD: THE EAGLE CLAN MOTHER

1. Zalman Schacter-Shalomi and Ronald S. Miller, *From Age-ing to Sage-ing* (New York: Warner Books, 1995), p. 190.

2. Ibid., *From Age-ing to Sage-ing,* pp. 187–210.

3. Brooke Medicine Eagle, "Grandmother Lodge," in *Women of the 14th Moon: Writings on Menopause,* ed. Dena Taylor and Amber Coverdale Sumrall (Freedom, Calif.: The Crossing Press, 1991), p. 260.

4. Schacter-Shalomi and Miller, *From Age-ing to Sage-ing,* p. 227.

5. Kathleen Wall and Gary Ferguson, *Lights of Passage* (San Francisco: HarperSanFrancisco, 1994).

6. Robin Heerens Lysne, *Dancing up the Moon* (Berkeley: Conari Press, 1995).

7. Joseph Epes Brown, "Becoming Part of It," in *I Become Part of It: Sacred Dimensions in Native American Life,* ed. D. M. Dooling and Paul Jordan-Smith (San Francisco: HarperSanFrancisco, 1989), pp. 15–16.

8. Sandy Johnson, *The Book of Elders* (San Francisco: HarperSanFrancisco, 1994), p. 194.

9. Brooke Medicine Eagle, "Grandmother Lodge," p. 260.

10. Eleanor J. Piazza, "Women of the Fourteenth Moon–The Ceremony," in Taylor and Sumrall, *Women of the 14th Moon,* pp. 263–66.

CHAPTER 7—THE USE OF THE USELESS: A TAOIST TREE

1. A statement quoted in Stanley Coren, *Sleep Thieves* (New York: Free Press, 1996), p. 249.
2. Martin Grotjahn, "The Day I Got Old," in *The Oxford Book of Aging* (New York: Oxford University Press, 1994), p. 10.
3. Thomas Merton, *The Way of Chuang Tzu* (New York: New Directions, 1965), p. 99.
4. Simone Weil, *Waiting for God* (New York: Harper and Row, 1951), p. 115.
5. Weil, Ibid., p. 111.
6. Weil, Ibid., p. 114.
7. Quoted in *Songs of Experience: An Anthology of Literature on Growing Old,* ed. Margaret Fowler and Priscilla McCutcheon (New York: Ballantine Books, 1991), p. 32. From an article first printed in *The Washington Post,* reprinted in the Congressional Record, April 22, 1975.
8. Quoted in Mark Dov Shapiro, *Gates of Shabbat: A Guide for Observing Shabbat* (New York: CCAR Press, 1991), p. 55.
9. Abraham Joshua Heschel, *The Sabbath* (New York: Farrar, Straus and Giroux, 1951), p. 8.
10. Heschel, *The Sabbath,* p. 32.
11. Heschel, Ibid., p. 14. From the *Zohar* I, 75.
12. As quoted in Heschel, *The Sabbath,* p. 23. From *Genesis rabba* 10, 9.
13. Maria Harris, *Jubilee Time: Celebrating Women, Spirit, and the Advent of Age* (New York, Bantam Books, 1995).

CHAPTER 8—COMPLETING THE PAST: SCROOGE'S GHOSTS

1. Robert N. Butler, "The Life Review: An Interpretation of Reminiscence in the Aged," *Psychiatry* 26 (1963): 65–76.
2. Arthur Schopenhauer, "The Ages of Life," in *Arthur Schopenhauer: Counsels and Maxims,* trans. T. Bailey Saunders (London: Swan Sonnenschein and Company, 1890), p. 151.
3. C. G. Jung, *Memories, Dreams, Reflections* (New York: Vintage Books, 1989), p. 326.
4. John Forster, *The Life of Charles Dickens* (London: Chapman and Hall, 1872–4), quoted in Charles Dickens, *The Annotated Christmas Carol* (New York: Avenel Books, 1976), p. 90.
5. See, for example, Sharon Salzberg, *Lovingkindness: The Revolutionary Art of Happiness* (Boston and London: Shambhala, 1995).
6. Zalman Schacter-Shalomi and Ronald S. Miller, *From Age-ing to Sage-ing* (New York: Warner Books, 1995), pp. 279–80.

7. Pierre Wolf, *May I Hate God?* (New York: Paulist Press, 1979).

8. *Alcoholics Anonymous* (New York: Alcoholics Anonymous World Services, 1939), p. 59.

9. William Shakespeare, *Macbeth,* act 5, scene 5.

10. Kenneth Kramer, *The Sacred Art of Dying* (New York: Paulist Press, 1988), pp. 134–35.

11. Schacter-Shalomi and Miller, *From Age-ing to Sage-ing,* p. 103.

CHAPTER 9—FACING DEATH AND THE DEATHLESS: A BUDDHIST MOTHER

1. St. Augustine, *The Confessions of St. Augustine,* trans. Rex Warner (New York: New American Library, 1963), pp. 74–75.

2. *The Bhagavad Gita,* trans. Eknath Easwaran (Petaluma, Calif.: Nilgiri Press, 1985), p. 154.

3. E. W. Burlingame, *Buddhist Parables* (New Haven: Yale University Press, 1922), pp. 92–94. Reprinted in E. A. Burtt, ed., *The Teachings of the Compassionate Buddha* (New York: New American Library, 1955), p. 46.

4. Sogyal Rinpoche, *The Tibetan Book of Living and Dying* (San Francisco: HarperSanFrancisco, 1993), p. 40.

5. Here I gloss over differences between the Hindu and Buddhist understanding. Most important, the Hindu recognizes a divine soul that reincarnates, casting off used bodies like threadbare coats. The Buddhists deny any such permanent soul. As a wave travels miles to shore without any single drop of water making the whole journey, so our karmic energy packet generates the next rebirth, though there is no abiding substance. Thus Buddha's Deathless Region does not imply any "thing" that lives eternally; he was resistant to this sort of metaphysics.

6. Ian Stevenson, *Twenty Cases Suggestive of Reincarnation,* 2d ed. (Charlottesville: University Press of Virginia, 1974), pp. 109–27.

7. *Journal of Nervous and Mental Disease* (May 1977). Most of this issue was devoted to Dr. Stevenson's work. *Journal of the American Medical Association,* December 1, 1975. These references are provided by Christopher M. Bache, *Lifecycles* (New York: Paragon House, 1990), p. 33.

8. See, for example, Ian Wilson, *The After-Death Experience* (New York: William Morrow, 1987).

9. Raymond A. Moody, Jr., *Life after Life* (New York: Bantam Books, 1975), p. 95.

10. Moody, Ibid., p. 97.

11. In addition to Raymond Moody's books, see, for example, Kenneth Ring, *Heading toward Omega: In Search of the Meaning of the Near-Death Experience* (New York: William Morrow, 1984); Melvin Morse, with Paul Perry,

Closer to the Light (New York: Ivy Books, 1990) and *Transformed by the Light* (New York: Ivy Books, 1992); Elisabeth Kübler-Ross, *On Life after Death* (Berkeley: Celestial Arts, 1991); Michael Sabom, *Recollections of Death: A Medical Investigation* (New York: Harper and Row, 1982).

12. Burtt, *Teachings of the Compassionate Buddha*, p. 50.

13. C. G. Jung, "The Soul and Death," in *The Structure and Dynamics of the Psyche: The Collected Works*, vol. 8 (Princeton: Princeton University Press, 1969), p. 407.

14. Rinpoche, *Tibetan Book of Living and Dying*, p. 23.

15. Thomas R. Cole and Mary G. Winkler, *The Oxford Book of Aging* (New York: Oxford University Press, 1994), p. 140. From a letter to his father, April 4, 1787. This letter can be found in *Mozart's Letters, Selected from the Letters of Mozart and His Family*. Ed. Eric Blom. Trans. Emily Anderson. (New York: Macmillan Press).

16. Rinpoche, *Tibetan Book of Living and Dying*, p. 26. From the Mahaparinirvana Sutra.

CHAPTER 10—SUFFERING AS GIFT: THE PASSION OF JESUS

1. Kathleen Fischer, *Autumn Gospel: Women in the Second Half of Life* (Mahwah, N.J.: Paulist Press, 1995), p. 143.

2. Miguel de Unamuno, *Tragic Sense of Life* (New York: Dover, 1954), p. 135.

3. Harold Kushner, *When Bad Things Happen to Good People* (New York: Schocken Books, 1989), p. 64.

4. Friedrich Nietzsche, *Twilight of the Idols* [published with *The Anti-Christ*] (London: Penguin Books, 1968), p. 33.

5. Ram Dass and Paul Gorman, *How Can I Help?* (New York: Alfred A. Knopf, 1985), pp. 19–20.

6. Carter Catlett Williams, "Salsify and Sacrament," *Aging and the Human Spirit* 3:1 (Spring 1993), published by the Institute for Medical Humanities, University of Texas Medical Branch at Galveston, quoted in *The Oxford Book of Aging* (New York: Oxford University Press, 1994), p. 133.

7. Teilhard de Chardin, *The Divine Milieu* (New York: Harper and Row, 1960), pp. 89–90.

CHAPTER 11—REBIRTHING THE SELF: SARAH'S LAUGH

1. Quoted in *The Torah: A Modern Commentary*, ed. W. Gunther Plaut (New York: Union of Hebrew Congregations, 1962), p. 143.

2. Deepak Chopra, *Ageless Body, Timeless Mind* (New York: Harmony Books, 1993), p. 67.

3. Gail Sheehy, *New Passages* (New York: Random House, 1995), p. 426.

4. Chopra, *Ageless Body, Timeless Mind,* pp. 69–70.

5. Chopra, Ibid., *Timeless Mind,* pp. 92–94.

6. Sheehy, *New Passages,* p. 258.

7. Robert N. Butler and Myrna I. Lewis, *Love and Sex After Sixty* (New York: Ballantine Books, 1976), pp. 15–109.

8. Butler and Lewis, Ibid., p. 281.

9. Rountree, *On Women Turning Fifty,* p. 141.

10. Sheehy, *New Passages,* pp. 159–175.

11. Sheehy, Ibid., pp. 199–222.

12. Sheehy, Ibid., p. 146.

13. Meister Eckhart, *Meditations with Meister Eckhart,* translated and freely adapted by Matthew Fox (Santa Fe: Bear, 1983), p. 32.

14. Florida Scott-Maxwell, *The Measure of My Days* (New York: Penguin Books, 1979), p. 13.

APPENDIX C—THE ELDERSPIRIT CENTER

1. Drew Leder, "Spiritual Community in Later Life: A Modest Proposal," *Journal of Aging Studies* 10:2 (Summer 1996): 103–16.

2. For further information about the materials and workshops offered, contact:
   Spiritual Eldering Institute
   970 Aurora Avenue
   Boulder, CO 80302
   (303) 449-SAGE

Index

About the Author

DREW LEDER, M.D., PH.D., is an associate professor at Loyola College in Maryland, where he teaches Eastern and Western philosophy. He is the author of *The Absent Body*, and has written and edited many works on the intersection of medicine and philosophy. Dr. Leder has a special interest in the spiritual dimensions of aging. Originally supported by a fellowship from Chicago's Park Ridge Center, he publishes and conducts workshops on this topic. He lives in Baltimore, Maryland, with his wife, Janice McLane, and daughter, Sarah.

Discover more of yourself with Inner Work Books.

The following Inner Work Books are part of a series that explores psyche
and spirit through writing, visualization, ritual, and imagination.

_____	The Artist's Way	0-87477-694-5	$14.95
_____	The Artist's Way Hardcover Deluxe Edition	0-87477-821-2	$24.95
_____	The Artist's Way Morning Pages Journal	0-87477-820-4	$20.00
_____	At a Journal Workshop	0-87477-638-4	$16.95
_____	Ending the Struggle Against Yourself	0-87477-763-I	$16.95
_____	Fearless Creating	0-87477-805-0	$15.95
_____	Finding What You Didn't Lose	0-87477-909-3	$15.95
_____	Following Your Path	0-87477-687-2	$16.95
_____	The Inner Child Workbook	0-87477-635-X	$15.95
_____	A Journey Through Your Childhood	0-87477-499-3	$10.95
_____	A Life in the Arts	0-87477-766-6	$15.95
_____	The Life We Are Given	0-87477-792-5	$15.95
_____	The Mythic Path	0-87477-857-3	$17.95
_____	Pain and Possibility	0-87477-571-X	$16.95
_____	The Path of the Everyday Hero	0-87477-630-9	$14.95
_____	The Possible Human	0-87477-218-4	$14.95
_____	The Search for the Beloved	0-87477-476-4	$14.95
_____	Smart Love	0-87477-472-I	$13.95
_____	A Time to Heal Workbook	0-87477-745-3	$14.95
_____	True Partners	0-87477-727-5	$13.95
_____	The Vein of Gold	0-87477-836-0	$23.95
_____	Writing from Life	0-87477-848-4	$16.95
_____	Your Mythic Journey	0-87477-543-4	$12.95

Subtotal $ _____

Shipping and Handling* $ _____

Sales tax (CA, NJ, NY, PA) $ _____

Total amount due $ _____

Payable by Visa, MC or AMEX only ($10.00 min.). No cash, checks or COD. Shipping & handling: US/Can. $2.75 for one book, $1.00 for each add'l book; Int'l $5.00 for one book, $1.00 for each add'l. Call (800) 788-6262 or (201) 933-9292, fax (201) 896-8569 or mail your orders to:

Penguin Putnam Inc. Bill my
PO Box 12289 Dept. B credit card # _____ exp.____
Newark, NJ 07101-5289   __Visa __MC __AMEX

Signature: _____

Bill to: _____   Book Total $_____
Address _____
City_____ ST____ ZIP_____   Applicable sales tax $_____
Daytime phone # _____

Postage & Handling $_____
Ship to: _____
Address _____   Total amount due $_____
City_____ ST____ ZIP_____

Please allow 4 - 6 weeks for US delivery. Can./Int'l orders please allow 6 - 8 weeks.
This offer is subject to change without notice.   Ad #___